Why on earth would anyone want to be an innkeeper?

Pretty much everything you need to know on how to find, buy, run, and sell the inn of your dreams.

by Jeff Bendis
(former innkeeper)

Why on earth would anyone want to be an innkeeper?
Pretty much everything you need to know on how to find, buy, run, and sell the inn of your dreams.

Amazon Edition

ISBN 978-1626130388

Published by ATBOSH Media ltd.
Cleveland, Ohio, USA

http://www.atbosh.com

Dedication

This book is dedicated to the over one hundred innkeepers I have met and the thousands I haven't who toil with uneven skill to provide the often weary, but often not-so-weary, traveler with lodging and sustenance,

&

to Bed and Breakfast, the cats who were rescued as kittens from the local animal shelter and who never understood why they were named Bed and Breakfast and who also never understood why they couldn't stay in the kitchen and help with the morning chores or romp unfettered about the inn,

&

to all of my friends and relatives who thought I was nuts to leave the executive, suburban lifestyle to move to Vermont so I could spend my early retirement years making beds and serving breakfast and cleaning bathrooms every day for a bunch of strangers,

&

to all of the guests who made the innkeeping venture all that I thought it would be and collectively may have unwittingly hastened the sale of the inn.

Table of Contents

Notes from the Author

The inn that I found, bought, ran and, eventually sold was named The Winslow House and it was located in the sleepy little hamlet of West Woodstock, Vermont. I refer to it by name throughout the book. Alas, however, it is no longer an inn. The folks I sold it to ran it for a while then converted it to a multi unit condo. Such is the life of some old properties – from a farmhouse to a small apartment building to an inn to a condo to a ...

Even though somewhere in the book I actually try to explain the difference between an inn and a bed and breakfast I will, solely out of convenience, use the word inn when I really mean bed and breakfast. I think the phrase "B&B keeper" is rather clumsy and conjures up, at least in my mind's eye, someone with insects buzzing around his head.

And, speaking of "his" head, I will use the words he and his when I really mean he and/or she and his and/or hers. Again this will be done solely out of convenience. There are many outstanding female attorneys, innkeepers, real estate brokers, accountants and so on and I mean them no disrespect. I just thought that it would get very tiresome to keep writing and to have you keep reading phrases like "he and she" or the terribly trying "he/she."

And, in the sections on finding and buying an inn, I will deal almost exclusively with finding and buying an existing inn. You obviously have the option of building your inn from scratch - although for insurance purposes you should really consider wood and bricks - or you could buy a big old house - or even a big new house for that matter - and make it into an inn. Regardless of which you choose, most of what's covered in this book will apply. Where it doesn't or where you might have to go beyond what's here, I'll give you fair warning and some worthwhile commentary.

And, although the title of the book and much of the stuff in it, might seem to be rather negative in nature, that's only done to keep you focused on the difficulties that you will face in your search for your inn and all of the other travails in making the purchase, running it, and eventually selling it. The reality is that the adventure was a very special one that I wouldn't trade for any other. Being an innkeeper is a very special calling and, done right, will be a very special time in your life.

Throughout the book, I use the phrase "more on this subject later" or words to that effect. I wrote the book in chunks and in that creative process some things may have ended up a little out of sync. I knew that more details on certain subjects were going to appear later in the book, but you wouldn't know that unless I told you. So, not wanting you be out there hoping for more information and not know that it's coming, I tell you each time that's going to happen - again and again and again. Live with it. You'll thank me later.

And, throughout the book I refer to your retirement income to make the economics of being an innkeeper work. Of course, there's no requirement that you be retired before you become an innkeeper, even though the vast majority of innkeepers that I've met are, in fact, retired. When and where you get your funding and how old you are when you make the decision to scratch the innkeeper wannabe itch, is entirely up to you.

You will undoubtedly make mistakes in your quest - everyone makes mistakes in their quests. My goal is to help you reduce yours to a manageable level.

Thanks for your understanding. Enjoy the book and good luck.

Jeff Bendis

I. It all began and should have ended…

It all began and should have ended, when the owner of the inn told us during the first lesson on innkeeping, "Don't confuse the life of the innkeeper with the life of the guest. All you have to do is sleep in the bed. I have to make it. All you have to do is eat the breakfast. I have to cook it."

Even though it seemed to be such sound and simple advice from someone who had apparently learned the hard way, the course on inn keeping (with all of its reality checks) rather than quashing our dream, actually was the beginning of an eight-year odyssey. An odyssey that culminated in the purchase of a charming, five-guest room bed and breakfast inn just outside of Woodstock, Vermont.

In retrospect, it would have been wise to pay more attention to all of the warning signals that the innkeeper/teacher was giving us. Why, pray tell, didn't we believe her?

But let's go back to the beginning.

We were fortunate that my life as a corporate executive allowed us to travel extensively - the fortunate part was the personal travel, certainly not the corporate travel.

Ah, yes. Corporate travel. What a joy! What's not to like about driving to the airport in what always seemed to be the middle of a stormy night or at least a stormy early morning; trying to find a parking space in one of those huge off-airport parking lots where there was never a space in the row the sign out front directed me to; waiting in the rain for what was already or would soon become an overcrowded little shuttle bus to finally make its way down my row (there should be a corollary of Murphy's Law addressing the fact that the time it takes an airport shuttle bus to get to a passenger is in direct proportion to the intensity of the storm the passenger is waiting in); sitting in stone silence with a bunch of strangers on the 10 minute ride to the terminal; standing impatiently in a line at the ticket counter with other harried business people who were also wondering if they were going to make their flights; racing down a crowded concourse barely missing the women and children who, with seemingly no particular place to go were meandering down the middle of the concourse in a poor imitation of the old Philadelphia Mummer's Parade; standing in line again at the gate with many of the same people who I just left at the ticket counter; finally boarding the plane only to find that I was sitting in a way too small seat next to someone with a raging head cold or an indescribable rash; wondering the entire time if my suitcase, which I last saw disappearing into a tunnel being slapped mercilessly by several hanging rubber straps, had through some miracle of baggage handling ledger domain made it into the same plane I was in (the reason for the rubber straps escapes me still, but if I really cared I would have asked someone by now); arriving at and wandering aimlessly through a strange, poorly-signed airport; finally locating the carousel from which my suitcase was supposedly going to emerge - amazingly, in my case, it always did even though it also amazingly was always the last one down the ramp and on to the baggage carousel; trying desperately to find the ground transportation area; waiting in a car rental line with many of the same people who were on the same flight that brought me to this point in my journey; finally getting out of the airport in a car that reeked of cigarette smoke and had such huge cigarette burns in the seat that I had to be careful where to place my attaché case lest in fall in one of the holes and become hopelessly entangled in the springs; arriving at my destination in sufficient time to begin my return trip to the airport for my return flight home; only to repeat the whole process the following week to another location on a trip of equally questionable value. And all of this was pre-9/11 which meant that I could actually keep my shoes on and my toiletries in my suitcase during the check in process.

Yes, corporate travel was certainly one of the many reasons that kept my part of our search for an inn alive and well.

But, back to our personal travel. How much easier it always was to simply pack our suitcases, hop in the car (or in our case a minivan since, in addition to sightseeing, we were always on buying trips to keep our antique shops well fed) and head off to the destination of our choice and not have to worry about being anywhere at any special time. And what a delightful change of pace it was to stay at a bed and breakfast inn during our first trip to Vermont over 30 years ago.

It was a picture book inn in a picture book setting during the picture book time of year. As we drove up to the inn, the innkeeper's goat (let me repeat that), the innkeeper's goat was tethered to the front step nibbling on a pumpkin. The trees on the hillside behind the inn were ablaze in color. Inside, a fire was crackling - thank goodness in the fireplace - and all seemed right with the world.

Our room was small, but delightfully furnished to fit the size of the room and the early farmhouse style of the inn. Breakfast each morning - it was advertised as a "full country breakfast" - was served in a charming dining room with yet another fire crackling in yet another fireplace. As best as I could tell, by the way, a country breakfast is a regular breakfast, which is served in the country. There was even an early morning frost on what was left of the pumpkins which were, fortunately, outside. Rumor had it that the innkeeper sprayed water on his pumpkins each morning to aid in the manufacture of the frost, but I'd like to think otherwise.

Needless to say, we were hooked from the start. Even way back then, we said to each other, "Someday." What we meant, of course, was that someday, we would have our own bed and breakfast inn, not that we would someday spray water on our pumpkins.

In the intervening years, we stayed in over 100 bed and breakfast inns all throughout the United States, Canada, and Europe. Some were country inns, some were small country hotels, some were city inns, some were just B&Bs, most were very old, a very few were not.

As an aside, talk about warning signs, my guess is that at least one fourth of the inns we stayed in were actively for sale at the time of our visit. And those that weren't actually on the market during our stay, were either about to go on the market or would be sold to us - virtually on the spot - if we had talked to the innkeepers long enough and had brought along our checkbook. More on this phenomenon later.

As veteran travelers, antique dealers, and history buffs, one of the beauties of staying in this type of lodging was that each one was completely different from all of the others - no cookie cutter Red Roof Inns here. Victorian, Georgian, Italinate, Colonial, Country Cape, Log Cabin, converted barns, rustic farmhouses - you name the architectural style and we stayed in at least one of them. And they varied in size from just one guest room to as many as twenty or so. Done right, they were furnished in period antiques and reproductions - except for the mattresses and the linens. Although in some cases the mattresses seemed to be original to the house.

As in all walks of life - some of the innkeepers had everything down pat - the decorating, the furnishings, the landscaping, the food, the service. Everything was just as you hoped it would be. Others didn't have a clue. So, when we began to think seriously about being innkeepers, we thought it would be a good idea to take notes. We entitled our notebook the "The Good, The Bad, and The Ugly." Certainly not an original title, but it captured the essence of what we liked and didn't like about staying in this type of lodging and what we would and wouldn't do as innkeepers.

Into the notebook went thoughts and experiences such as:

✓ Don't let your grandchild pedal his tricycle into a guest room while the guests are in their room. True story and, as an inn guest, a rather delicate one to resolve - I mean what exactly were we supposed to do with the kid?

- ✓ Think twice about using last names and hometowns when you introduce your guests to each other. Some people on 'getaways' would clearly rather remain somewhat, if not completely, anonymous.
- ✓ Don't tell your guests that you only change the sheets and towels upon request because you're trying to protect the environment from those nasty little soapsuds. They will think you're only being cheap and they will probably be right.
- ✓ Don't slide a note under each of your guest room doors each morning with that day's weather forecast. It seemed like a good idea when the Michigan innkeeper provided us with this supposedly helpful bit of information, but since the forecast was lousy, he ruined our day even before we came down to breakfast.
- ✓ Never ever go into any of your guest rooms without knocking even if there are no cars in your inn's parking lot. She may have gone shopping and he may be lying naked on the bed taking a nap and your entry into the room may wake him up. True story as told to us by a mortified female innkeeper.
- ✓ When you think you've finished cleaning a guest room, check under the bed. Whatever thought just ran through your mind regarding what might be found there, it probably has been including an uncompromising Polaroid photograph of the previous night's guests.
- ✓ Think twice about having a book in each room where your guests can write about their stay. You might not like what some of them have written and

a page torn out of the book speaks volumes. Worse yet is the page you left in the book, which should have been torn out.

✓ Until you've eaten at an area restaurant more than once while it's busy, don't recommend it to your guests. You have enough to worry about without being called to task for someone else's lousy food and/or service.

✓ Occasionally, spend a night in each of your guest rooms. The value of doing so will become obvious when you realize that your guests have been unable to reach one of the end tables or that another wastebasket in the bedroom would have been very helpful, or that a guest stole all of the hangers in the closet or armoire, etc.

✓ Don't talk politics, gender, race, or religion with your guests or, if you must, don't ever take a stand on an issue.

✓ *Never tell a dirty joke*, - 'nuf said.

✓ Iron your pillowcases. That way your guests who are staying more than one night will know that they have been changed.

✓ Only use white linens and towels. You can bleach the hell out of them and you will have to.

✓ Don't have the room number and the name of your inn on the room key tag that your guests will use. It is axiomatic that at least one guest per month will loose her key and you probably don't want keys to your rooms out there in the public domain. Oops! Did I say her?

✓ If you are a pet friendly inn don't ever baby sit a guest's pet while they're out doing whatever it is guests do. If you don't think this is an important tip, think of the fun you'll have trying to explain what that lump of fur in the road is all about when your guest returns to the inn. True story.

✓ If you accept children, don't discipline them even when you see them throw their gum under the dining room table or their bacon under the dining room heat run. True stories.

✓ Try to keep the minimum age for children just over the age when they stop throwing their gum under the dining room table, their bacon under the dining room heat run or, worse yet, their scrambled eggs around the dining room when your dining room is full. Yet another true story.

✓ Make sure the innkeeper's quarters (why do they call them quarters?) have their own entrance. If all of these notes, thoughts and ideas were put in order of importance, this could be number one. More later.

✓ Make sure the innkeepers actually have decent sized quarters. You wouldn't believe (trust me, you actually wouldn't believe) what some innkeepers do to themselves as far as living accommodations go.

✓ Make sure that all of the bathrooms in your inn can be used by above average sized adults standing upright, (see the chapter on bathrooms for many more helpful hints on bathroom related matters).

✓ If you're a bible-toting preacher man who sells vitamin supplements on the side, don't burden your guests with your religious rantings or your sales pitch during breakfast or at any other time for that matter. Amazingly, another true story. And, it turned out that he was also a religious bigot. Nice combo.

✓ If you end up catering to a slightly older clientele, but every now and then will have younger guests, don't leave hot water bottles hanging on the back of your bathroom doors. I'm really not making this stuff up. A true story from an otherwise lovely country hotel in Scotland.

✓ Don't subject your guests to a prayer before breakfast. Not that there is anything wrong with a prayer before breakfast, but not everyone is in to that method of starting their day. Those who want to will do it on their own - hopefully, unobtrusively.

✓ If a guest room's private bathroom is actually down the hall from the bedroom, provide your guests with that important fact when they make their reservations so they can bring along their bathrobes or you should have clean, fluffy bathrobes available for your guests to use. A true story and we weren't told in advance and we didn't have our bathrobes with us and the innkeeper didn't provide any for us to use. Are you picturing this?

✓ It is not a good idea to con your guests by telling them that the bathroom has a shower, when in reality it only has a bathtub and a long hose with a shower head on the end and the only way to take a shower is for each of you to hose down the other while you are also soaking the entire bathroom - 'each of you' being you and your traveling companion, not you and the innkeeper. And, what are you supposed to do if you're traveling alone?

- ✓ Clean the common areas of your inn and police your grounds everyday - as in *every single day* - even if you don't think they need it, they do.
- ✓ If you have an extremely squirrely personality and generally don't like people, don't become an innkeeper. It is truly shocking that some innkeepers I have met actually thought that they were cut out to be in this business.
- ✓ The day before you become a curmudgeon sell your inn - everyone will lose if you wait for the day after.
- ✓ Do not bore your guests with tales of your innkeeping adventures or misadventures or your pre-innkeeping adventures or misadventures unless they comfortably fit into a conversation. Remember it's not about the innkeeper, it's about the guest.
- ✓ For those who are heavily into Victorian frufru and find it necessary to have pillows and lace and little stuffed things all over the place, make sure that you leave some room for your guests and their luggage and their toiletries.
- ✓ If you are a retired British military commander and also a retired school headmaster - what a combination - and you think everything must be run by the clock, think twice before you knock on a guest's door because they're five minutes late for breakfast. Most inn guests are, in fact, on holiday (as the Brits say) and, yes, this is another true story.
- ✓ If your full service inn (which means that you provide dinner along with a bed and breakfast) is a working farm in Devon, England and you slaughter

your livestock to provide the main course for dinner, don't tell that to your guests while they are petting the animals in your barnyard. This also really happened.

✓ Periodically check your front room for homeless people who may be sleeping on your sofa - it can be slightly disquieting for early morning guests who are going out for a jog. If I was a creative writer by profession, I couldn't have dreamed this one up.

✓ Even though you may have an unpretentious inn, you should never go barefoot while you are serving breakfast while balancing your new baby on your hip. She was delightful and the baby was cute and her feet were probably clean, but come on.

The list went on and on and, of course, included many very good ideas, which are covered throughout this book and actually became the basis for the way we eventually ran our inn. Again, in hindsight, perhaps the negative entries on the list should have told us to look elsewhere for the best way to spend our early retirement years. But, there were more positives than there were negatives and I wouldn't trade our time as innkeepers - as brief as it was - for anything.

Before we get into the nuts and bolts of how to find, buy, run and eventually sell the inn of your dreams, here are a few stories, which might help put your innkeeping dream into perspective.

II. Why on earth would anyone want to be an innkeeper?

A question that I asked myself too many times after we launched our innkeeping venture. As you will see from the following tales, this business is chock full of surprises - but, in hindsight, that should not be surprising since we were dealing primarily with people. Oh, sure - an occasional plumbing or heating issue, but primarily people. I have been around long enough and seen enough human foibles that nothing should surprise me anymore. The only difference here is that now I was seeing them from the perspective of someone in the hospitality game. It may be a new playing field, but the players are very much the same as in every other game. So read on and pay careful attention.

"Is the orange juice fresh squeezed?" was the reply to my regular morning question, "Can we start you off with a glass of orange juice or apple juice?" He had apparently never heard the old adage, never answer a question with a question.

I could have said "It was once," hazarding a guess that most of the orange colored stuff in the frozen concentrate container came from real oranges that were squeezed at some point along the way. But, always wanting to be truthful with our guests, I said, "No."

"Then I'll have the apple juice," he said. I didn't bother to ask how he thought the apple juice got out of the apples or how long ago it may have happened.

Having been advised - in an impromptu gathering of guests in the Sitting Room of our restored farmhouse the night before - that the main course for breakfast was going to be our famous pumpkin pancakes with bacon strips, a selection that met with universal approval, he now advised us that he wasn't much of a pancake eater and asked if would be possible to "scramble up a couple of eggs." I smiled, reminded myself that I was in the hospitality business, and said, "Of course I can."

"Could you make them with just the egg whites?" he asked. "Of course I can," I said never having made scrambled eggs with just the egg whites, but guessing that you could and wondering what I was going to do with the left over yolks.

I then boldly turned to his wife not knowing what to expect. The good news was that previously frozen orange juice was just fine with her as were pumpkin pancakes, but "I'm a vegetarian," she said so "I can't have the bacon." This tidbit also never came out in our chat the night before. Rather than dream up and prepare a non-meat side dish I decided to simply give her an extra pancake.

The offer of coffee or tea brought a not so surprising response. "Do you have (and here he named a tea which I had never heard of and that probably only exists in some remote village in China)?" "No," I said, "but try this selection," as I handed him our regular basket of teas including Earl Grey Regular, Earl Grey Decaffeinated, Cinnamon Apple Herbal, Quietly Chamomile Herbal, Cozy Chamomile Herbal, Green Tea with Mint, Green Tea with Mango, Green Tea with

Lemon, Green Tea with Peach, Green Tea Decaffeinated, Orange Pekoe, and many others.

He thumbed through the basket with a "if-this-is-all-you-have-I'll-see-what-I-can-do" look of resignation and, without comment, found one that he apparently thought he might be able to choke down.

But, let me go back again to the night before when this couple from California - it probably went without saying that they were from California with all due respect to my relatives and other lovely guests we had from California - spotted our vacancy sign and, as we say in the trade, "dropped in."

"Do you have any rooms?" they asked. "Of course we do, we're an inn," I said with a smile, giving them my standard smart ass, but light hearted reply, "What type of accommodations are you looking for?"

As our conversation unfolded while we toured the available rooms, he told me that he was a graduate student - having recently gone back to school after a career in another field - and, therefore, didn't have much money. Unfortunately, I missed this warning sign.

It turned out that they had already stopped at a nearby motel and quoted me the motel's recently reduced off-season rate and boldly asked me if we could match it. I was tempted to ask how it was that they could even afford any kind of vacation much less fly to Vermont from California and rent a car, but I didn't. In hindsight, I should have sent them back to the motel. However, being a new innkeeper and wanting to build the business, I quoted them our standard off-season rates making sure that they knew that my rates included a full breakfast - unlike the motel.

Even before I had finished speaking, he gave his wife a rather classic "Honey, I-really-want-you-to-have-the-best-of-everything-and-staying-in-this-lovely-inn-would-be-the-crown-jewel-of-our-little-getaway-but-you-know-we-can't-afford-to-stay-here-on-out-meager-income" look. There was no doubt that the look was also intended for my eyes. He then made me an "offer."

Against my better judgment and ignoring the advice I had been given in innkeeper's school, I began a little round of negotiations - it was, after all, a quiet time in our neck of the woods (hence our lower rates) and the room they had chosen was going to be vacant that evening if I didn't bag them as guests.

After we settled on a price much closer to my rate than the motel's, he had the nerve to ask for a AAA discount. Enough was almost enough. I advised him that he couldn't have both the negotiated rate and the 10% AAA discount. He actually looked at me like I was somehow screwing him and the little woman, but they decided to take the room.

In each of our guest rooms was a hard plastic sleeve that contained a sheet of information about our inn. Things like check out time is 11:00 a.m., park your car facing the west side of the inn, we charge $10 for lost room keys, let us know if there are any dietary restrictions, etc.

Even though guests nod politely when I ask them to read the list as soon as they get settled in and many of them actually do, so many didn't that I began placing the plastic sleeve on the middle of the bed saying to them with a smile, "Sooner or later you're going to have to move this and hopefully when you do, you'll take a moment to read it." If the California couple read any of our "rules of the inn," they obviously ignored the one about notifying the innkeeper about dietary restrictions.

Soon after they moved their stuff into the room, they cranked up the heat, left the room door open and went out to dinner. Fortunately, I saw this happen so I turned down the heat and closed their room door.

The next morning, after they finally finished their made-to-order breakfast, the 'missus' asked me if it was all right for them to check out about 1:30 or so that afternoon since they wanted to get in some cross country skiing and would like to take a shower before heading on to their next destination. I can only assume that this one-two approach to negotiating what I thought was the last ounce of service from us was pre-planned. He, after all, had negotiated the room rate and the special breakfast. Now it was her turn to beg for more time. And now I also understood why they didn't stay in the motel.

Applying one of my personal standards of always taking the high road, I said that a 1:30 check out would be fine. The room wasn't rented for that night anyway so I could afford to be a nice guy and we'd still have time to get it ready for another drop in. Who knows, I thought, maybe these jerks have nice friends and relatives who will find out how gracious we were.

With the heat back on high even though they would be gone for several hours, they went skiing. At least this time they had closed the door to the room. However, having previously experienced their unabashed energy inefficiency, I went in to their room and again turned down the heat. We were, after all, living in the Northeast and we were on the news every night from November until March with a lead story about our rising energy costs.

Early that afternoon, they returned from skiing. Naturally, 1:30 became 2:00 and 2:00 became 2:30 when they finally got ready to leave. As they were walking out the door they turned and asked if I knew the whereabouts of an auto mechanic since their car's washer fluid reservoir was leaking. Since it was a rental car they were reluctant - no surprise here - to spend much money on fixing it. Having had more than enough of them, I politely gave them the name of *and directions to* the local service station that usually had a mechanic on duty. Of course, rather than leaving, they went back into their room to call the service station.

It probably won't come as a shock for you to hear that they packed up and left without saying good-bye or thank you. Lying atop the dresser in their room was our inn's brochure that I had given them the night before - so much for them telling their family and friends about us. I decided not to spend a lot of time looking around the room for a tip. There are a lot of "takers" in this world and we had just found the authors of the book.

"I shut off the water to the toilet when it began to overflow," said the good doctor when he and his family came down to breakfast. The gang from Connecticut was absolutely charming. He was a dentist by profession and a darn good photographer by avocation. She was the quintessential housewife and mother. The young twin daughters - about 12 years old or so - were cute and extremely well mannered. Even their dog - we took pets under certain controlled conditions (more about that later) - was a delightful guest. They stayed with us during Fall foliage when we were always booked solid and charged the big bucks. As an aside, if you're an innkeeper in Vermont and you're not full during "foliage," you're in the wrong line of work.

A full house for us meant 10 for breakfast - or, to put it another way, depending on what we decided to serve - 10 glasses of previously frozen (see previous story) orange juice or apple juice, 10 bowls of fruit, 30 pancakes (you had your choice of hand-picked blueberries, chocolate chip, banana, or plain if we weren't serving our signature pumpkin pancakes that morning), 30 strips of bacon, probably 20+ cups of coffee, and a large quantity of maple syrup. And, we did this every morning during foliage. I repeat, *every morning.*

And, of course, during "foliage," everyone wants to eat relatively early and get on with the business of "leaf peeping." The word frantic comes to mind.

In the wonderful world of inn keeping, "my toilet is overflowing" ranks right up there with "I smell smoke," "there doesn't seem to be any heat in our room," and "can you scramble just the egg whites?" The only good thing about a blocked toilet is that it usually happened during reasonable hours. After all, most folks, at least those under 50, don't go during the night and if they do go in the middle of the night in an 18th century farmhouse bed and breakfast, they must not flush until morning. But let's not dwell on that thought.

So I located my plunger and bucket. Fortunately, we had a back stairway so I didn't have to parade through the packed dining room with my plumbing tools - another thought to keep in mind in the design or layout of your inn. My goal was to solve this problem while everyone was at breakfast.

Unfortunately, the plunger gods were not with me that morning.

Try as I might, whatever was blocking the toilet was really blocking the toilet. Sweating like the proverbial stuck pig (boy, is that a saying that begs for an explanation), I came back downstairs, stood around for a couple of minutes so I would stop perspiring, washed my hands, and continued to assist with the breakfast chores wondering what I was going to do about the Connecticut family since each of them was probably going to have to "take one for the road" before they left.

Under the category of "good things happen to good people," the couple in the room across the hall had breakfast earlier than the Connecticut Yankees and were leaving before them. It didn't take many of my persuasive powers to convince Doc, the little woman, and the kids to use the bathroom in the room next door - after a quick cleanup, of course.

That bit of fortuitous timing may have solved their immediate problem, but it did little to solve mine - the toilet, you see, was still blocked. Now, however, I had time on my side. So, after everyone had either checked out or left the inn for their personal walk in the woods or to stroll through one of Woodstock's many antique shops, gift shops, and art galleries, I went back in the bathroom armed, this time, with liquid drain opener along with my not-so-trusty plunger and bucket.

A few minutes after pouring in the drain opener, the bathroom began to resemble a scene from the movie "Mister Roberts" when Ensign Pulver, played brilliantly by a very young Jack Lemmon, exploded his homemade stick of dynamite in the ship's laundry. Soapsuds everywhere and I mean everywhere.

The blockage had apparently been caused by one of our small bars of soap somehow landing in the toilet and now you and I both know what happens when a bar of soap is attacked by liquid drain opener. It's not a pretty sight. Or, actually, it might be considered a pretty sight under slightly different circumstances.

The bad news was the quantity of suds. The good news was that the conversion of the soap from a bar into suds unblocked the toilet. Perhaps, also, it was God's way of telling me to clean the bathroom floor - as in *really* clean the bathroom floor.

One day during Fall foliage we had what appeared to be the innkeepers dream situation - a full house and everyone who had stayed with us the night before was staying over. No guests were going to be checking out and no new guests were going to be checking in and it was going to be a sunny day. So we told our guests at breakfast that they would not have any innkeepers that afternoon. They were welcome to come and go as they pleased, but they shouldn't waste any of their precious tourist time knocking on our door because no one would be there to answer.

After we prepared, served, and cleaned up after breakfast and freshened the guest rooms, our plan was to get away from the inn for a while. Our own leaf peeping tour of the Vermont countryside was in order along with a sandwich from one of Vermont's delightful "ma and pa" country stores.

One of our guests that weekend was a couple from Nevada who at first seemed pleasant and talkative - innkeepers usually like talkative guests because they keep the conversation going at breakfast. If you've ever seen or been part of a group of ten strangers sitting at a table having a meal in stone silence you know how valuable a talkative guest can be.

However, the Nevada couple, it turns out, was on the high maintenance side - quite demanding and rather full of themselves. The stories they were telling at breakfast of where they had traveled and where they had stayed when they got there had us wonder how it was that they ended up staying in our lovely, but unpretentious, country inn. It seemed that it was going to be their mission during breakfast to convince the other guests that under normal circumstances they would be staying in a much fancier place. Even though it appeared that all the other guests were on to their game, it was disquieting to hear them treat our dream inn with such disrespect. And, of course, we were powerless to stop them without risking a scene.

When we got back from our outing there was a note and a room key on the dining room table. It didn't come as a shock to find out that it was from the Nevada couple. It seems as though she had an allergic reaction to something or other - perhaps the pet that one of the other guests had with them, the note opined - and they would not be able to stay with us the second night. The note went on to say that it would be nice if we could re-rent the already paid for room, but they would understand if we couldn't on such short notice.

Thank goodness for rule number one on the sheet in the plastic sleeve that requires the guests to pay for the balance of their stay as soon as they arrive. The excuse we gave on the sheet in the plastic sleeve was that our mornings were rather chaotic what with doing breakfast and guests coming and going, but the real reason is that we didn't want to subject ourselves to, "It's not what I expected" or "The bed was too hard (or too soft)" or "I had an allergic reaction to the guest in Room 4's Rottweiler" or "You're scrambled egg whites were too runny."

The ball, therefore, was in our court. She had her supposed allergic reaction, but we had their money and if we chose not to rent the room, we would be cooking two fewer breakfasts the next morning and the best news was that we (and the other guests) wouldn't have to listen to them trash our place anymore. It would have been appropriate pay back for us to do nothing.

However, as I said before, good things happen to good people. Once again, in this case, we were the good people and, once again, we decided to take the high road and tell the local Chamber of Commerce that we had a room available. The Chamber had, in our brief tenure as innkeepers, referred several potential guests to our inn. It was our turn to do the Chamber a favor and help out some "what were they thinking" tourists who had, somewhat unbelievably, arrived in Vermont during foliage without a lodging reservation.

Just to give you some idea how precious a commodity an available room is in Vermont during foliage, I will digress and share with you what happened next.

Moments after I called the Chamber, my portable phone rang. As an aside, I learned quickly that an innkeeper cannot be more than 4 to 5 inches from a phone at any time. So mine was always - well, almost always - hooked in the rear pocket of my blue jeans. (Yes, blue jeans. Having left the corporate world behind, I had decided that blue jeans would best present the down home unpretentious image we wanted at our inn.) The Chamber was calling to tell me that they had just sent a couple to inquire about our vacancy. Even before I had a chance to hang the little flaps over the word NO in NO VACANCY on either side of our roadside sign which would tell the world - or at least the small part of the world that drives by our inn - that we had a vacancy, a car pulled into our parking lot.

In the car was a rather bewildered looking couple holding one of our brochures, which they had obviously obtained from the Chamber. They told me that the Chamber had sent them, but there must have been some mistake since our sign said NO VACANCY. I informed them that I was just about to cover the NOs. So, leaning in their car window, I began to describe the available room and how much it would cost them.

In the middle of our conversation, my phone rang again. It was the Chamber asking whether the first couple had showed up and whether they were taking the room because they had another couple to send over.

I explained that the first couple had arrived and that I was still talking to them. Sensing the urgency, I asked the couple in the car if they were going to take the room. Sensing the urgency, they said yes. I told the Chamber that the room was no longer available and said to the couple in the car, "Let me show you the room you just rented." And, so it goes during Fall foliage in Vermont.

To close the loop on the Nevada couple, we sent them a credit for the second night of their stay and, to their credit; they e-mailed us a thank you note.

The nervous-sounding man said he was calling from a town in eastern New York State and was inquiring about a room for the upcoming Saturday night. After describing our available rooms and their features and their rates, we closed the deal. The room was for him and his friend and they would be arriving late Saturday afternoon.

When the 30s something couple arrived, he was quite pleasant and she was seriously on edge. It didn't take a genius to figure out what was happening here.

Early the next morning when I was getting the newspaper - I never did get used to this rural newspaper delivery service that being a plastic chute out by the street which required me to trudge out in all manner of weather and clothing to round up the paper for me and the guests - he was in the parking lot having a smoke. Another bullet point on the information sheet in the plastic sleeve in our guest rooms informed the guests that ours was a non-smoking inn, but they were welcome to smoke in the parking lot or in their cars.

During our brief chat, it came to light that his companion was originally from Seattle. I told him that we really do live in a small world because one of the other guests currently staying in our little five guest room inn was also from Seattle. I then went back inside to help prepare breakfast.

After all of the guests had finished eating, except for New York State who never came down to breakfast, I noticed that their car was not in the parking lot. You guessed it. They had left without eating or saying goodbye apparently while everyone else was at breakfast. It was up us to wonder whether it was the fear of meeting someone from "back home" that sent her on her way, but I would guess that is exactly what happened. I went in the kitchen and threw away their food.

The mother from New Jersey and her three daughters - ages 8, 11 and 13 - had stayed in our inn before we became the owners. She was very pleasant on the phone as we made the reservation for a three-day skiing and "boarding" getaway for her and the girls. She said that she looked forward to meeting us and seeing the changes we had made to the inn.

The day before their scheduled arrival, she called to tell us that one of the girls had a fever and they were going to have to cancel. She seemed legitimately apologetic. I told her that I would waive our cancellation policy because she was a former guest - otherwise she would have owed us for one night's stay - and suggested that she consider just canceling the first night and if the daughter was better they could still come up for the second two nights. It was both a serious suggestion and an attempt to smoke out perhaps the real reason for the cancellation. She decided to accept my offer.

The next morning she called and launched into a convoluted tale which included being stopped by the police for running a stop sign while on the way to the doctor's office with her sick daughter, having her car impounded by the police because her driver's license had expired, being dropped off at the doctor's office by the police, and having been driven around town to solve the expired license and impounded car problems by another patient's mother who overheard her story in the doctor's waiting room. It was too far fetched not to be true.

Convinced that this was all a preamble to canceling the rest of the reservation, I was pleasantly surprised to hear the end of the story. The daughter was better and they were on their way. "We might be a little late," she said, "but we'll be there."

Let me interject here that our official check in time was anytime after 3:00 p.m. Most guests arrived in the late afternoon after either driving directly to the inn or sightseeing or skiing in the earlier part of the day and arriving at the end of the day when those activities were over. This gave them time to check in and then go out to dinner. The bottom line is that most guests arrived between 3 p.m. and 6 p.m. give or take a minute.

Long about 10 p.m. when all of the other guests were back from dinner and tucked snugly - we could only hope - in their beds and, some of them probably asleep, and I was thinking that we were going to have our first "no show," the door bell rang.

In charged the New Jersey mom and her kids and their ski boots and their luggage and their stuffed animals. They were pleasant and respectful of the inn and our furnishings, but their arrival was extremely chaotic considering the time of day, or rather the time of night. Naturally, their room was on the second floor which required them to pass every other guest room door on the way to theirs. There must be another corollary of Murphy's Law at work here. The girls were personable, but wired. They must have been overtired or it may have been caused by something they had for dinner.

Our decorating scheme included several small antique items scattered about the inn that often became the subject of the guessing game "What is this?" Of normal course and at normal times we thoroughly enjoyed playing that game with our guests. A real icebreaker. This, however, was not normal course or normal times. But, the kids were full swing into the "game" anyway and playing at a rather high decibel level. "What's this?" " What's this used for?" Mom was oblivious.

It took a great deal of my wit and charm to calm everyone down without insulting them. Then, to quote Samuel Pepys, "And so to bed."

The next two days were rather uneventful. Except for the fact that in a couple of chance conversations, I did learn more about mom and her relationship with her ex than I needed to know, but I have learned that the innkeeper, the bartender, the barber, and men of the cloth have to share at least one trait in common - that of being a good listener. It is rather amazing how quickly friendships can develop and how intense they can become in a two or three-day period.

With thanks for a delightful stay all around, mom and the kids left after their second night. Their plan was to ski or board most of the day and head back to New Jersey by late afternoon. So we cleaned their room - in this case changing the linens on two beds since they had stayed in the guest room with the hide-away - mopped the floor, scrubbed the bathroom (four women had used this one bathroom for two days) and got the room ready for a new guest. We didn't have one booked, but the room was ready. Let me tell you how much more of an effort this is than merely freshening an occupied room.

Almost the moment we walked out of the room having checked under the bed as we did so, the phone rang. Mom had just learned that none of the kids had school the next day thanks to the government proclaiming the third Monday in January Martin Luther King, Jr. Day - one would have thought that mom would have known this, but one would have been wrong - and she was wondering if it was possible to come back to the inn for another night.

Again, reminding myself that we were in the hospitality business, the answer, of course, was "Yes, we'd be delighted to have you back." So, here they came - luggage, boots, stuffed animals, et al for a one-night's stay.

It was obvious by the sounds coming out of Room 1 what was going on in there. Knowing that you're in an old farmhouse, you'd think that you would try to keep your groaning and moaning to a minimum. Not so in this instance. The problem was that I was standing in the front entrance hallway just outside Room 1 with a lovely middle-aged couple who was just checking in.

To pretend that nothing was happening would have been foolhardy. To try to quickly spirit them into the Sitting Room and away from the sounds of ecstasy would have been clumsy at best. What to do? What to say?

Holding out my hand in a gesture designed to casually direct them toward the Sitting Room, I said, "We do have very comfortable beds." The ice was broken and we all had a mild chuckle.

Ours was a pet friendly inn. We allowed pets in certain rooms and under certain conditions. We actually had another smaller plastic sleeve that we put in the room when we had a guest with a pet. It contained our four pet rules. 1. The pet could not be left alone in the room except during breakfast. 2. The pet could not sleep on the bed on sit on any other fabric furniture. 3. The pet should only be walked on a certain path behind the inn so nobody had to pick anything up. And 4. When the owner and the pet returned from one of the walks, both the pet and the owner had to wipe their feet.

We certainly didn't expect the average - even the above average - pet to be able to wipe its own feet, so we kept a basket of towel scraps by the front door. The sign above the basket stated:

PLEASE USE THESE LITTLE
TOWEL PARTS TO WIPE
YOUR PET'S FEET
THEN
PLEASE USE THE RED
RUG BY THE DOOR TO
WIPE YOUR FEET

Thank You
The Floor Cleaner

Credit where credit is due. The day we moved into the inn and for the next three days my brother Jon and his friend Barbara came up from New York to help us get settled in. They also brought Jon's two - not one, but two - Golden Retrievers. Naturally it was raining. It rained or snowed so often when we had guests with pets, that the local weatherman called us before he gave the forecast knowing that we could predict it better than he could. It was brother Jon's idea to create the basket of towel parts and it worked very well.

The young couple from New York City was booked into our most luxurious room for a four-night stay in peak time at our highest rate. Life is good, I thought. This was one of the reservations that we inherited when we bought the inn and the reservation slip simply had a check mark in the space next to the word Pet(s). In came New York City with a one-year old Rottweiler, which had never seen or at least had never tried to navigate a set of stairs before. Why is it that everybody in New York City - all of whom live in apartments - have pets? Big pets? Perhaps for protection?

Any way, for a young and powerful dog, Mocha was well trained, especially when she took her owner for a walk. Mocha, you see, went wherever Mocha wanted to and at Mocha's pace.

After they had brought in enough luggage to set up a wilderness homestead if they ever got stuck out on the road, he went back to the car and brought in a huge folding wire cage, a massive quantity of dog food, a dog bed, dog toys, dog dishes, and a dog blanket. Mocha wanted for nothing - except perhaps for the pleasure of another Rottweiler.

It was then that we decided that we would no longer allow pets in our only fully carpeted guest room.

The next morning at breakfast brought the usual full house chaos. Guests coming and going. Food coming in and out of the kitchen, etc. So it was almost by happenstance that I noticed that the New York couple and Mocha were getting into their Mercedes SUV - *before they had breakfast.*

Guessing that perhaps they didn't understand that when you stay at a bed & breakfast your breakfast is included, I ran out to the car to ask if everything was all right.

"We really don't like eating our meals with other people," he said. "We'll just grab a cup of coffee and a roll somewhere in town. But, thanks anyway."

We knew they came and went because every now and then we heard Mocha try to climb the stairs, but we never saw them again - literally never saw them again. I'm not sure if they did it on purpose, but it seemed as though they timed their coming and going to coincide with when we were otherwise occupied with breakfast or other guests' needs or simply not around.

That is until the morning after their third night. He caught my attention from the Sitting Room as I was serving breakfast and he signaled me over. I excused myself from the other guests for a moment and met him in the front hallway.

"The weather's kind of crappy," he said and he was right, "So we're going to head back to the city. Thanks for everything. We've had a very relaxing stay." And, with that, they were off. They had already loaded the car - again when we weren't looking. He didn't ask for a refund for their fourth night's stay and they left so quickly that I didn't even have time to offer him one.

I have no idea what they did each day, where they had dinner, or why they stayed at a bed & breakfast. Perhaps it was because we were pet friendly. My only hope is that they didn't tell anybody they met wherever it was that they had breakfast each morning that they were staying at our bed & breakfast.

He was just plain fat. Oh sure, I could dance around the issue and try to be politically correct, but at the end of the day, the only proper word for his condition was fat. And his girlfriend hadn't missed too many meals either. The couple from upstate NY had booked a four-night stay just after foliage season and they were our only guests the day they checked in. When they asked where the best "color" was, I assumed correctly that they were referring to foliage and told them that it was probably in

Connecticut. They had to know that they were past prime time for Vermont color, but they apparently didn't know how far past they were.

I carefully explained to them that God had created November specifically for Vermont innkeepers - a period of no snow, no leaves, and no guests - a time to relax a bit and paint a room or two. It was also the reason that their room rate was substantially less per night than it had been the week before. "There's a reason for everything," I said. The good news was that this did not appear to be too disturbing. They were on a getaway and the quantity and the color of the leaves was not of primary importance. Everything seemed to be on an up tick.

Then came their first breakfast. We thought that we had figured out the proper portion control so that our guests didn't leave the table hungry and so that we didn't throw away a lot of eggs or pancakes or anything else for that matter. Rarely did we get a request for another pancake or English muffin and it wasn't because the food wasn't tasty or because we didn't ask. Almost every one of our guests was a member of the clean plate club. We had seemingly figured out this part of being innkeepers.

However, having inhaled his entire breakfast in record time, Upstate NY asked for more. And not just a second helping of part of the meal, he boldly asked for a complete second breakfast for each of them - starting with the juice, then the fruit, then the hot entree. The coffee, cream, and sugar were also being consumed in great quantity. So back to the kitchen I went and started all over again.

Betting that they wouldn't want a second breakfast two days in a row, we served our usual quantity on day two. But, alas, a second breakfast was, indeed, requested. And, again, on day three. One guest couple - three mornings - six breakfasts.

Once again, however, this story has a relatively happy ending. Our heavyweight guests found out during the third day of their stay that he had to get back to work a day early. Not only did they tell us to keep the fourth night's payment, but they also left us the largest tip we ever received. It wasn't enough to change our lifestyle, but it was gracious and entirely unexpected.

"We're over at Bentley's," a restaurant in the village approximately one and one-half miles from our inn "and I can't get my husband away from the TV. His alma mater is playing in the XYZ Bowl" - here she named either a fruit, or an insurance company or some type of telecommunications outfit or whoever was sponsoring the game. She seemed truly apologetic, but she was obviously not in control of the situation.

It was already early evening and the other guests were starting to come back from dinner and would soon be either going to sleep or doing whatever it is that guests do in the evenings when you no longer hear any noise coming from their rooms - except perhaps from Room 1 when you're standing in the hallway just outside the door.

I told her that we prefer that they check in before 10 p.m. out of respect for the other guests and, at least partially, out of respect for the innkeepers. She said that shouldn't be a problem, but she was apparently unaware of how long a college football bowl game can last what with the extended half time shows and all.

So long about 10:30 and with this couple from Virginia - who were only staying with us for one night - nowhere in sight, I boldly called the restaurant, had them paged at the bar where the TV is located, and asked as nicely as I could if they could find it in their hearts to grace us with their presence within the next few minutes. I even told her - it was not surprising that she took the call lest her husband actually stop watching his precious game for even a few minutes - that I would have the TV in their room turned on so that he could watch the game while she was checking in. I opined that they could probably make the trip from the restaurant to the inn during a time out and that if the football gods were on his side, he might not even miss a play.

Obviously embarrassed, she said that they would be there in a couple of minutes. And so they were.

He walked right past me into their room without acknowledging my presence and started watching the game. He paid no attention as I showed them the room's features - a little walk-through that I developed to make the guests comfortable with the inn and their room. We'll cover this in some detail in a later chapter.

The next morning, when all of the other guests had finished eating and either checked out or gone about their day's activities, she appeared in the dining room - alone. Either she had been listening at her door or her timing was just fortuitous, because this way she didn't have to apologize to anybody but us as to why Mr. Virginia Tech wasn't making an appearance.

All things considered, she was quite pleasant and talkative after we got past her half-hearted explanation as to why he wouldn't be joining her for breakfast - something as I recall about him not being a breakfast eater. My guess is that she has spent a rather unfortunate percentage of their time together apologizing for this jerk for one misstep or another and she had the routine down pretty good.

Needless to say they left without saying goodbye although I'm sure - class act that she was - she would have preferred to acknowledge our existence as they were leaving.

Imagine living with this guy, much less going on vacation with him. He had to watch the game with no concern about her, us or the other guests in our inn - and I'll bet that he only had one drink at the bar that he nursed the whole time he was there - left her to explain his boorish absence from breakfast, left her to eat alone, and, probably, wouldn't let her say goodbye, lest she have to actually face us and explain why he was already in the car with the motor running.

Perhaps he had some very good reason for acting the way he did, or perhaps - as Bill Bryson (in his marvelous book *In a Sunburned Country*) characterized a tourist he ran across in Australia - he was just an asshole.

She had just moved to Vermont, she said, having recently begun working as the personal chef for a couple with residences in California and Vermont - this was the beginning of the six-month Vermont stay - and she was anxious to get away for a day as well as see some of her partially-adopted state. She also had a tiny little dog - a Yorkshire Terrier as I recall - with a stupid little ribbon tied on the top of its little head.

She was our only guest in what is affectionately known in Vermont as Mud Season. Mud Season (March through early May when everything is melting and the roads run with mud) is the flip side of Stick Season (November). No snow, no leaves, no guests. One wonders why her employers decided to come to Vermont at this extremely bleak time of year. Our guest was pleasant and appreciative of my help in suggesting what to see and how to get there. She took copious notes and extremely detailed directions - she was apparently geographically and directionally challenged, but at least had the courage to give it a go.

The mild surprise came at breakfast the next morning. "I don't feed Isabella dog food," she said, "So could you please scramble up an egg and an extra strip of bacon?" Since she was our only guest, I said of course we could and we did and we put the dog's breakfast in the little dish she brought with them.

Shame on us in retrospect. We didn't ask her if Isabella liked her eggs hard or soft scrambled.

There you have just a few day-in-the-life-of-the-innkeeper anecdotes. Trust me, there are enough of them to fill a book and I was only an innkeeper for two years. When you're dealing with people and things mechanical, the anecdotes and the challenges that come along with them just keep on coming.

III. So, if despite all of those warnings…

So, if despite all of those warnings, cautions, hints, and anecdotes you still want to be an innkeeper - What size inn should you buy? What type of inn should you buy? Where should it be located? What do you expect from it in terms of income and lifestyle? How long do you expect to be an innkeeper - remembering that this is an extremely high burnout profession and your chances of lasting five years or more while maintaining even a semblance of your sanity not to mention your marriage (or should I say your relationship with your significant other to be politically correct?) are very remote? How much of your savings or your early retirement buyout are you willing to throw at your dream? How much of your social life and personal travel are you willing to give up? Are you really a good enough plumber, electrician, painter, plasterer, landscaper, graphic designer, interior decorator, bookkeeper, customer service wizard, advertising executive, cook, purchasing manager, space planner, accounts payable clerk, work flow scheduler - I could go on, but you get the picture - to do all of these tasks for a living? And, finally, how do you go about finding, buying, and running the inn of your dreams?

So if you really believe that you are mentally, physically and financially ready to take the plunge, let's try to answer the first question - what size inn should you buy?

A. The size of your inn...

The size of your inn is a reflection of a whole bunch of factors. Pay close attention.

To begin with, the size of your inn really depends on how much money you intend to make (pardon me while I stop laughing and climb back up into my chair) and how much time you want to spend unblocking toilets. There are absolutely no rules here, but until you get to the eight to ten guest room size, don't expect the inn to do much more than cover its own expenses. Therefore, if a four or five guest room inn sounds just charming and would appear to be the right workload for your early retirement years or your dream life as an innkeeper, you will probably need some level of supplemental income to make your life worthwhile. As you do this financial analysis, keep in mind that if you structure your inn correctly from a tax standpoint, a good deal of your living expenses like insurance, real estate taxes, utilities, mortgage payments, etc. will be covered by the inn. And remember also that you won't have to spend much money on personal entertainment and travel because you will never be able to go anywhere. So here's a look at the different size inns that you might consider.

We once stayed at a lovely inn just outside of a small town in southern Ohio that had one - count 'em folks, one - guest room. The house was owned by a charming, middle aged English couple, who at the time we stayed there had been in this country a dozen years or so. Clearly, they had no intention on funding their retirement with the proceeds of their inn venture, but they were having fun and they were enjoyable hosts. They also were able to eat out and travel because they had outside income.

As an aside, there is a What a Small World We Live In story that comes along with the mention of this inn. The place was named White Tor. Imagine that - they actually named a one-guest room inn. But, that's not the story. Tor is what the English call a hill that is something more than a mound and something far less than a mountain. In the evening of our stay in White Tor, we were sitting on a small couch in the private sitting room next to our bedroom looking through what turned out to be the owner's family photo album. And there, standing on White Tor in Tavistock, Devon, England were our innkeepers. Turns out that they were both born and raised in Tavistock. The remarkable part about this story is that we had actually been to Tavistock on one of our trips to England and we had seen White Tor. Think about that for just a moment. A couple originally from Cleveland, Ohio travels to Tavistock, Devon, England on a trip to the English countryside, stares for a few moments at a hill known as White Tor and several years later stays at a one guest room inn in rural Ohio named after that very hill by the English couple who own the inn and were born there. Where's Rod Serling when you need him?

One small step up from White Tor and its one guest room - but not a giant step for mankind - was an inn in another small Ohio town that had two guest rooms, which shared one bathroom. There was absolutely no reason for anyone to ever visit this particular town, so how on Earth did we end up there, and more importantly why on Earth would anyone open an inn there? Well, we were there because we were visiting friends of ours who were in the process of building a getaway cabin on a nearby 100 acre site that they had recently purchased for something like $17.95 (and, seemingly worth every penny of it) and, thank goodness, the trailer they were temporarily living in wasn't big enough for the four of us. And, thank goodness, there was an inn in the nearby town. This innkeeper couple actually had another residence in Baltimore, Maryland and shared their time between the two cities. I don't recall if their Baltimore home was also an inn. Clearly, there was a tax dodge at work here although she was very gracious, served us a respectable breakfast, and hugged us goodbye when we were leaving as though we had become fast friends during our two day stay - which we had not

A lovely couple from Newport, Rhode Island stayed with us one night. He was 6'5" and had to stoop over to see his face in the bathroom mirror. You'll hear more about them later in the section on bathrooms. For now, I mention them because they were retired and had a three-guest room inn. Just large enough they said to be busy and make some additional money during Newport's busy season and just small enough to enable them to close up and travel about since they weren't in the business on anything close to a full-time basis. Hence their trip to Vermont. If all you're looking for out of your inn venture is what these one, two, and three guest room innkeeping couples were - God bless you. If you need or want more than that - like you really want to be in the innkeeping business - you'll need to think about five or more guest rooms. Although, having said that, these folks - even on a very small scale - were, in fact, in the hospitality business and had to do or should have been doing all of the things covered in this book to attract guests and make them comfortable. They just didn't have to do them as often.

The next, and painfully obvious, step up from a three-guest room inn would be a four, five or six guest room inn. Depending on its location and, therefore, its drawing power, an inn of this size should be able to at least cover its own operating expenses and, perhaps, part of your living expenses as well. If the inn is located somewhere that has a busy season or two, it will really keep you hopping as our five guest room inn in Vermont did during the summer and Fall foliage tourist seasons. With a fair amount of hard work and a lot of pre-planning, we were able to run our inn all by ourselves. The only outside help came in the form of a snowplow contractor - I wasn't completely insane and Vermont is Vermont - and, on very rare occasions, a repairman. Otherwise, we did it all - cooking, laundry, painting, ironing, room cleaning, lawn care, advertising, room booking, plumbing, etc.

The next step up is a very big one. When you start getting to the seven, eight or more guest room inn you will undoubtedly need a staff. Is that a Pandora's box, or what? Running help wanted ads, interviewing, hiring, training, motivating, supervising, payroll, payroll taxes, employee benefits and, of course, the dreaded unemployment compensation premiums so that your state of residence will have a fund through which your former employees - who you canned for very good reasons, but not good enough to beat back their claim for benefits - will be able to sit back and do nothing but collect some of your tax dollars and, of course, the equally dreaded worker's compensation premiums so that your state of residence or your insurance company will have a fund through which your injured employees - who hurt themselves doing something really stupid - will be able to sit back and do nothing but collect some more of your insurance premium tax dollars. And, what to do in the meantime - the meantime being that time between firing the incompetent bed maker and hiring the next incompetent bed maker? Or the time between the day the klutz who injured himself bending down to pick up a scrap of paper and wrenching his back in the process and his completion of the 18-week chiropractic regimen after which he was able to return to work with limited duties. Guess what happens in the meantime - you make the beds, you clean the bathrooms, you vacuum the floors and rugs, you do the dishes - you do everything you would do if you had purchased the smaller inn only now you have to do it for ten rooms give or take a room. Not exactly what you bargained for in your retirement years, is it? So be careful when you think about the larger inn. Yes, it should produce more income, but at what price? Think about the difference between serving ten people a full breakfast and serving twenty people a full breakfast. Go ahead. Think about it. Then think about making ten beds instead of five and think about cleaning ten bathrooms instead of five and think about doing the laundry - twenty bath towels, twenty hand towels and twenty washcloths - every day - in addition to the bed linens. Mind boggling you say. We'll you're right. Then think about the marketplace for help. Is there a sufficient pool of menial task type folks in your potential inn's location to provide you with an endless supply of incompetent workers? More on this phenomenon later.

This shouldn't be a separate paragraph, but the last one was probably getting too long to hold your attention. During our busiest season - Fall foliage - we could run 30 consecutive days or so at full capacity. That figures to 300 guests in 30 days (assuming two guests per room). Yes, most of them stayed at least 2 and sometimes 3, 4, and even 5 days, but with the exception of not having to change the bed sheets every morning, all of the guests had to be fed and their rooms had to be re-toweled, re-toilet papered, re-soaped, re-pillow slipped, vacuumed, and re-customer serviced. Guests checking in. Guests checking out. Toilets to unblock. Eggs to scramble. Pancakes to flip. Orange juice to squeeze - yeah, right. Now double that for the ten-room inn - *600* guests in 30 days passing through your door and flushing your toilets. Wow! So the size of your inn is an extremely important consideration.

If you really want to become an innkeeping "captain of industry" - or in this field maybe it should be spelled *inn*dustry? - you could go all the way and purchase a 12, 15 or even a 25 room full-service inn. The difference between an inn or a bed & breakfast and a full-service inn is dinner. The full-service inn serves dinner at least to its own guests and sometimes to the public. We won't go into that arena for one main reason. I know virtually nothing about what it takes to run a full-service inn - at least the food service part. Everything else is pretty much the same regardless of your inn's size. By design we chose not to even think about doing dinners. If you are a chef or want to hire one - after another - after another - you're way beyond any help that I can give you.

So, it all goes back to the basic question of what you want out of your life as an innkeeper. If your inn needs to support itself and you, then - based on its location and income or income potential - you'll have to look at the larger inn and subject yourself to the rigors of really running a business. Probably doing all of the business things you foolishly thought that you were leaving when you accepted that early retirement package or finally decided to spend some of your hard-earned savings and kiss the corporate world or your legal practice goodbye.

The size of your inn can be deceiving, however. We are aware of six and eight room inns that run at staggering 65% occupancy levels and, therefore, need a substantial staff in addition to a major league commitment on the part of the innkeepers. I'm not sure that they wanted to be that successful when they launched their ventures, but there can be a fine line between being too busy and not being busy enough. For your information, the national average occupancy level for inns is something like 35%. I say "something like" because very few innkeepers tell the truth about their actual occupancy percentage until they pay their taxes or put together their marketing package in preparation to selling their inn. And, even then, the truth may not come out. More on that later in the section on buying your inn.

One of the keenest minds I have ever had the pleasure of dealing with was possessed by one Sid Lewine. Sid was, for many years, the head of a major medical center in Cleveland, Ohio. When he finally decided to retire many of his business associates begged him to provide their companies with consulting services. So Sid became a reluctant, but excellent consultant in the health care field. I once asked him how his consulting practice was going. He replied, "When the phone rings, I'm a consultant. When the phone doesn't ring, I'm an unemployed gardener and grandfather." The same can be said for innkeepers. When the phone rings, you'll be an innkeeper. When the phone doesn't ring, you'll be an unemployed retiree with a very large mortgage payment. You might also be a gardener and grandfather, but that's not the point of this part of the story. We'll deal more in this area later when we talk about advertising and promotion, but for now, be aware that, in the main, there's not much that you can do to create customers if you're running a rather small inn. Therefore, your percentage of occupancy, which will dictate your income, will be pretty much out of your hands.

There is one other factor that may assist you in determining the size of your inn - government regulations. Again, we'll deal with this delightful phenomenon in greater detail later, but you should be aware of the fact that the village of your dreams where you always wanted to open or buy the inn of your dreams may have a funny regulation or two that will turn your dream into a nightmare. Maybe the town fathers think that too many of their fine old homes are being converted into inns and have passed legislation that makes buying and owning an inn quite problematic. Or maybe the village doesn't have any challenging restrictions, but the state does. Again, we'll deal more with this issue later.

B. The location of your inn...

The location of your inn will be critical to its success. If you're more than say twelve years old, you probably have heard the old real estate adage that the value of a piece of property is based on three factors - location, location, and location. Well of course that adage also applies to the value of inns. With very few exceptions, your inn will not be an end destination in itself - the place people go because your inn is so special that its location doesn't matter. It will either be a stop along the way or a place to stay when your guests get to where they were headed - like Vermont in the Fall. So its value, like most other pieces of real estate, will be determined by its location. And if its value is a function of its location, where should it be located?

You will now begin to see that several of the issues we will be dealing with are interrelated. The size of your inn as we learned in the last section will be, at least in part, a reflection of how much money and time you want to throw at your dream. By the same token, as you are about to learn here, the value of your inn will be, at least in part, a reflection of its location. There are general rules of thumb that should determine the price of an inn - things like so many dollars per guest room (some wizards say that a range of $80,000 - $120,000 is appropriate) or a multiple of the inn's gross income (some of the same wizards use 6 or 7). Whereas, those numbers may hold for an established inn in most markets, there is also a vanity factor that may come into play. It goes something like this, "If you want to buy an inn in a really special place that has a lot of charm and travelers, you're going to pay through the nose. So you can ignore the rules of thumb."

There are actually two questions that are triggered by the last paragraph. What is a "rule of thumb" any way? And, how and why do we actually "pay through the nose" for something? But, once again, I digress. The point is that you may end up paying a vanity premium for the privilege of being an innkeeper in selected markets. This goes back to the point that you should not even think about going into this business to make money.

But, let's return to the issue of your inn's location. The real first question that you need to answer is "Where do I want to live?" Because at the end of the day and actually at the beginning of the day as well, you will become a resident of the community in which your inn is located. And, here you really have to do a lot of homework. I'm talking about some serious, in depth, sweat bullets, cram for the final exam type homework. The following issues are not in order of importance and the list is probably not complete, but you should spend a lot of time dwelling (no pun intended) on them and maybe adding some of your own.

Assuming that you currently live in a large town and your inn will be in a small town - because most of them are - you have to answer this basic question. Do I really want to live in a small town? Small town issues include the fact there may be only one Chinese restaurant (our town didn't even have one); there may not be a movie theater (this is not as important as it used to be what with cable television and VCRs and DVDs, but it is something you may want to consider); speaking of VCRs and DVDs, there may not be a rental store within an acceptable driving distance (although this may not be an issue what with the ability to get them through the mail); everybody in the town will eventually know your name - perhaps that's a good thing - and everybody will immediately know your business - that may or may not be a good thing (we had people we barely knew tell us that business must be pretty good because they saw cars with out of state license plates in our parking lot - and these were not other innkeepers scoping out the competition, they were just town folk driving by); depending on the town, there may not be enough for you to do in the off season - assuming that your inn will have an off season - to keep you out of trouble and your mind occupied; since you're not going to serve lunch or dinner in this innkeeping scenario, you need to be sure that there are good quality restaurants in various price ranges nearby; unless you are truly a jack of all trades, there must be a substantial cadre of modestly-priced tradespeople within spittin' distance of your inn - remembering that some of them may have to get to your place very quickly and at odd hours; unless you're really good with a hose and, of course, own your own pumper, you will have to rely on the local fire department and, hopefully it's the full time paid variety (as an aside, I have to admit that I've never been totally comfortable with the concept of a volunteer fire department for the same reason that I've never been totally comfortable with the concept of a volunteer dentist or a volunteer open heart surgeon - there are some things that just cry out for a paid professional and besides, why do they call it a fire department rather than a put out the fire department?); since this list can go on and on, I'm going to stop here and start another paragraph on the same subject.

Depending on the size of the town, there may be only one road in and one road out and it will probably be the same road which makes driving about rather boring; on the positive side, you won't have to join all of the local chapters of the various civic organizations - Rotary, Lion's, Moose, Elk and whatever - in order to make friends because the membership of each club will be the same 12 people; the touring company of Les Miz probably won't make it to your town, so be aware of the fact that you may have to travel some distance for cultural events unless, of course, you consider the annual local talent show a cultural event - perhaps fearing the worst in attendance, the local talent show in our town was called The Community Showcase, but alas "a rose by any other name..."; depending on how healthy you are or how lucky you feel, you should give a lot of points on your weighting scale to the quality of health care which will be available - we actually had the choice of several full-time dentists, but the nearest oral surgeon who I never gave a crack at my apparent root canal, was several miles away in a not altogether large town; your choice of barbers and hair dressers could be more limited than your choice of doctors and may be a more important consideration - the good news here is that everyone will look as bad as you do which helps to reduce the embarrassment factor. I hope that I've made my point with these examples. There are several excellent books on the nuances and culture shock of moving from a large town to a small town and I strongly suggest that you read every one of them.

If, for some reason, your lifestyle change to becoming an innkeeper will have you moving *from* a small town *to* a large town, please read the last two paragraphs backwards. Actually, I've never seen any books on the subject of moving to a large town probably because nobody ever moves from a small town to a large town so who would buy the book, but it could happen and I would imagine that the culture shock would be just as severe.

If you want to avoid all of that culture shock business which would then allow you to concentrate on becoming an innkeeper, if you currently live in a small town, look for an inn in a small town and if you currently live in a large town, look for an inn in a large town. Believe it or not, there are actually inns in large towns and many of those that we visited were extremely nice and catered to an interesting clientele. We stayed in a lovely Italianate town house inn in Columbus, Ohio which at any given moment could play host to visiting professors and the like as well as tourists - yes, tourists actually visit Columbus, Ohio - and it all made for interesting breakfast conversation. In a similar vein, we stayed in a charming, albeit somewhat Victorian, townhouse inn in Richmond, Virginia right in The Fan as they call a section of the old city. So it can be done and done successfully giving the innkeeper as well as the guests all of the culture, traffic lights, Chinese restaurants, and dentists that they could want.

C. North, south, east or west ...

North, south, east or west are other factors to consider. In the previous section we talked about whether your inn should be in a small town or a big town or a resort town and things like that. Now you need to focus on the area of the country you want to live in so your search can begin to take shape. Here are some factors to help you in this process.

How much do you like to shovel snow? If you have never lived in the north and have fantasized about charming New England Currier & Ives winters - wake up. They are, admittedly, lovely to look at, but consider what you will be faced with as an innkeeper. Guests arriving late or not at all because of severe weather conditions; vehicles stuck in your parking lot or driveway or down the road and your guests calling you for help; guests' vehicles smacking into each other in your parking lot and you, in the onset of your retirement, getting a serious workout either moving the snow or paying for someone else to do it. Here in Vermont we experience 12" to 18" to 24" snowstorms. And the overnight temperatures can hit 25 degrees below zero and they can hit it several days in a row. And, of course, there are always those breathtaking ice storms. So, even if you have lived in the north and think you can handle all of this, why would you want to? You'll have enough to do just running the inn of your dreams.

On the positive side is the fact that depending on where you are - like in Vermont - of all these winter challenges may be offset by a bunch of winter guests who come to ski and snow board. So if you're going to live in the north and subject yourself to the slings and arrows of winter, you might as well live near some really top flight skiing and boarding.

How much do you like to sweat as in South Carolina in August sweat? Take everything I wrote above and flip it around for the inn of your dreams being in a serious southern clime. Of course, in the deep south, your guests' vehicles won't slide into each other in the middle of winter, but they might get slammed up against your inn during a hurricane. And, think of the fun you'll have doing the yard work in 100 degree plus afternoons.

And, in the far west, your inn may get thrown into the ocean by an earthquake. The phrase "pick your poison" comes to mind. I've exaggerated (except for the ferocity of Vermont winters) for emphasis, but you get the idea. Weather will dictate much about your life as an innkeeper - when guests will arrive, how much work you will do or pay to have done and when you will be able to take your own time off. All things to carefully consider before you begin your search.

And speaking of how weather conditions dictate much of what your innkeeping life will be about, during your search try to see the inn of your dreams at different times of the year. Don't just visit an inn in the coastal Carolinas in late spring and early summer. The local highway department posts those hurricane route evacuation signs on certain roads for a reason. Don't just visit an inn in Vermont during Fall foliage. Try Vermont in what is affectionately known as "mud season"- late March through early-May. If you never thought about what happens to all of the snow and ice that has had tons and tons of sand poured on top of it for traction all winter long, come to Vermont in April. It is seriously ugly and seriously bleak, and seriously filthy. And now try to traverse that lovely unpaved country road that leads your guests from the "big road" to your charming inn tucked away in the countryside.

There is a reason for everything and the reason that there are down times in the tourist traffic in almost every place you will look is invariably weather related. If no one wants to go there at certain times of the year, why would you want to live there? But, you may want to live there because no place is perfect and you need the downtime to get away and/or paint a room. Just be aware of the year round weather conditions and their impact on your new life not to mention your workload and your expenses.

Weather isn't the only geographical factor to take into consideration, however. I met an innkeeper couple from somewhere in New Jersey who bought the inn of their dreams in a small town in Ohio. They had done a serious rip and tear on a charming Victorian home which she was running as a four guest room inn while he was running an old fashioned ice cream parlor around the corner on Main Street - it really was named Main Street. When I asked how they had ended up in Ohio, they said that Ohio wasn't necessarily their goal, but it was within a one-day's drive from her mother who still lived in Jersey. That was their geographical criteria. They had actually begun their search by drawing a circle on a map with a 600-mile radius from mom.

Maybe you want to be within so many miles of a major city so you can travel there every so often to refresh your memory on what traffic jams are like and in the process remind yourself how wise you were to leave them behind and live in the country or in a small town. Maybe you want to be within so many miles of an international airport so it will be easier for you to take those vacations you planned to take in your retirement. Never mind the fact that as an innkeeper you will never be able to go anywhere. Maybe you want to be within so many miles of a major medical facility as you come to the realization that you really aren't as young as you used to be. Maybe you want to be within so many miles of a major highway interchange so guests can get to you more easily and so that you can plan your own periodic escapes more easily. Maybe you want to be within so many miles of a McDonald's restaurant although I can't imagine why. And, so on. Think about the things that are really important to you and factor them into the geography of your search.

This is your chance to combine the best of all of your worlds, so take it. Keep in mind that you will probably be buying an inn that people will be going to on their vacations. How cool is that? You will actually be living in a place that folks pay to travel to. How fortunate you will be to live in a vacation destination, but you need to plan wisely and factor into your search all of your personal likes and dislikes. Being an innkeeper in a location that doesn't fit who you are and what you want is a sure recipe for disaster. And, even if it all does fit, remember that as an innkeeper the time that you will have to be able to enjoy everything around you will be severely limited.

So after you've decided to live in a small town or a large town (or maybe even a medium size town or maybe out in the country) and where that town should be located or how far out in the country you are comfortable, you can really begin to think about the other location considerations relative to your dream inn. I mentioned earlier that there are three types of inn locations - an end destination (your guests will go to your inn for the sole purpose of going to your inn), a stop along the way (your guests will go to your inn because everybody has to sleep and eat somewhere and you happen to between where they were and where they're headed) or a place to stay when they get to where they're going. It's your choice, but it's a major one that will have serious ramifications on the price, location, workload, number of guests, and a host of other factors.

D. The end destination inn...

The end destination inn is probably the most challenging - unless of course you happen to get very lucky and completely misjudge who your guests will be and where they will come from. Dear friends of mine (they actually let us baby sit their inn for some much needed practice when they took their yearly getaway) established an inn in an old farmstead replete with a barn and chickens and goats and hens and roosters and a couple of horses in a National Park south of Cleveland, Ohio. In their pro forma which was designed to convince the banking community that their venture had every chance to be successful, they wrote that their guests would be travelers between New York City (give or take a mile) and Chicago (give or take a mile). In other words, a stop along the way. However, as it turns out, they were dead wrong. Their inn has been remarkably successful for many years primarily as an end destination. People go there just to go there. It helps of course that they are within a 45-minute drive of the 10 octillion people who live in Northeast Ohio who think that the "country" begins at the end of any freeway ramp that doesn't have three gas stations and four fast food restaurants. But, they also happen to run a fine establishment that is within a very few miles of many excellent eateries and cultural attractions. They also have a modest, but pretty waterfall next to the inn. And, of course, they have farm animals. Ignoring the facts that farm animals require constant maintenance, they smell, they poop a lot, and they die, city folks just love to be photographed standing next to them.

Using this as a perfect example of a successful end destination inn even though it's successful in spite of the innkeeper's best guess, think of the three main factors that make it so - the aforementioned location, location, and location. A National Park, a waterfall, restaurants all over the place, a whole lot of people within a 45-minute drive, cultural attractions, and a zoning ordinance that allowed barnyard animals.

This very same farmstead inn, run by the very same charming and experienced innkeepers, but located in the middle of nowhere, would surely have died a rapid and perhaps painful death. In fact, it most likely wouldn't have even gotten off the ground. As another aside, my computer's thesaurus doesn't seem to mind the word 'gotten', but rest assured my junior high school English teacher is rolling over in her grave knowing that she had somehow failed to get across to me the point that "gotten" should never, ever be used.

The end destination inn may not be subject to the vagaries of seasonal travelers. People - especially city folk - always need to get away. So if there are enough of them nearby, your inn can be their getaway haven. That's a good thing if you want guests all year round or a bad thing if you want some extended down time. It's early May as I write this section of the book and I just happened to talk to the farmstead innkeeper couple I just told you about. His most memorable comment in that conversation was, "We've had our last day off until November." The reality is that many innkeepers including those in Vermont can say the same thing in May. But we'll deal with that later. Think about it though. NO DAYS OFF from May to November - NONE. You may not be full every night, but you will, hopefully, have at least one guest so you have to be at the inn and be ready to take care of them and of course be available to take reservations for the rest of the year.

End destination inns can be successful even without all of the location, location, location factors working for them, but they require a lot of other special factors, such as relatively easy access (some of your guests may already be wondering why they're going to your place to begin with so they shouldn't be challenged by how to get there), exceptional decorating, common rooms with many worthwhile activities (way more than a 1,000 piece jigsaw puzzle on a card table), outstanding cuisine (this actually gets into the matter of having to serve dinner so you may want to give up on the idea of having an end destination inn right now if serving dinner is not what you're after), lovely scenery or grounds, a peaceful, quiet setting, etc.

One of the huge pluses for an end destination inn is the fact that satisfied guests will refer their friends and neighbors and family members to your inn. And since it's easy to find your place and you are relatively convenient to a whole lot of them, they may actually make a reservation. I'm sure that many of our guests told their friends and neighbors and family members about us, but not that many folks from Ohio or Nebraska or Wyoming or a bunch of other places I can name, find their way to Vermont. So relying on referrals ain't going to make you rich - in fact, as I've said more than once already, innkeeping ain't going to make you rich no matter where you're located or what type of inn you buy or how many referrals you get.

E. The stop along the way…

The stop along the way, as the name implies, is an inn that travelers stay at while going from someplace to someplace else. Either there are no motels around so they have no choice or they just like the inn experience. These travelers will rarely stay more than one night so you're not going to get to know them well, if at all, and, depending on why you want to be an innkeeper, that may or may not be a bad thing.

Most likely, you won't get a lot of referrals from your guests either. Not unless, their friends and relatives are going to travel the same route to get from someplace to someplace else. Your guests' neighbors could actually take the same route since, by definition, they live near your guests, but don't expect a lot of them to show up at your inn. The odds are simply against it.

Your stop along the way inn still has to have a lot of things going for it. It really has to be along the way to things that people actually go to. It has to be relatively convenient to the road they are taking from where they came from and the next place they are heading toward. And, it has to be near eateries. Notice how, in this instance, I said eateries rather than restaurants. Travelers who are just booking in for a place to stay overnight are probably not interested in a major meal, so the quantity and quality of the area eating establishments is not a major factor, but there has to be some.

And, of course, you still should want to make their stay comfortable and enjoyable. So everything in this book on how to set up and run an inn applies to the inn along the way, or at least it should.

One final, but important consideration about the inn along the way is the fact that you will be living there - it will actually be your home, your community. So, you should ask yourself why is it only a stop along the way? Why don't people want to come and visit your adopted hometown? The inn may be the inn of your dreams. It may be just the right architectural style, just the right size, in excellent repair, priced right, etc. But it just might be in the wrong location for you as a place to live. You should spend a lot of time scoping out the community before deciding to purchase an inn along the way or any inn for that matter.

F. A place to stay when you get there...

A place to stay when you get there, is by far the most common inn for several reasons. First and most important is the fact that it has the greatest chance to be successful. And, if the location is extremely popular, you just might be successful in spite of yourself. During Fall foliage in Vermont or on Dartmouth College graduation weekend if you are within 20 miles or so of Hanover, New Hampshire, you are going to be full. And, if you have your wits about you - and that may be debatable since you are contemplating being an innkeeper - you will be charging the big bucks and have a very stringent cancellation policy. More about that in the section an actually running your inn.

Even though the place to stay when you get there inn has a lot of pluses - traffic (inn traffic, not necessarily road traffic), a nice town to live in, many and varied restaurants (notice how I'm back to calling them restaurants rather than eateries), manpower (or should I say people power?) to help you run the place, local services like a newspaper, a grocery store, a pharmacy, etc. you still should pay attention to everything in this book on how to do it right. You don't want to be an embarrassment to your innkeeping brethren and you should want your guests to be happy and refer people to you. Even in the best of locations, a poorly run, poorly maintained, and poorly decorated inn is going to fail. And, selling it will be a major problem.

G. Your income and lifestyle...

Your income and lifestyle goals have to be taken into consideration in this entire process.

Don't be mislead by the word income and don't confuse the word income with the word profit. As I've said elsewhere in this book, you should not go into your innkeeping venture with a profit goal in mind - there will be more later on the economics of innkeeping in the section on running your inn. What we're after here is an understanding of what, in general, you want to accomplish financially as an innkeeper. If you're after the big bucks, keep your corporate job or your law license. If you really want to be an innkeeper, read on.

As we said in the previous section, the size of your inn will determine, somewhat, how much help you will need to run the place, how much outside income you will need to eat out, travel, and go to the movies - assuming that there is a movie theater and at least one restaurant in your new small hometown, how much of your personal time you want to devote to unblocking other people's toilets, etc. All of which points to the conclusion that income and lifestyle are very much intertwined for the innkeeper.

If you want time to enjoy your new town, engage in community good works, join the local Rotary Club, volunteer for the board of trustees of a non-profit organization or two, or even throw your hat in the ring for election to the select board, or the zoning commission, or the planning commission, or the how-high-can-the-fences-be-in-our-town commission, you will need downtime from innkeeping. To do all of these outside things, you can buy a small inn where you do everything and still have time available to do other stuff or buy almost any size inn you can afford and staff it so that you have time available to do other stuff.

A key point to consider in the tricky blend of an innkeeper's duties and having a life outside of the inn is the matter of timing. Most likely, when you want to travel so will everybody else and., if you're lucky, at least some of them will want to travel to your inn. Most likely, when you want to go out to dinner your guests will be descending upon you for dining recommendations and to ask for your help in making reservations. Most likely, when you want to go to the movies or to a local play or some sort of community social event, one of your arriving guests will call to tell you they are on the way, but they were held up in traffic and will be three hours late and beg you to wait for them. Most likely, when you want to… Get the idea. Your time won't be your own.

The point here is to keep in mind that income and lifestyle matters should be factored in to your buying decision. As I pointed out before, the small inn needs outside income to sustain even a modest outside-of-the-inn lifestyle and it will give you extra time to do other things besides innkeeping. The larger inn should be able to support itself and you, but if you have to staff it to the point of giving you extra time to do other things besides innkeeping, you might back yourself into the financial corner of needing outside income to sustain even a modest outside-of-the-inn lifestyle. Hopefully that's clear to you. If not, read it again until it becomes clear because it's a very important inn buying factor - maybe the most important inn buying factor of all. Then, of course, comes the fact that you probably won't have time to do what you want to do when you want to do it anyway.

H. How long you intend to own...

How long you intend to own the inn of your dreams is another very important consideration, but one that defies any attempt at up front determination.

Remember that this is a very high burnout profession. It is a lot more work, aggravation, and stress than most innkeepers bargained for - even those who really thought about it, studied it, practiced it, took courses in it, and did everything else possible to know what they were getting into. So, chances are that you are not going to be an innkeeper for very long. I read somewhere that the average length of owning an inn is something less than five years. Sounds about right. And keep in mind that five year period includes the length of time that it takes to sell your inn once you have put it on the market. This means that you may be an innkeeper for longer than you want to be and for the period of time between putting your inn on the market and selling it, you might not be a very happy innkeeper. Innkeeping is a tough enough business to be in when you enjoy it. It's even tougher when you don't enjoy it or when personal circumstances require you to sell.

When I first became an innkeeper, I was asked by those who were questioning my sanity and who cared about my well being what my Plan B was just in case innkeeping didn't agree with me or me with it. My cavalier response was that I would come up with a Plan B when I needed a Plan B, because I was not going into this venture expecting to fail and didn't want to already have a fall back plan in place, which could have a tendency to make "failure" too easy. What an idiot I was. What I failed to take into consideration were the myriad ways that an innkeeper can fail. So let's spend a moment doing that.

As an innkeeper you can **fail** to achieve a satisfactory occupancy level. You can **fail** to achieve a satisfactory income level. You can **fail** to achieve a satisfactory level of personal fulfillment. You can **fail** to understand how much work is really involved and the strain it can put on your marriage or whatever type of relationship you have with your innkeeping partner. You can **fail** to achieve a satisfactory level of joy in your new small town or new big city environment. There may be others, but let's jump ahead to the most important "failure" of all. Assuming that you are going into your innkeeping venture with a partner and because innkeeping is such a monumental lifestyle change for most people, you could **fail** to understand the real possibility that one of you will love it and one of you won't. And by "won't" I mean really hate it. Hate it so much that you have to get out of the business as quickly as possible. Whoa!!! Then what?

Well it points to the need not only for a Plan B - what are you going to do when your innkeeping days are over - but an *escape plan* as well - how are you going to run your inn when you come to the realization that innkeeping doesn't agree with you. And the sooner you have your escape plan in place the better off you will be financially, emotionally, and in every other way. So, how do you plan to be a success and a *failure* at the same time? Well you shouldn't plan to fail, but you should be a realist and know that you might and have your Plan B already in place just in case failure becomes the order of the day. Remember, your Plan B is what you will do after you have sold your inn. Your escape plan is how you will run the inn during the extremely challenging period of time mentioned above - the time between when you decide to sell the inn and the close of the sale. There you are living in the inn of your dreams in the perfect little village of your dreams completely fried, spent, drained, and very mad at your partner for ever suggesting that you should buy an inn in the first place, much less forcing you into actually doing it. But you have to keep running the inn. And, you have to run it well so your "numbers" remain strong which will help facilitate the sale. This is what was affectionately known as a conundrum - which we now call a Catch-22, since the book and movie made that phrase so popular.

Given all of these potential problems, your escape plan should, at the very least, include funds to hire some folks to run - or help you run - the inn. So don't put your last spare dollar into buying and outfitting the inn. Hopefully, there was no need for me to tell you that, but consider it a little reminder to keep your head on straight in the inn-buying process. More on that topic in the section on how to actually buy an inn.

I would love to provide you with all of the excruciating details of the ideal escape plan, but I'm not going to because I can't. Your escape plan has to be your escape plan. It will be created to resolve the issues that you and your partner face as innkeepers. For example, if you always loved to cook when friends and family were coming over and you thought that this would translate into you being the perfect breakfast chef, but you come to the stark realization that you hate cooking breakfast for a bunch of strangers day after day after day, then you have to hire a cook or teach your partner to cook and, hopefully, like it. If your partner has always kept an immaculate house and loved doing it and you both thought that this would translate into him or her keeping an immaculate inn, but your partner comes to the stark realization that he hates to clean a slew of bathrooms day after day after day after they have been used by a bunch of strangers, then you have to hire a housekeeper or you have to learn how to clean and, hopefully, like it. Get it? Your escape plan will be a function of the factors that have you decide to sell the inn of your dreams. The point is that you might need a lot of money to throw at your escape plan or you and your partner will have to engage in a major shift of duties.

I really don't want to mention this next point, but I must. A harsh reality when you go into a small business venture with only one partner is that you or your partner could end up with a serious injury or disease or even, heaven forbid, die. The proper amount of life or "key man" insurance should enable the still upright partner to hire the needed help in the event of an incapacity or death, but this isn't what you had in mind when you embarked on this venture now is it? So a sale of the inn will be the order of the day, but sometimes they don't sell all that quickly and here you are in a terrible situation. Sometimes life sucks.

On the positive side, of course, you and your partner might remain healthy and absolutely love innkeeping and, as a result, you will be innkeepers for the next 10 or 20 years. But, even in this most glorious of situations you must still be aware of the fact that inns don't always sell quickly. So if you plan to be an innkeeper for let's say five years or ten years or until let's say you are 65 or 70, don't wait for year five or year ten of your career as an innkeeper or for your 65th or 70th birthday to put your inn on the market. Start when you're in your fourth year or ninth year of innkeeping or when you're 64 or 69 or so. The worst-case scenario here is also, perhaps, the best case scenario. You might get lucky and find a buyer right away. Selling your inn a year before you planned to is far preferable to selling it a year after you planned to.

I really didn't know where to put this next item, so I'm, obviously, putting it here. If at all possible, there should be a separate entrance to your personal space - or quarters, if you must. This will let you take your groceries and hardware supplies and whatever directly to where they belong without having to traipse through your guest entrance and through your sitting room. Having your own entrance will also give you a sense of privacy and just might make your whole innkeeping experience much more enjoyable.

I. How much you will spend on your dream…

How much you will spend will depend on several factors. No surprise in that statement is there? There is no magic formula - only a host of variables for you to ponder. I have touched on some of these variables elsewhere, but not directly in relation to their impact on your personal finances and the finances of your inn. So put on your pondering hat and try on some of these.

How much you will spend on your inn is a function of how much money you will have left over after you have completed your multi-year, multi-state search. Don't forget this part. The time and money you will spend in your search can be significant. The search can be enjoyable - and, in fact, it should be since your inn-buying trips may be your last trips for a long time - but it will take time and money.

How much you will spend on your inn is a function of how much money you have or is at your disposal. This may sound frighteningly obvious, but think of how many variables go into figuring this out. Where is your money coming from? A cash investment account earning some modest interest rate, but that doesn't lose any money either; a stock portfolio that might currently be in the toilet and cashing it in will require you to shift your paper losses to realized loses; a retirement plan that may, depending on your age, include a penalty for taking out the funds early; the equity from the sale of your home which may require a contingency in the inn purchase agreement which the sellers may not be willing to grant (more on this later); a loan from your favorite uncle who won't consider you his favorite niece or nephew when the loan payments cease while you go about the business of paying for the installation of a new furnace or a new roof for your inn; the proceeds from a bank heist; or an inheritance or some other type of windfall that is just this big old pot of money that you can throw at your inn venture without concern of whether you ever see any of it again - as in, maybe you are just stinking filthy rich.

If you don't have that big old pot of money, how much you will spend on your inn is a function of how much the local banks are willing to finance. And, this is way out of your control. The local banks may already be stretched to their limit with inn loans; they may have soured on inn loans as a result of previous failures; there may not be any local banks large enough to even entertain a loan request - the small town in which your dream inn is located might just be that small; general loan making conditions and interest rates might not be favorable when you are in the market for a loan; and your personal credit history may make you the poster child for those debt consolidation outfits that haunt the Internet and the late night cable channels.

How much you will spend on your inn is a function of how much you will need to activate your escape plan. Remember to figure out how much extra money you will need to run the inn after you decide that you have made a huge mistake and that you really long for the big city, corporate life style after all or that the fates have conspired against you - injury, illness or death - and selling the inn becomes necessary. Please don't work up your escape plan numbers and figure that you will put some money away each month into some sort of rainy day fund. It might start raining the day you take title. An innkeeping friend of mine broke her ankle as the moving van was pulling up to their newly acquired inn. Hubby was left with the tasks of moving in and running the place for quite a while as she sat on the couch in the sitting room with her leg in a cast. And, yes, he had to hire someone to help with the chores.

How much you will spend on your inn is a function of how much you will need to furnish the place assuming that it isn't a complete turn key sale. If you don't know what that means, don't worry; we'll cover it later.

How much you will spend on your inn is a function of how much you will need to make necessary repairs and redecorate whatever needs redecorating from the get go. The chances of buying an inn that doesn't need anything done to it are the proverbial slim and none.

How much you will spend on your inn is a function of how much you will need to prepare and print all of your advertising and promotion stuff - brochures, envelopes, website, business cards, reservation forms, etc. Nothing, well almost nothing, is worse than a guest or potential guest receiving a brochure with the former innkeepers' names crossed out and the new innkeepers' names written in. Unless you buy your inn on the spur of the moment and have no choice - and please don't buy your inn on the spur of the moment - you should have sufficient time to have these things prepared and ready the day you take over. This may not be a crucial matter if the former innkeepers didn't include their names in their brochure or other advertising stuff, but the chances that you will want to use there material are also slim and none so you'll need some funds to replace it all.

How much you will spend on your inn is a function of how much you will need to move to the new small town or big city of your dreams to take on your innkeeping chores. This number can really knock your socks off. If you're moving from a house - and you probably will be - and your house is several hundred miles away - and it just might be - the physical move itself could set you back $10,000 or more. Then there are things like utility deposits and connection charges, transferring vehicle registrations, state vehicle inspection fees, etc. Oh, and how will you get both of your vehicles from there to here? And another. How will you get your pets from there to here? If it's been a long time since you've pulled off a major move you're in for several shocks and a heavy outlay of cash.

How much you will spend on your inn is a function of how much you will need to pay for administrative things like attorney's fees, accountant's fees, and inn inspection fees. Inn inspection fees you ask? Oh yeah. More about these later.

How much you will spend on your inn is a function of how much you will need to cover transition costs like a bridge loan if your house back there doesn't sell in time for the close. Along with these costs will be the joy of trying to maintain and sell your old place while you are trying to find the dry cleaner, drug store, and everything else you will need to find to function in your new town, not to mention running your inn.

Finally, there is a very unique and hidden cost that must be accounted for in determining how much you will need to finance your grand adventure. Boy are you going to be glad that I told you about this one. Chances are extremely high that you will be closing on the purchase of your inn in the middle of your inn's slowest time of year. That's because the sellers, if they have their wits about them, will want to delay the close until after they bag the last of the big bucks of their innkeeping career. The good news about this is that you will be able to adjust to your new environment and paint a room or two without worrying about those pesky guests getting in your way. The bad news is that you will have little or no income to pay for things like your mortgage, your electric bill, your gas bill, your phone bill, your cable television bill, your … Get the idea. You had better establish a pretty hefty reserve to get you through this slow period. And, by the way, this slow period happens every year so you have to be ready for it every year.

Separate from all of these economic factors which all have to do with buying an existing inn are the costs of buying a vacant piece of land and building an inn and furnishing it or buying an old home and converting it into an inn and then furnishing it. These are harder to determine up front. If you look at an ad for an inn you will know that barring some really strange circumstances, that's the most you will pay. Oh, there will be some add-ons, but for the inn itself, you pretty much know what the ceiling is. If you're building new or doing a conversion, virtually all of your costs won't be known until you find the parcel of land, design the inn, meet with architects and builders, and determine the costs to build it and furnish it or find the old home that you're going to convert and meet with architects and builders and determine the costs to convert it and furnish it. This is a long and complicated process. But then there is no specific time pressure because you won't have any arriving guests until your inn is ready to open for business.

Since you're not going to remove emotions from the purchasing decision – at least not in their entirety - you are simply going to spend more than you planned to on the inn itself - trust me on this. We'll touch on this later in the section on buying the inn, but suffice to say that you will undoubtedly pay more for your inn than you should and this will throw all of your projections into a cocked hat. Which, of course, leads to the two-part question, what is a cocked hat and why do we throw things into them?

IV. Stuff to look out for and think about…

Stuff to look out for and think about when you start to actually look at inns on the market is the subject of this chapter. The internal debate was whether this wealth of information should be presented here or in the section on conducting your inn search. But, alas, I chose to present it here.

What follows is a room-by-room discussion of things your inn should include and things your inn should not include if they can be avoided. It's a wish list and as with most wishes they all won't be achievable. However, you should give it your best shot, keeping in mind that even if the inn of your dreams doesn't include all of this stuff at the time you buy it, there may be space, time, and money enough to add them in the future.

You may notice that throughout this section some elements of running your inn have crept into the text. I couldn't help myself. But if you think about this book as an innkeeper's handbook, you will make notes in the margins, dog-ear or bookmark some pages, and otherwise make it useful as a ready resource. The point is that you will refer back to various sections often so where they are in the book is irrelevant. Most of the stuff presented here also applies to your situation if you are building a new inn or converting an old home into an inn. Here goes.

A. The bathrooms are by far...

The bathrooms are by far the most important rooms in the inn - at least from the standpoint of an innkeeper and the innkeeper's guests, not to mention the innkeeper's plumber. Someone once told me that the kitchen was the most important room. It was probably the same person who said that breakfast was the most important meal of the day. After all, the reasoning probably went, shouldn't the most important meal come from the most important room? However, let me respectfully disagree.

Guests will put up with almost everything and anything you can throw at them - a lumpy mattress, dust bunnies under the dresser, a burned out light bulb in the reading lamp on the bedside table, runny scrambled egg whites, a malfunctioning remote control unit for the TV (although in some households I am aware that this could be considered the beginning of the end of civilization as we know it) - but give them a dripping faucet or a slanted ceiling that doesn't allow them to stand upright while shaving or taking care of other bathroom necessities or a running toilet or an errant shower spray or a partial roll of toilet paper with no backup roll within easy reach of the commode and you have yourself a real unhappy, one-time guest.

So when you are scoping out your inn, pay particular attention to the bathrooms. And, if you actually become an innkeeper, keep your bathrooms in perfect working order and well stocked. It may not sound like the best advice you will ever receive and you probably won't tell your friends and relatives that you spent a good part of your innkeeping day tending to your bathrooms, but you'll thank me for this bit of advice many times over.

Once, during our travels we stayed in an inn that had a shared bath arrangement. The good news was that during our two-day stay there were no other guests using the bathroom. And, the more we thought about that, the more we realized that it was a very good thing - especially in this day and age of just plain uncomfortable rashes that can be transmitted in all manner of ways not to mention life-threatening diseases. It also occurred to us that most people have a hard time sharing their bathroom with their "significant other" not to mention a couple from Topeka, Kansas. No offense Topeka.

So, unless the inn of your dreams has one bathroom per guest room and they are all preferably en suite (for those of you who don't speak French, that means they ain't down the hall) or if there is insufficient room to add them, I would strongly suggest you continue your search. To quote Grand Daddy Maverick, "There's a better one in the deck." And, when I say a bathroom or space to add them, I'm talking about a real live, full-size, man-size, stand-up-while-you're-taking-a-leak or a shower size bathroom.

The International Association of Builders, Owners and Architects Who Convert Old Farmhouses into Inns (I don't know if there such an association, but there probably is and they probably have a monthly magazine and a website not to mention an annual convention in Las Vegas) should present an annual Screw the Guests Award to honor the designer of the bathroom who can fit a shower stall, commode, and sink into the smallest possible space. And, if they decide to give the award retroactively, they should send me a handful of contest enrollment forms - I can think of several prime candidates.

If your inn happens to be a restored farmhouse or a restored inn or a restored mansion or a converted barn - anything that required or will require adding bathrooms - be wary. Describing your rooms as cozy might seem enticing in the brochure or on your website, or even when your guests first arrive and you are showing them their home away from home for the next day or three.

However, when he stands up from the commode and smacks his head on the slanted ceiling reaching back to activate the flush handle or takes a shower stooped over under a spray of water barely strong enough to extinguish one of those little striped birthday candles or they don't have any place to put their toothbrushes, shaving cream, curlers, hair dryer, and all of the other bathroom stuff that we find it necessary to take with us on our travels, don't expect them to be smiling when they come down to your lovely, tasty, and candle-lit breakfast.

Not only doesn't the candlelight make your food taste any better, it doesn't make the lump on his head any smaller. The only way to make sure that you won't have any of these problems is to have proper sized bathrooms and the only way to make sure that the bathrooms in the inn you are considering are the proper size is to use them all - before you buy the place. Assuming, of course, that you yourself are proper size.

So during the purchasing process while you are arranging financing with the local bank whose loan officer may sound pleasant, but is probably and correctly convinced that you are very close to being out of your mind and while you are taking care of all of the other matters covered throughout this book, you should make it your business to spend at least one night in each guest room in the inn even if it will take you an extra couple of trips to accomplish this task.

And while you're 'test driving' the rooms, pretend that you are a guest of the inn on your long-anticipated vacation.

Pretend that you've made arrangements to have your cats looked after by that weird cat lady who lives by herself in the big old house at the end of the block. Pretend that you've canceled your newspaper so they don't pile up on your doorstep (forget about the fact that the guy in the circulation department and your paper boy - or should I say paper person - now knows that you are going away and for how long). Pretend that you've offered your neighbor's teenage son an outlandish sum to mow your lawn while you're away, which really upset your neighbor, because the little jerk won't cut his own lawn. Pretend that you've bought a new set of luggage so you won't be embarrassed when the innkeepers come in to clean your room each morning (although you will find out later that innkeepers have far more to worry about than their guests' luggage).

And when you arrive at the inn, continue to pretend that you are a guest. There will be more on this inn visiting later. But, for now let's get back to the bathroom.

Flushing the toilet to test the water pressure at two o'clock in the afternoon while you're touring the inn with the real estate broker or the seller is pretty much a waste of time not to mention a waste of water. Flushing the same toilet at 7:30 in the morning while your spouse and a bunch of other guests are in the shower (not, we hope, in the same shower) and toilets are being flushed and showers are in use all over the place is the real test. The problem with a failed test, however, could be a scalded spouse. Some would suggest, however, that this is a small price to pay to find out whether there really is sufficient water pressure and hot water to make your guests happy.

Even if you are only staying one or two nights (on each of our inn buying trips, you should prearrange with the sellers to stay in a different room each night), spread out your bathroom stuff like you will be staying for several days. And if you're the type of traveler who doesn't spread your stuff out, spread it out anyway. The simple question you want answered is, is there room for everything? And, if the answer is no, what can be done about it? A tasteful shelf. A charming small stand. A lovely vanity. And with one or more of these in the bathroom, will there actually be room for a guest - or two - to do bathroom things?

Also, check to make sure that everything is at the right height. One of our inn's bathrooms had a relatively low ceiling caused by a low budget renovation project during one of the inn's previous lives - either during its transformation from a farmhouse to three apartments or from three apartments to an inn.

Being of average height myself, everything seemed okay when we stayed in this room (although I should have been wary because I am one of a very few adults who fit relatively comfortably in the coach seat on an airplane) and there was more than enough space to hang a beautiful pine mirror above the sink - a touch we added to all of the bathrooms.

Everything was okay until a very pleasant innkeeper couple from Rhode Island stayed with us one night - I mentioned them before in the section on the size of inns. He was 6'5" if he was an inch and the next morning he came to breakfast with tiny pieces of tissue paper stuck all over his face - either he was trying to kill himself a little bit at a time or he had the shaving experience from hell. He took me into the bathroom and showed me that while he was trying to shave standing upright, he was staring directly at the top of the pine frame. Bending over to finish the task obviously lead to all of the nicks and cuts.

Unfortunately, not all problems have easy solutions and this was one of them. We couldn't raise the mirror any higher because there was a light fixture above the mirror and we couldn't raise the light fixture any higher because there was a ceiling right above the light fixture. Raising the ceiling would require, among other things, removing the existing ceiling. Then, of course, would have come the rerouting of the plumbing lines that were running around above the ceiling that served a former kitchen and now a bathroom on the second floor. This would have required the creation of what is known in the construction industry as a pipe chase (a framed-in space with pipes in it), which would take up more room in an already smallish (or as the inn books would say "cozy") bathroom. The other solution was to place light fixtures on either side of the mirror, but, alas, there wasn't really sufficient room.

So without embarking on a major rip and tear project, we did the next best thing - we left it alone. Of course, we could have asked anyone inquiring about that room how tall they were, but that type of question would have sent up red flags that all was not right with our inn or at least with that room. And, we rationalized, that since most people don't use a razor anymore, aren't 6'5" and somewhat challenged in their shaving skills, what are the chances that we would encounter this problem again? As luck would have it, it never became a problem. This would fit in the category that it is often better to be lucky than good.

The point, however, is that all elements of your inns bathrooms must be carefully explored including:

All of the fixtures (the faucets, the commodes, and the parts inside them) should be the best - or almost the best - money can buy. It goes without saying, but I'll say it anyway, that you don't want or need the hassles of making plumbing repairs - even if you're good at it. Likewise, your guests would rather not ask you to make a repair - especially if it needs to be done late at night.

When you're inspecting your inn - we'll deal a lot more in the area of inspections later - pay particular attention to the condition of the flooring around and beneath the commodes. Discolored tiles or partially rotted wood are rather obvious signs that there is or was a problem. And, besides, I'm sure that your guests will be leery of using a commode that looks like it might crash through the floor into the guest room below with them on it.

Make sure that all rusted nuts and bolts and other corroded parts are either replaced or that you plan to have replacement parts on hand and, more importantly, that you have the ability to install them under the watchful eye of an aggravated guest at all hours of the day and night. Or, as a back up plan (I chose this as my primary plan) that you have the phone number of a local plumber who has promised you that he will respond to your middle of the night panic phone calls at reasonable rates.

And while we're talking about commodes, give serious consideration to outfitting your inn's bathrooms with slow-closing toilet seats. I love those.

Make sure that the water lines throughout the inn have either been replaced or at least inspected to determine their condition. The old water lines and fittings might be seriously corroded decreasing your water pressure and they may also be made of or contain lead. You wouldn't want to have a guest drop over at breakfast with lead poisoning - especially in front of other guests.

Without question, make sure that the hot water tank is of sufficient size to handle the worst possible situation - the one morning that every one of your guests decides to take a shower at the same time you're running a load of laundry and, perhaps, washing the dishes you forgot to wash the night before. To avoid at least part of this problem, we made it our business never to run the dishwasher or washing machine when guests might be showering.

A shut off, for those of you who are plumbingly challenged, is that little faucet handle looking thing located between the place where the water line enters the bathroom and the fixture itself. Its sole purpose in life is to enable you to shut off the water (hence its name) to that leaking or overflowing fixture during the time of a leak or overflow without having to shut off the water to the entire bathroom, or perhaps, to the whole house. And good luck finding or reaching that whole house shut off when you're racing around your inn in your pajamas at some ungodly time of the night and you're not thinking all that clearly. If each of your bathroom and kitchen fixtures isn't equipped with a shut off, make it your business to have this omission rectified the day before your first guest arrives. Come to think of it, if you don't know what a shutoff is, put down this book and think seriously about whether you are really cut out to be an innkeeper.

And, while we're on the subject of shut offs, there should be several more of them in the basement which serve to shut off the water to the entire house (see the previous helpful hint), or just to a part of the house, or to each individual bathroom, or to the kitchen, or to the laundry room. When you have nothing else to do, but preferably just before your first leak bursts forth, find out where these are and, for heaven's sake, label them. If your inn doesn't have a bunch of shut offs, call your plumber immediately and have them installed.

For those of you who have gone through life without paying attention to exhaust fans (and I would hazard a guess that includes most of you), those located in bathrooms serve two purposes. The most obvious and, one could suggest, the most desirable purpose (I certainly fall into this camp) is to direct bathroom odors to the outside. Where the odors go from there is anybody's guess, but at least you don't have to endure them anymore. The second purpose is to send at least some of the moisture generated by the taking of a shower or the steam generated by shaving to the same place that the odors go. Once upon a time I looked into the possibility of purchasing a charming and very old home long before I succumbed to the temptation of becoming an innkeeper. For some inexplicable reason this home didn't have an exhaust fan in the bathroom. You wouldn't believe what the moisture had done to the walls and woodwork over the years. And, if your inn doesn't have exhaust fans it's probably in violation of a housing code or two and this should have been noted on your pre-purchase inspection - more on this later. When you go to buy your exhaust fans, once again, you should buy the good ones. Not only will they last longer, but they will be - or should be - much quieter. Keeping noise down to a minimum is a good thing especially when several people who don't know each other and use their bathrooms at different times of the day - and night - are sharing the same home.

Once, a very long time ago on a trip to England, we visited Stonehenge (and, by the way, that's how it's spelled and no it wasn't built by the Druids). The only reason that I bring this up is because in the public bathroom nearby I came across the worst toilet paper imaginable. I'm sure that the local carpenters stopped there to pick up a sheet or two when they ran out of sandpaper. And, believe it or not, each and every sheet was imprinted with a regal-looking crest and the phrase "Property of Her Majesty's Government." It comes to mind that some bloke (I would have said "guy" if this were an American anecdote) who probably toils at minimum wage in the quality control department of Ye Olde Royal Toilet Paper Manufacturing Plant spends his day making sure that each sheet has the proper wording and crest on them and that they are properly centered on the sheet. What do you suppose he says to the little woman when she asks the time-honored question over dinner each night, "What did you do at work today, honey?" But, I digress. The real issue here is the texture of the toilet paper. Once again, for your inn, you should only buy the good stuff. Whereas, your guests will never compliment you on the softness of your toilet paper - I mean how could that possibly come up in conversation and surely you wouldn't want it to at the breakfast table - rest assured that they will tell their friends, family and co-workers, not to mention their dermatologist, if they leave your place with a chafed butt caused by cheap, harsh toilet paper. Oh, and have an extra roll somewhere near at hand in the bathroom.

The same goes with facial tissue. I would have said Kleenex, but then I'd probably have to put that little encircled "c" next to the word Kleenex. Buy the good stuff. The difference in price is marginal and your guests' noses and selected other body parts will appreciate your thoughtfulness. Oh, and have an extra box somewhere in the bathroom or guestroom.

Back to your toilet paper for a moment. Please make sure that the roll in mounted in the holder so that the toilet paper comes over the top rather than from underneath the roll. This isn't really a requirement. It just happens to be a personal preference. And, after you've finished cleaning your bathrooms, fold under the corners of the next sheet on the roll so that it makes a point. This subtle move let's your guests know that you've addressed everything.

Don't have a toilet brush in your guest bathrooms - even if it is in one of those dare I say charming plastic holders with pink flowers printed on the sides. The message sent here is that you either expect your guests to scrub their own toilet (and if you do, don't go into this line of work) or you're too lazy to bring a brush with you along with your other cleaning supplies when it's time to freshen or seriously clean the bathroom (and if that's the case, don't go into this line of work).

Your shower curtains or shower doors should be opaque. Most people don't like to be on display while they are showering (and, in most cases and with all due respect, that's probably a good thing) and the person who cleans your bathrooms (who just might be you) will appreciate how much easier it is to clean an off white shower curtain or shower door as opposed to clear plastic or clear glass. And, if you wisely decide to follow this advice, please, if only for my sake, stay away from those little fish patterned curtains or doors. I hate those.

Whether your bathrooms have stall showers or bathtubs, you should have those non-slip strips installed - or install them yourself. It was such an easy task that I actually did it myself where they were needed. Your guests and your insurance carrier will love you for it.

And as for the soap in your guest bathrooms, think about the fact that if most people liked to use glycerin soap or soft soap, those would be the big sellers. But, they're not. So use regular small bars - one size for the sink and a larger size for the shower or bathtub - and for heavens sake, throw out any opened bars after that guest leaves no matter how little of the bars have been used. This is one area where quality isn't that important. Guests who are fanatical about what brand or type of soap they use, will bring their own. Oh, and watch out for the overly scented soaps.

Unless you really like to do laundry (and if that's the case call me for a recommendation of a top notch psychiatrist), I would suggest that you only have one washcloth, one hand towel, and one bath towel per guest in your bathrooms. There is actually a corollary of Murphy's Law that addresses the fact that the number of towels that inn guests will use is in direct proportion to the number of towels directly at their fingertips. If they really need more, they can ask you and believe me they will.

And unless you like to spend a lot of time and money purchasing towels, all of yours should be white - fluffy, but white. Usually, you can bleach them until hell won't have it and most stains will come out. Don't try this bleaching trick at home with your fancy towels that are the same colors as your designer sheets and drapes. Even this tip is not foolproof, however. It may seem hard to believe, but one of our guests wore more makeup than the late Tammy Fay Baker and used a face towel to remove it. It was so bad, that we didn't even cut it up to use in our basket of pet foot wipes.

If only some of the doors in your inn actually shut tight - and they all should - make sure that they are your bathroom doors. I could go on a bit on this issue, but why bother?

Here's a good one. Make sure that your guests can comfortably reach the toilet paper holder while they remain seated on the commode. The aforementioned International Association of Builders, Owners and Architects Who Convert Old Farmhouses into Inns could give an annual Creative Positioning Award for the most bizarre placement of toilet paper holders. What on earth were some of these people thinking of when they began to screw the holder into the wall across the room from the commode? And, if for some reason, there is no wall by the commode, for heaven's sake, buy one of those freestanding paper holders. And, for heaven's sake buy the good ones that are heavy enough not to fall over when the guest tears off a sheet or two or seven of paper.

Not quite as bad as the toilet paper being just beyond your guests' reach is the towel bar or towel ring located across the room from the shower stall or tub. But it is a very close second. What do these people do, just find a blank space on a wall and start screwing things into it? One of the first things I did when I moved into our inn was install a towel ring right outside the shower stall in each bathroom. Why should a guest have to drip his way across the room to reach a towel or yell out to his significant other to hand him one? And, after all, we're the ones who had to mop the floor. And, every now and then, there wasn't a significant other.

I could come up with several sarcastic and a bunch of off color reasons why so many accidents happen in the bathroom, but one legitimate reason that is easily corrected is the lack of a night light. And, if you really have your guests' well-being at heart, buy the ones that have a little photocell in them so they come on automatically when it gets dark. What we're trying to avoid here is the guest who stumbles out of bed in the middle of the night and realizes all too late (that being just after he's smacked into the wall and crashed to the floor) that he is in a strange place and worse yet, that he's in a strange place in the dark.

A brief anecdote on entering a bathroom in the middle of the night. One of our bathroom doors had to be held open by a doorstop - these things happen in old farmhouses. It just so happened that we had a medium

95

sized porcelain cat doorstop, which worked very well and fit nicely into the room's decor. A charming guest actually admitted at breakfast that when he had to use the bathroom in the middle of the night; he bent over to pet the cat, which, it turns out, looked remarkably like his pet cat back home.

And speaking of light, make sure there is plenty of it in your bathrooms remembering that there is a fine line between not enough, just enough, and too much. Few of us - in actuality, none of us - look good in those Hollywood make up lighting arrangements especially considering that your bathrooms will be used primarily by travelers who will already be traumatized by far too many bad hair days as it is and probably don't want to begin their mornings or end their days examining every pore on their faces. On the flip side, subdued romantic lighting has its place, but not in an inn's bathroom - unless you end up or are planning to cater to a different kind of traveler than most innkeepers. And don't just address the lighting by the mirror - think of the need for an overhead light in the middle of the bathroom and perhaps one in the shower stall as well.

This is a good time to reemphasize how important it is to stay in each of your guest rooms periodically. If you have a hard time putting on your makeup or shaving, by golly, so will your guests.

As a relatively inexpensive guest convenience, you may want to consider installing one of those clotheslines that stretch across the bathroom and retract into a little chrome housing when not in use. Most folks won't need them, but the ones who do will probably include you in

96

their will. Even those who don't use it will probably comment on it favorably to each other.

If this list was presented in any kind of order - as in most important to least important (and it's not) - this item would be near the beginning. Spend an extra buck or two and get high quality showerheads that give the showeree (yes, I made that up) the option to have a shower massage. If you don't want to go that far (thinking that you will be encouraging your guests to take long showers and, thereby, increasing your utility costs), at least get good quality shower heads that provide a steady and even stream of water. Nothing - well, almost nothing - irritated me more in my inn traveling days than a puny and erratic shower spray.

Whereas most folks won't use them - I know that I never did - your bathrooms should have mung-free, wall-mounted toothbrush holders. Our inn had holders, but since we never used them ourselves, their location was of no concern. Shame on us. After we installed the large pine framed mirrors there wasn't enough room in one of our bathrooms for a toothbrush to fit into the holder. We actually had a regular guest (a regular guest is one who stays in your inn on a regular basis - not to be confused with a guest who is regular) tell us rather nicely about this problem. We relocated the holder to the wall just to the right of the sink, took a photo of our handy work and mailed it to the guest with a note thanking her for her suggestion. Guests apparently use these little bathroom accessories after all.

This next tip actually was given to us by another innkeeper guest who stayed with us for a couple of nights and who I boldly asked to critique our inn. Considering the fact that I was a raw rookie at the time, it was pleasing to have them give me just two recommendations - and they were marginal ones at best. She suggested that after the bathrooms are cleaned, the shower curtain be left partially open so air will be able to circulate through the shower stall. Certainly not a powerhouse thought and I debated even including it here, but what the heck - they can't all be pearls of wisdom and it does make sense. Their other suggestion appears in the chapter on bedrooms and is equally mundane.

Here are some additional items: A hook on the back of the bathroom door; a wastebasket with a plastic liner; an area rug with a non-skid backing or it should be tacked down; your choice on whether you want to invest in those tiny toilet articles with or without your inn's name on them.

Keep your bathrooms absolutely, completely, utterly, and totally clean at all times. Get the picture?

Well, I bet that you never would have thought that I could fill up that much space on just bathroom-related stuff, but I did. And if you're serious about being an innkeeper - at least an innkeeper who wants to actually have repeat guests and referrals - you should take all of these suggestions to heart. To do anything less would be unfair to your guests and to your innkeeper brethren - at least those who are trying to do it right.

B. On to the bedrooms...

On to the bedrooms which are the second most important rooms in your inn. Most of this stuff will seem pretty obvious and after you've read this section you'll probably say to yourself something clever like "Oh sure, I would have thought of that." But I can only assume that a lot of these gems weren't obvious to many of the innkeepers we met otherwise they would have done them.

Remember as you go through this list that your guests are quite interested in having a good night's sleep. Therefore, the number and size of the dust bunnies under your beds aren't nearly as important as the quality of your mattresses not to mention the size and quality of your blankets and pillows. As an aside, however, it wouldn't be a bad idea to keep the dust bunnies down to a bare minimum. I mean, let's not push it.

It shouldn't come as a surprise that several of the ideas presented in the last section on bathrooms apply to your bedrooms as well - size of the rooms, ceiling height, lighting, etc. Your bedrooms should be spacious enough to accommodate all of the furniture that a normal bedroom usually contains - if there is such a thing as a normal bedroom - as well as some of the extra goodies that a traveler might expect. And the ceiling height should be a consideration especially if you or your predecessor innkeeper added bedrooms in the eaves where slanted ceilings can, at one and the same time, create charming rooms with nooks and crannies and also result in serious concussions. What is a cranny anyway?

There should also be sufficient lighting to do everything that a normal guest will want to do in a bedroom. If there is such a thing as a normal guest.

So here are a host of thoughts, comments, ideas, and recommendations.

You shouldn't buy high quality mattresses because they will take a lot of abuse. The reality is that no more than one couple per night, usually, will be sleeping on each of your mattresses - 'bout the same number of people who sleep on your mattress at home when you think about it. And chances are that you will only have an annual occupancy rate of 35% to 40%. So your inn mattresses won't be used nearly as much as your own mattress. But, you should buy high quality mattresses because they will last longer and, hopefully, provide your guests with a good night's sleep. This will put your guests in a better mood during breakfast and depending on how good a cook you are and whether it's raining in the morning that could be very important. Also, you should buy the kind of mattresses that do not - ever - require flipping. They're out there, they're good and they work.

If your rooms are large enough - and you should make sure that they are - you should opt for at least Queen size beds - Kings would be better. The only down side to Kings or Queens is that you will have more bulk to kind of muscle around when you're making them. But it's a lot nicer to be able to advertise that you have King or Queen size beds especially if you want to be able to charge the big bucks.

One of the bedrooms in the inn we ended up buying had the bed coming out of the corner of the room with the room's only bedside table no where near the side of the bed. When the former innkeeper dropped over one day and saw that we had placed the bed in that room with its headboard actually up against a wall with a bedside table on each side of the bed, he told us that some of his guests had repositioned the bed like we had and moved the lone bedside table next to the bed. My immediate and not all that perceptive reaction was to say, "Don't you suppose that they were trying to tell you something?" Imagine a guest having to push the furniture around the room to make it more 'user friendly' and the innkeeper not catching on. The bottom line here is that your rooms should be big enough to have a bedside table on each side of every bed and each of your bedside tables should have a reading lamp on them. If for some serious space reasons this isn't possible, think about a shelf and a wall lamp.

And speaking - or actually writing - about bedside tables (or shelves), they should be big enough to hold a pair of reading glasses, a book or a magazine or an iPad, and a glass of whatever in addition to the lamp. At first it was amazing to see what our guests brought with them to consume in the evenings - even those who were only on a one night's stay. But as time went on, nothing surprised us. Wine, cheese, crackers, all manner of dips, soda, bottled water, pasta salad, couscous, fixings for making cocktails, things they bought during their travels like fudge and doggie bags from that evening's dinner. You name it and guests will bring it along or buy it and eat it in your rooms. So you might as well provide them with a table to put it all on.

Part of being prepared for your guests' snacking pleasure should include having a little refrigerator in each room. I'm talking here about those mini ones with tiny freezer sections and those precious little, but almost useless, ice cube trays. Our inn had those and they were not only a tremendous selling point, they were used by the guests - a lot. Unfortunately refrigerators have to be cleaned and scrubbed all the time and those with freezer sections have to be defrosted every now and again. Those are all small prices to pay. But please don't forget to look in them when you're getting your rooms ready for the next guest. Here again, you will at first be surprised at what your guests placed in them and you will also be surprised that they left this stuff behind. But, don't worry that level of surprise will wear away in time.

If you don't want to or can't fit a little refrigerator in each guest room (ours were strategically placed under the luggage racks) - and if you can't your guest rooms are obviously way too small - have a large refrigerator available somewhere in your inn's common areas for all of your guests to use. Be aware, however, that there are at least three problems with this approach.

First of all, how can you make a refrigerator of sufficient size to serve all of your guests unobtrusive? And you will or should want to make it unobtrusive. A big refrigerator sitting in the upstairs hallway, for example, is probably not the ambiance you're after - at least it shouldn't be. And what about those guests on the first floor who have to traipse upstairs to refrigerate and then retrieve their goodies?

Second, how will you know which items still in the refrigerator were left behind by a guest who just checked out and which ones belong to a guest who just checked in or is staying over? Trust me, they're not going to label their stuff no matter how many times or how politely you ask and they will leave stuff behind.

Third, as an innkeeper you will have enough to worry about without being confronted by a guest asking you what happened to their cherished bottle of wine. And what are you as the innkeeper going to do about it? You don't have to stretch your imagination to believe that a guest might steal a bottle of wine, or even a bottle of beer for that matter, from another guest.

There are undoubtedly other problems with having a common refrigerator, but you get the idea. However, if this approach is the only one available - take it. Then try to have your guests cooperate with one another by placing a tasteful sign by the refrigerator that reminds them to only consume their own goodies - good luck wording that so it's not insulting - label their stuff and to take their leftovers with them when they leave. You could facilitate the labeling process by providing some labeling material by the refrigerator.

Even if your guest rooms have individual heat control you should have an extra blanket stashed in a dresser drawer or, perhaps, in the bottom of an armoire. A quality, clean blanket that goes with the room's color scheme. This, of course, assumes that your inn isn't in the tropics and that your rooms have a color scheme. Don't try to dictate your guests comfort level. Your job is to provide them with everything they might need or want.

Picking up on the individual heat control idea, I have absolutely no clue what it costs to get there, but it should be seriously explored. Our inn was so equipped and it was, as my mother who was not all that religious would say, a Godsend - for two reasons mainly. The obvious first reason was that it allowed each guest to set the temperature wherever they wanted without affecting any other guest. Just because the charming early middle aged lady in Room 4 is having hot flashes and doesn't want the heat on even in the middle of a Vermont winter's night, shouldn't mean that the guests in Room 5 have to pile on the blankets or, worse yet, knock on your door at three in the morning begging for more heat. The second reason for having this type of heating control is that it allows you to turn down the heat in occupied rooms during the day and in unoccupied rooms during the day and night. We learned quickly that sticker shock in Vermont isn't when you go to a new car showroom; it's when you get your first heating oil or propane bill.

Buy large, chubby, well-made pillows with removable, bleachable pillow covers and have at least two extra pillows per room. Most of your guests will use the extra pillows to enable them to read sitting up in bed. You don't or shouldn't want to think about what your other guests will do with them. But, remember, as an innkeeper you are in the hospitality business. Ah, but where to put them? We decided that it wasn't in our best interest to store them in our laundry room and require our guests to ask for them, so we placed them in dresser drawers in the guest rooms. This seemed like an obvious location, except for the fact that here they could get in the way when guests actually wanted to place their clothes in the dresser drawers. However, like other problems that seem to defy resolution, this one had a way of working itself out. No guest ever complained that there were too many pillows in their room or that they had to put them on a chair or love seat - or perhaps actually on the bed - in order to use the dresser drawers

During all of our travels we never put one thing in a dresser drawer - no matter how long we stayed in the inn or hotel or motel - but some of our guests literally moved in. Clothes hung in the closet, toothbrushes in the toothbrush holder, clothes placed neatly in dresser drawers. So here's what you have to do to accommodate these folks:

Have a dresser in each bedroom. Seems rather obvious doesn't it? But you'd get eyestrain reading the list of places we stayed whose owners didn't think about this.

Make sure your dresser drawers are clean and, perhaps, lined. And if you're going to line them, do it with something that can be easily replaced or cleaned. And then, remember to periodically replace or clean them.

For heaven's sake, check the drawers when you are preparing the room for the next guest. We could have had a monthly charity clothing drive with the items left behind by our guests. By the way, if it seemed like the item left behind was important or costly, we always tried to contact the guest and make arrangements to send it to them. The heaviest and most difficult to package up and the most costly to ship was a pair of ski boots. How could a skier who is into the sport enough to have his own equipment and fanatical enough to bring his boots inside each night so they won't be cold when he hits the slopes in the morning, forget them? But, he did, and he was very thankful to get them back. He sent a very nice note and a check, which was in an amount way more than the shipping costs. Finally, on this stuff left behind point, our common sense told us that it was better to simply toss some of the items rather than call the guests and embarrass them by the mere mention of the unmentionables. We must have guessed right, because we never got a call regarding any of these items.

Hopefully, your rooms are big enough to have a closet or an armoire. If they are and they do, the same rules apply. Keep them clean and check them after each guest leaves. We always threw out any hangers left behind by our guests so the closets and armoires only had the matching hangers that we provided. It may be a small point, but it made it seem as though we cared - and we did. We placed four padded and four plastic hangers in each closet and armoire and we actually made mention of the quality of our hangers in our advertising. None of those skinny wire hangers that leave peaks in the shoulders of your clothing, we said. The problem was that the plastic hangers kept disappearing even though we jokingly asked our guests to leave them behind for the next guests - see the list of "rules" which appears later in the book. Even though it was always upsetting to have these hangers "stolen" by our guests, at only 8 or 10 cents each, we kept on providing them. If your guest rooms are too small to have a closet or an armoire, either buy another inn or have some hooks or pegs mounted on the wall. And please don't use those little wire screw-in hooks. Let's show a little class and decorating style here.

Buy good mattress covers and keep them clean. Many guests - well, not many, but some - actually stripped the bed on the last morning of their stay. How embarrassing it would be to have them take this helpful step only to find themselves staring at a ratty and stained mattress cover or, worse yet, at a ratty and stained mattress. As an aside, it was surprising how many guests made their bed on the last morning of their stay. Did they think that the next guest was going to sleep on the same linens they just used? In hindsight we could have told them in yet another bullet point on the sheet of rules not to make their beds, but at the time, we obviously didn't think of that.

Your sheets and pillowslips should be of good quality, but I would strongly suggest that you stay away from silk or flannel. If most folks liked them, most folks would buy them. But, alas, they don't. Your linens should also be white. If your inn were ever featured in Inns Beautiful (or whatever the latest inn journal is called), you'd probably like to have them mention and picture your designer sheets, but after you toss your first set in the rubbish because you can't bleach the stain out, you'll thank me for this tip.

If you really have time on your hands, you should iron both your sheets and pillowslips. If you only have limited time on your hands, you should just iron your pillowslips. Depending on the size of your inn and the amount of your previously hard-earned cash you want to throw at your inn's operating expenses, you might be able to find a laundress or laundry service nearby. We changed the pillowslips each morning when we freshened the room for a guest staying over. If they stayed more than three nights, we changed the sheets after the third night. When you think about it, you probably don't change your bed linens at home that often.

Like we said in our brochure, "All of our guest rooms are air conditioned to keep you cool during those three hot days in August with ceiling fans to keep you comfortable the rest of the year." Our air conditioners were through-the-wall units in the bedrooms. Obviously, the amount of air conditioning and the number - or even the existence - of ceiling fans will depend on where your inn is located. Being in Vermont with relatively mild summers, central air is not the order of the day - not to mention an extremely costly proposition to add to an old farmhouse. But having air conditioning does sound good to wimpy city folks who came up here on vacation.

Even though today's younger travelers usually showed up with those duffel bag looking things, most of our guests still brought their stuff in regular suitcases. Therefore, somewhere in the bedroom should be a luggage rack. We opted for wooden racks - painted to match the room's trim - and placed them over the mini refrigerators, thereby conserving valuable space. One constant maintenance problem, however, was the wall behind the luggage rack. Whereas I'm sure they didn't mean it, many guests banged their suitcases against the wall when they swung them up onto the rack. The only two conditions noted by the state inspector when we took over our inn were a hairline crack in a toilet flush handle (that cost me $1.39 and about 10 minutes to correct) and a "dirty" wall behind a luggage rack. The poor inspector obviously had failing eyesight since that's all he noted, but more on that later. Keep extra room paint handy and make sure it is labeled - you know, wall, ceiling, trim, room number, etc. Always remember and never forget that latex paint sitting around even in a tightly sealed can will lose some water content thereby changing the color slightly and the paint on the walls or trim will also discolor from sunlight. You may end up repainting an entire wall or a doorjamb just to get rid of a smudge or two - such is the life of the innkeeper. Another solution to this smudged wall problem is to install a piece of clear plastic above the luggage rack. We didn't do it, but it should work and probably wouldn't look bad.

Keep in mind as you furnish or refurnish your bedrooms that many guests don't "move in" but rather just open up their suitcases on the floor and spend their clothes changing time plucking things out of and tossing things back into them. They need floor space to accomplish these important tasks. Therefore, you may want to furnish your rooms rather sparsely or sparsely enough to allow for this. Any negative feelings that your guests may have when first seeing a relatively barren room will be replaced by positive feelings when they realize that they can actually move around in the room without crawling over the bed and stumbling over their luggage, not to mention each other. If floor space is at a premium, make sure that your dresser tops aren't cluttered with your grandmother's thimble collection so that they can be used for suitcase placement among other things.

Again, don't underestimate the importance that lighting in the bedroom has on the comfort of your guests. We already mentioned the need for lamps on your bedside tables, but I neglected to mention the need for light bulbs in them. And, don't skimp here. As a matter of fact, don't skimp anywhere. Go with at least 60-watt bulbs unless you have antique lamps that can't tolerate that much wattage. Regardless of the size of the bulb, however, you should lie down on your beds - at night - with the overhead light off (assuming you have overhead lighting) and try to read a book. The light should be bright enough and the lamp should be tall enough to make this a pleasant experience. That, of course, assumes that the book is worth reading.

In our inn, the overhead lights in the bedrooms were part of a ceiling fan arrangement and the reality is that neither one (the fan or the light) was used that much. But they looked good and they were a nice touch when we were explaining our guest room features to prospective guests or introducing an actual guest to the room. "Each room has a ceiling fan," we would say. And it sounded like we had done everything possible to make their stay a truly memorable one. But, ceiling fans or not, you should have some lighting in addition to the bedside lamps. Floor lamps would be fine as long as you promise me not to use those $19.95 discount store black plastic numbers.

Each of our guest rooms had a clock radio. Once again, it sounded like we were really on top of all possible guest comforts. However, it seemed as though the only time they were touched was when we dusted them or when the power went off and we had to reset them. There must be yet another corollary of Murphy's Law that addresses the fact that the length of the power outage is in direct proportion to the time it takes for all of your digital appliances to begin flashing 12:00. My assumption is that most guests who don't want to just wake up when they're done sleeping - even though that should be one of their vacation goals - bring along their own little travel alarm. As far as listening to the radio - forget it. Does anybody ever listen to the radio except when they're in their car? Or in the case of a teenager, when they're sitting in algebra class? Therefore, it might be wise to have CD player/radio/alarm clock units in each room.

All of the windows in our guest rooms - bathrooms, bedrooms and private sitting rooms - had window shades. Here again is your opportunity to do the right thing on behalf of your guests and buy room-darkening shades, not just privacy shades. Depending on the time of year and the direction your rooms face, the early morning sunlight could be hazardous to your guests' sleep. You won't score a lot of points here, but the very occasional "thank you" will be worth your trouble and, indeed the extra expense. And since you're not going into this business to make money anyway, you have to go for all of the "thank yous" that are out there regardless of the cost.

Because we had a country inn, we opted for country quilts with matching pillow shams. They really made a pleasant decorating statement and our goal was to give each room its own "wow" factor. We literally wanted the guests to say "wow" when they first walked into their room. The challenge was to buy the good stuff while recognizing that they might not be treated very kindly and would have to be cleaned and then replaced every now and again. Pillow shams really set the room up nicely, but they do require you to buy yet a third set of pillows for each room - one set on the bed, one set in a dresser drawer, and one set in the shams. You could get away with only two sets of pillows if you want your guests to use the pillows that are in the shams as their extra pillows. This means that they are going to have to either remove the pillows from the shams to use them or, heaven forbid, use the shams with the pillows still in them. This could leave you with wrinkled and stained (with God knows what) pillow shams. Did you follow all of that? Whatever you use should be of good taste and blend in with the style of your inn.

Regardless of your decorating style, you should consider bed skirts or dust ruffles. Those are the things that hang down from the mattress to the floor and prevent dust from getting under the bed - yeah, right. It's more like they prevent you and your guests from seeing the dust that will end up under the bed no matter what you try to do to prevent it. Most of the time you will see these in a House Beautiful spread in a country-decorating scheme, but they make simple ones that will fit into any decor. They do give a room a nice finished look whether your rooms are carpeted or have wood floors. But remember - now pay attention to this warning - you still have to look under and occasionally dust or vacuum under your beds, not to mention periodically cleaning the dust ruffle itself.

Most inn guests come from the big city and they can't fathom leaving their precious belongings in an unlocked room. To be honest, even as innkeepers, it was hard for us to get used to the idea of not double locking every door and window when we would go shopping or to our once every three months dining out adventure. So, in order to assuage our guests' concerns and to keep the good folks at AAA on our side, we had dead bolt locks and regular passage locks on each room door. It must give a New Yorker or a Bostonian a good feeling to have a bunch of keys in their pocket even though they have just left all of their stuff under the care of someone they don't really know who has duplicate keys to their room.

112

Each of our guest rooms had its own TV for several reasons:

Our inn only had two rooms that served as common areas - the Sitting Room and the Dining Room. If we had put a large TV in the Sitting Room there wouldn't have been any place for us to comfortably check in guests or work with them on planning their days or evenings - much less just having a place for them to sit and relax.

Even if we did have the space, we learned from experience. Several inns we stayed in only had one TV in a common room. Is it fair to your guests that the first one who made it to the TV after dinner was able to watch his or her cooking show or boxing match or football game all evening?

When I owned my inn you could buy a 13" cable ready color TV with remote control for something less than $100. Now that all TVs are digital, a 15" widescreen flat-panel TV is around $150 and takes up even less space in the room. And what a great advertising piece - "Each of our guest rooms has its own extended cable color TV with remote." Just what the city folks didn't expect in a country inn. And speaking of cable, it cost us about $45 per month for our guests (and their innkeepers) to have extended cable as in 75 channels or so. Small price, big benefit. This assumes, of course, that your inn is serviced by cable. If it isn't, you might want to seriously consider installing your own satellite dish, or, if roofs aren't your favorite place to hang out - having one installed for you. Be careful, most cable and satellite providers specify a maximum number of TVs that you can have on an account so be specific about how many TVs you have and work out the best package for your needs.

Three of our guest rooms were actually three-room suites - bedroom, bathroom, and a small private sitting room. You would be very fortunate if your inn had the room for this luxury, but if it does, you're in luck. This enabled each "roommate" to do a different thing without bothering the other one. One could read a book in bed while the other one watched TV in the private sitting room, or one could go to sleep while the other one read a book or watched TV in the private sitting room, or - well, you get the idea. Later in the book you will see our brochure and how we worded this luxury. Oh, and all of your guest rooms should be able to access WiFi and if not, there should be access in your sitting room or some other common area.

Here are a few other miscellaneous items that you should factor into the furnishing and decorating of your guest bedrooms: If your rooms aren't carpeted, you should have some area rugs and they should either have non-skid backings or be tacked down; each room should have a fire extinguisher and it should be visible and there should be instructions on how to use it; a full length mirror would be nice; a wastebasket with a plastic liner; a box of facial tissues; a flashlight - check periodically to make sure it still works; and a list of emergency phone numbers - even if there is no phone in the room, most of your guests will have cell phones. Speaking of phones, our inn had an outgoing only phone system. This might not seem too important in the cell phone age, but many areas - like small towns - are still not serviced by cell towers and guests need to make calls every now and again.

Finally, I would strongly recommend that you have appropriate - and I stress the word appropriate - lighthearted - and I stress the word lighthearted - reading material in your guest rooms. It never ceased to amaze me that some of the inns we visited had War and Peace and other heavy tomes in their guest rooms or in the living room or in the sitting room. Which chapter did they expect me to read during my stay? And, why would I bother? Here are some titles that we had lying around: Robert Fulghum's classic "It Was On Fire When I Lay Down On It" (by the way, that's an actual quote from a guy who was asked by the firemen how his mattress caught on fire); Art Buchwald's "Whose Rose Garden is it Anyway?" "The Sayings of Bernard Shaw" by guess who (this book was returned to us with a kind note by a guest who found it in their luggage when they got back home); "The Portable Curmudgeon" edited by Jon Winokur; "Flash Fiction - 72 Very Short Stories" edited by James Thomas, et al; "Landscapes of Scotland;" "Villages of France;" You get the idea. Your guests might not want to watch TV. You know that they aren't going to listen to the radio. And this type of entertainment is the perfect alternative to talking to their spouse or roommate.

Oh. I almost forgot. Remember the innkeeper couple I told you about who gave us two ideas neither one of which were barn burners - although I should be careful using that expression in rural Vermont since a neighbor's barn literally burned to the ground during our stint as innkeepers. Their first idea was to leave the shower curtain open a little so the shower stall could air out. Here's the second. He happened to suffer from sleep apnea and in order to plug in his nighttime breathing unit he had to unplug one of the bedside table lamps. At least on that wall, we were underoutletted. (My computer's spell checker just informed me with a red underline that I have made up yet another word - in this case, underoutletted and, I love this part, underoutletted is apparently so far away from anything my computer has in its word bank that it had no correct spelling suggestions). So this guest's suggestion was that we should have sufficient electrical outlets for our guests with sleep apnea. Even though I'm taking bets that you will probably never have a guest with sleep apnea, you should make sure that your bathrooms, bedrooms, and private sitting rooms (if you have them) have sufficient outlets - properly grounded of course - for your guests to plug in darn near anything and that the outlets can actually be reached.

Speaking of the barn that burned down - there are two interesting animal related tales to tell about it. It was farmer MacDonald - yes, it really was farmer MacDonald and you can bet that his family and friends called him Ol' - whose barn caught on fire. Also, it seemed that Ol' MacDonald had a "600 to 700" pound pig that stayed in that barn. Small wonder that it stayed in the barn and small wonder that he didn't know how much it actually weighed. Turns out that the pig kept trying to go back into the burning barn until someone (either a firefighter or neighbor) put a garbage can over its head. During all of the commotion in trying to put out the fire, the pig ended up in the river that ran behind the barn and had to be pulled out by several local volunteers *the next day* about *a half-mile* downstream. Farmer MacDonald was quoted in the local paper as saying, "He's a good pig…a smart pig, too…except when it comes to swimming." It remains to be seen, at least in my eyes, how smart he is if he kept going back into a burning barn. Here's the other animal tale. The list of what was lost in the fire included the phrase, "…and possibly some barn cats." Possibly? They didn't know? Even if you're not a cat person, that's really kind of sad.

Here's a totally unrelated pig story. A fellow on a ride in the country spotted a pig with a wooden leg. Unable to help himself, he drove up to the farmhouse to ask how that came about. The farmer told him that this was not an ordinary pig. "One day," the farmer said, "I slipped off my tractor and hurt my leg and do you know that pig ran back to the house and squealed until my wife and son came to my rescue. Then, just a few months later our Christmas tree caught on fire and that very same pig rushed out of the barn and banged up against the front door of the house until everyone was awake. We were able to put out the fire and save the house." "But," the traveler said, "what about the wooden leg?" "Well," said the farmer, "you wouldn't eat a pig like that all at once now would you?"

So there you have my thoughts and comments on pigs and your guest bedrooms. And now that I reflect on the treasures included in this section, I'll bet that you aren't saying to yourselves "Oh sure, I would have thought of all that." The only thing that should hold you back from implementing all of these suggestions including the ones in the previous section on bathrooms is space - not money.

Think back on all of your personal inn or bed and breakfast experiences - or even your motel experiences for that matter or even staying at your brother-in-law's or your mother-in-law's for that matter - and remember the overnight stays that you truly enjoyed. Then try to remember why. Chances are they were the sojourns where everything was just plain comfortable. Your innkeeper and your brother-in-law gave a damn. Perhaps your mother-in-law did too.

C. The dining room ranks third...

The dining room ranks third right behind the bathroom and bedroom as the most important room in your inn. You are, after all, in the food service business as well in the lodging business. But, the level of food service that you provide will be - or should be - far above the level of food service we have come to know in 21st century America - or 21st century world for that matter. Pity the child who has grown up in the sandwich generation.

I'm reminded of the tale of the businessman who was bragging to a friend about his son's early career accomplishments. The lad had become a doctor or an investment banker or something else that dad thought was worthy of mentioning. The other fellow's son, however, was still slaving away in the local Burger King as a night shift leader flipping burgers. Not wanting to be outgunned, however, he informed his associate that his son was in management in the food service industry.

Whereas, you and Burger King may both be in the food service industry, I can only hope that as an aspiring innkeeper, you will think way beyond Burger King when you think about your inn's dining room and what will take place there and what will be served there and what will be consumed there. This is of course with all do respect to Burger King.

For many of your guests, the breakfast and the camaraderie that surrounds it are the main reasons that they stay in an inn to begin with. It, therefore, becomes part of your job as an innkeeper to set the tone - and the table - in a way that facilitates the achievement of those goals.

If you haven't stayed in many inns, you probably haven't spent much time thinking about the options that are available regarding the breakfast half of the bed & breakfast experience, so much of the following will be new to you. If you have thought about the options, only some of the following will be new. In either case, pay attention.

Depending on your personal breakfast goals or, perhaps dictated by the size of your inn and your inn's dining room, you have many choices that all spin off of the layout of the room, the time you serve, and what you serve.

If you can't serve all of your guests at the same time - as in you have seven guest rooms that can hold 14 guests and a dining room that can seat 10 people - what are you going to do? In my opinion, only serving breakfast to the first 10 guests who come down to eat, is probably not a very good idea. So the first decision that you have to make is whether you will serve breakfast during a certain period of time - say 8 a.m. to 10:00 a.m. - and hope that by luck of the draw your guests will trickle down to eat and you won't have to deal with a rush or whether you will have two or more seatings and by luck of the draw all of your guests will get the time they want. If you're going to serve during a set period of time, you may end up with a jam - that's jam as in traffic jam as opposed to jam for the toast. What then do you do to make everybody happy? If you're going to have seatings, how will it be determined who gets which seating? The first guest who makes a reservation? The first guest who checks in? The guest who yells the loudest? And what in this scenario do you do about the guests who are unhappy with their breakfast time? We were able to serve all of our guests at once, but that would really make the Dining Room rather crowded and we didn't want to require specific seatings because it was a forgone that folks were simply going to miss their appointed times and, thereby, wreak havoc with the schedule. So we served breakfast from 8 - 9:30. When too many people showed up at once, we poured a cup of coffee or tea for those who couldn't be seated at the table and had them wait in the sitting room listening to light classical music - it was always on during breakfast anyway. They could also read some general light picture book type stuff or travel material we had lying around or the morning newspaper or - and here's a novel early morning thought - converse with one another.

If your dining room is large enough to seat all of your guests at the same time in comfort, is your kitchen large enough to make breakfast for all of them at the same time? And, if your kitchen is large enough to make breakfast for all of them at the same time do you really want to make everybody's breakfast at the same time. If it isn't or you don't want to, your guests are just going to sit around anyway. If, your dining room is large enough to seat all of your guests at the same time and you want to make everybody's breakfast at the same time you are, perhaps, in luck.

Having said all of that, we stayed in several inns, which had separate seatings, and, as I recall, there were very few fistfights before, during or after breakfast. In my experience, however, separate seatings is not the ideal situation.

Then comes the seating arrangement. Regardless of whether you are going to drive yourself completely crazy by serving all of your guests at the same time or only drive yourself partially crazy by serving them in shifts, you have to decide whether you are going to seat all of them at the same table - thereby kind of forcing them all to talk to each other - or seat them at two, three or perhaps even four separate tables - thereby forcing only little groups to talk to each other. This decision will depend as much on the size of your dining room as it will on how many conversations you will feel like starting and stoking each morning. If you are leaning toward the multiple table approach, keep in mind that you will often end up with a single guest or one couple at a table all by themselves looking, perhaps, bored and lonely. In addition to being their cook and server, you may also be called upon to be their breakfast companion. You should also be mindful of the groups of three - mom, dad, and their kid or the charming couple and her mother - that might create chaos with your seating arrangement.

Understand that there are no right or wrong answers to these perplexing issues, but they have to be addressed.

Having come to grips with the seating times and table arrangement matters, you will now have to address the style of breakfast that you will be serving. The options are somewhat endless.

You can - heaven forbid - serve store-bought Danish along with a selection of those little individual boxes of cereal - you know, the kind with the perforated sides that you can punch open so that they become a cereal bowl. We actually stayed at an otherwise delightful inn whose owners thought that this type of breakfast would endear their guests to them and to their inn. At least in our case, they were wrong on both counts. This was far too reminiscent of what one would expect from a motel chain that advertises a free breakfast. Whereas, in some quarters, this would be known as a continental breakfast, it really fell far short. Regardless of what you call it, in my not so humble opinion, you should never serve those little cereal boxes. Cereals yes, but not from those little boxes.

The next step - or actually what I would consider the first rung on the breakfast ladder - would be a true continental breakfast. This is the least that you should offer your guests if you truly think of yourself as being in the specialty end of the hospitality industry. A selection of fruit juices; home baked pastries; cereal out of their boxes and presented in large glass containers including, perhaps, your own granola mix; and milk, tea, and coffee - make sure that you include decaf (both tea and coffee) in your offerings as well as both low fat milk and cream for those guests who will feel better about themselves when they wash down one of your pastries with a cup of tea or coffee seriously whitened by a non-fattening dairy product. For those guests who know what it means to be on vacation, you should also serve the loaded with fat milk and cream. And make sure that at least one of your cereal selections doesn't have nuts in it. A whole bunch of folks are allergic to nuts or simply can't eat them because of some sort of medical condition.

A meaningful step above the continental breakfast, yet one that will not necessarily tax your culinary skills, would be to add a hot entrée served buffet style to everything included above. This will allow you to make up a breakfast casserole the night before and heat it up in the morning and serve it on a warming tray. The biggest problem with this type of breakfast is the look of the casserole dish when the second wave of guests comes down to breakfast. (By the way, one or more of your guest rooms might be on the first floor so everyone may not be coming "down" to breakfast). There's almost nothing less appetizing to a guest than serving up their own breakfast from a casserole dish that has been attacked by a ravenous bunch of strangers or a ravenous bunch of relatives for that matter - food stuck to the serving spoon, food dripping over the sides of the dish, food dribbled all over the side board - you get the picture. An option, of course, is too not serve it in a dish for all of your guests to attack, but to plate it up individually in the kitchen. This way the only people who will see food stuck to the serving spoon, food dripping over the sides of the dish, and food dribbled all over the kitchen counter top will be the innkeepers. Either way, portion control can be a problem with this type of breakfast. How much to make? What do you say to the guest who asks for a second helping when there isn't anything left? Too little food is obviously unacceptable and leftovers get tossed - or perhaps eaten by the innkeepers for lunch.

The next rung on the ladder takes you to the same breakfast-served-to-all, but cooked to order approach. This is what we did and it worked extremely well. We began the breakfast by offering each guest a choice of apple or orange juice - orange juice was the clear winner by maybe 10 to 1. As an aside, the apple juice industry shouldn't be overly concerned with these numbers because this was hardly a scientific survey. It was cute to watch some of the guests ponder this decision as though the future of the free world would be impacted by their choice. We then served small individual bowls of fruit or our famous sectioned pink grapefruit served warm with a topping of brown sugar. The half of a red cherry that was placed in the center to cover up the not-all-that-attractive gathering point of the grapefruit sections usually was still there at the end of the breakfast, but it was a nice touch and added color to the plate. I'm pretty sure that this dish would have worked just as well with regular - non-pink - grapefruit, but we'll never know. Sometimes the fruit serving - such as an apple French toast turnover or simply a half peach also with a soon-to-be-returned half of a red cherry floating in the middle - was included on the plate with the hot entree. The bottom line here is that there was always a side dish of fruit.

During the summer and fall, we tried serving - no, we actually did serve - mini muffins or fruit breads. I can vouch for how tasty they were because most of them were brought back to the kitchen untouched by human hands, except for the human hands that placed them in the basket in the first place. Not so during the winter however. The skiers inhaled them. They must have needed the energy boost for those long afternoons awaiting for the ski lift or sitting around the ski lodge. So you need to think about adjusting your breakfast with the seasons and the type of activities your guests will be pursuing.

After the fruit and breads came the main course hot entree. And each morning everyone got the same thing. We may have been partially nuts to go into this business in the first place, but we weren't completely nuts. One morning the entree might be a wonderful creation of ours - pumpkin pancakes or it could be the guests' choice of blueberry, banana, chocolate chip or plain - or any combination thereof - pancakes. These were always served with a side of bacon or ham or sausage. The only problem here was the "I don't eat meat" guests. More about them a little bit later. Other hot entrees included scrambled eggs - usually with Vermont cheddar cheese and again with a side of meat and an English muffin - don't forget to put a small sprig of parsley on the scrambled eggs for color; one of many tasty, filling and very fattening breakfast casseroles; plain or stuffed thick sliced French toast - the "stuffing" was almost anything you could comfortably cram into a sliced open chubby slab of bread - bananas come to mind. Again, stay away from nuts - too many guests have nut-related diet problems. And, of course, tea and coffee. Except for the casseroles, these breakfasts were cooked separately for each guest - no warming trays here.

On top of the ladder are the fancy puffs and soufflés and/or the truly cooked-to-order breakfast. We steered clear of all of these under the guise that ours was an unpretentious country inn serving an unpretentious, but hardy and tasty country breakfast. In reality ours was, in fact, an unpretentious country inn serving an unpretentious but hearty and tasty country breakfast. And it sure made our lives easier - at least at breakfast time. But if you want to slave away over various high-end concoctions, have at it. There are endless breakfast cookbooks and several cooking shows - if your inn is actually serviced by cable TV - featuring an endless array of recipes. But just remember one burned flan can really upset your guests not to mention ruin your morning.

We always tried to determine during the check in process if any of our guests had important dietary restrictions and in case we forgot to ask, we included the need to let us in on these little secrets on the infamous list of "rules and regulations" strategically located on the bed in each guest room. Check in was also a good time to ask whether they preferred tea or coffee with their breakfast and, if coffee was the drink of choice, whether real, a.k.a. regular, or decaf was the order of the day. A small point you may say, but this enabled us to have the right amount of each brewing in the morning. Also, having learned in advance who the vegetarians were helped us decide what to serve the next morning. This plan was not fool proof - witness the idiotic situation we went through with the boorish California couple we talked about earlier (the ones who wanted their egg whites scrambled and had other dietary issues that they didn't share with us until breakfast time) - but more often than not, it gave us valuable information and made the breakfast more enjoyable for the guests and for the innkeepers.

Previously we addressed the need to have quality products in your guest rooms - toilet paper, mattresses, and pillows for instance. Don't forget quality when it comes to the food you'll be preparing and serving. And if you think the guests won't know the difference now is probably the perfect time to drop your plans to become an innkeeper. Remember, you can fool some of the people some of the time, but you can't fool the fat couple from upstate New York at breakfast. Our coffee blend, which included one-quarter hazelnut, was hugely popular. Some guests actually told us that it was the best coffee they ever tasted. When asked what it was, it would have been embarrassing to give them the name of a discount brand that we bought at a big box retailer in 55-gallon drums. Of course, we could have lied, but if it's your intention to lie to your guests, now is really the perfect time to drop your plans to become an innkeeper. By the way, we brewed the hazelnut blend in both regular and decaf. No little decaf packets for our guests.

To make the breakfast time somewhat easier on us, we had the coffee and tea on top of an antique dry sink in the dining room so the guests could pour and refill their cups themselves. It saved us the bother and gave the breakfast a rather convivial atmosphere. "Here, let me refill that coffee cup for you," one guest would say to another and this would kind of open up a breakfast chat among strangers. The following is a total digression from this topic, but it just came to mind. During one late afternoon in the Fall, two couples were checking in at the same time. One had advance reservations and the other was driving by and saw our sign. It turned out that the second couple had made reservations at another inn, but when they got there, the innkeeper was away, the place was locked up, there was a rather unfriendly "welcome" note on the door advising them to come back later, and a relatively vicious dog was snarling at them. Did you pick up on the several lessons to be learned here? There was such instant rapport between theses two couples that had just met in our sitting room, fostered, no doubt, by their charming innkeepers, that they ended up going to dinner together. It was one of those lovely moments that kind of made you think that this inn keeping business can be truly enjoyable. A tasty breakfast served in a delightful setting with amiable hosts and friendly guests can have the same effect - starting a traveler's day off just right.

We ironed the napkins - which were white for the same reason that our bed linens and towels were white - and we had cloth place mats that were machine washable. Plastic place mats would have cleaned up easier, but we saw ourselves as having friends over for breakfast, not running a diner. So plastic was out. We wore aprons with the name of the inn on the front - just a little gift I bought for both of us before we left the big city where you could buy such things - and we kept them sparkling clean. Maybe nobody noticed that they were clean, but you can bet your ass that they would have noticed if they were dirty.

Breakfast was always served by candlelight even when it was already daylight and we always had light classical music playing in the sitting room, which could be heard in the dining room. As our brochure said, the candlelight didn't make the food taste any better, but it was a nice touch. The real question here is when do you replace the candles? We used hand-dipped colonial candles in traditional colors. It would have cost us a small fortune and would have been extremely wasteful to replace them each morning. On the other hand, we didn't think that our guests would be impressed with little stubby candles flickering there way to extinction before their very eyes. There is no magic answer to this question. But, to help you through this, we learned that an already lit candle looks much better than an unlit candle. Our job, therefore, was to light the candles just before our first guest arrived at the table. As for the classical music, the high brows enjoyed playing the name-that-tune game and we felt that it was our duty to introduce the low brows to a little culture. It also provided some background noise between the time that the breakfast chitchat stopped and we could get back to the dining room to stoke the conversational fires.

We found out that clearing the dishes from the table was both an art and a science. Whereas you shouldn't leave dirty dishes in front of a guest for too long a period of time, taking them away too soon might give the impression that breakfast is officially over and it's time for the guests to be on their way. As a restaurant patron, I always thought that it was awkward - if not downright rude - for a waiter or busperson to remove all of the dishes, let's say, but mine when my co-diner or diners had finished eating. It made me feel like I was dining alone and I ended up rushing through the rest of my meal. Breakfast was always an important part of our bed and breakfast experience as travelers and I wanted to give our guests that same feeling. Let them eat at their leisure and enjoy a second or third cup of coffee or tea - unless, of course, there were other guests waiting in the sitting room for their chance at our pancakes. We apparently made some of our guests feel so much at home during breakfast that occasionally some of them would actually begin to stack the dishes in preparation to taking them back to the kitchen. We quickly let them know that if they insisted on continuing with this irrational behavior they would be expected to clean and dry them as well.

There is - or should be - yet another corollary of Murphy's Law that deals with the truism that if an innkeeper's dining room has one large table set for 6 or 8 or 10 people for example, the first guests who come to breakfast will sit in such an arrangement as to leave only one open seat on each side of the table usually somewhat diagonally across from each other. Therefore, one of our jobs as innkeepers was to re-seat our guests without being obnoxious about it so that the late arrivals were able to sit next to or directly across from each other assuming that they wanted to.

Something that you might consider to be too minor to address, but I obviously don't, is that we had the morning newspaper available for the guests during breakfast. If we only had a couple of guests, we placed the paper on the corner of the dining room table. If we had a crowd and needed the table space for things like dishes and food, we placed the paper on the sofa in the sitting room. In either case, we only had one paper so it was up to the guests to share it. To their everlasting credit, they were always able to accomplish this task without causing any serious incidents. The credit, I think, goes to the women - if I may be a bit of a sexist for a moment - who were able to convince their men folk that a fifteen or twenty minute wait for the sports section would not, in fact, ruin their day. Of course, we could have had six papers delivered each day - one for each guest room and one for the innkeepers - but we knew that we weren't going to be full each night and our approach solved what turned out to be a very minor problem, saved a fair amount of money, and a host of trees.

It didn't take long for us to realize that without leaving the door between the kitchen and dining room open - and, trust me, you don't want your guests to be able to see into your kitchen - we had absolutely no idea when our guests had arrived in the dining room. The simple solution was to install a peephole device in the dining room door. This was also used to determine when the last guest had left the table allowing us to spring into action to clean up the room. As another aside, make sure that you place the peephole at the right height so both of you can use it comfortably - assuming that there will be two of you. Did you catch on to a clunky, but not too serious oops here?

We did stay in a couple of inns that featured open hearth cooking. The big old fireplace replete with trammel was right there where we sat and the innkeeper or hired hand cooked the breakfast right before our very eyes. This approach, of course, allowed the guests to see the kitchen because they were sitting in it. If you want to be on display and have your breakfast prepared in a tavernesque environment, have at it. To each his own.

All of our dishes as well as our napkins were housed in the dining room in a beautiful antique jelly cupboard. The problem here was getting access to the cupboard with a partially filled dining room so we could re-set the table for the second wave of guests. The simple solution was to bring the extra dishes and napkins into the kitchen when we were setting up the table for the first wave. No big deal, you say? Our first breakfast as innkeepers was for 10 people. We were almost completely clueless and would have paid dearly for this tidbit of advice. Another solution would be to store your dishes and napkins in the kitchen.

Then comes the real juggling act. All at the same time, some guests would be finished eating and were going to be checking out and saying their good byes and were requesting our services in helping them plan their day. Some guests would be finished eating and were requesting our services in helping them plan their day. Some guests would be just beginning their breakfast and required our relatively undivided attention, as well they should. This always led to a flurry of activity. What to do? Easier said than done is that you have to take care of everybody in a timely manner with wit, charm, and grace. Anybody who told you that being an innkeeper was going to be easy was either a former innkeeper who was lying, a current innkeeper who was trying desperately to sell his inn, or a friend or co-worker or family member who either didn't have your best interest at heart or who had no idea what they were talking about.

Well, there you have some of the nuts and bolts (remember to go easy on the nuts) of being an innkeeper during breakfast. Hopefully, you now have an understanding of what you are up against during the key part of your day, not to mention a key part of your guests' day.

In the welcome center in Charleston, SC in the section on lodging where a traveler could find brochures on all of the inns and motels in the area, was a rack card that simply said Bed, No Breakfast. The card went on to extol the charm, cost, and location of a home with two guest rooms, which shared one bath - period. That's all you got - a bed and the shared use of a bathroom. In retrospect, it appears that they may have been on to something.

Later on when I address actually running your inn, I'll deal with things like setting up your dining room and kitchen for breakfast, buying food and supplies, preparing the meal, cleaning up after the meal, etc. The real fun part of being in this business - he says sarcastically.

D. Next comes the Sitting Room...

Next comes the Sitting Room or the living room or the common room or the front room or whatever you call the first room your guests will see (besides the front or side hallway) when they enter your inn. Throughout this section, I will refer to this room as the sitting room for two reasons. First of all, that's what we called it in our inn. Second, I feel like it and I'm the author.

If your inn is already set up, you may not be able to take advantage of all of these pearls of wisdom, but you should try to adopt as many as you can assuming that there is sufficient space available. If you are establishing your inn, you should incorporate as many of them as you can. Assuming that your inn has a modicum of "curb appeal" - that's the real estate industry's version of what Hollywood would call "sex appeal" - the real first important impression your guests will have of your inn after seeing it from the street or your parking lot, will be that initial step over the threshold. Trust me, I'm not discounting the importance of curb appeal. We'll address it later.

You just might be asking yourself, "If the sitting room is the first impression, why are we only dealing with it now?" Well, I look at it this way. You are running an inn, not a sitting room. Whatever, problems or challenges your guests may encounter in your perhaps less-than-perfect sitting room, will be forgotten with a perfect bathroom, bedroom, and dining experience.

Our inn began its life as a farmhouse in 1790 or so and, it would appear that Jesse Safford wasn't a wealthy man or perhaps he was wealthy, but cheap. The original house was quite modest. And, even as the house went through its various career changes - from a farmhouse to three apartment units and finally to an inn - it still only had two common rooms - the dining room and the sitting room. Many places we stayed in were quite a bit larger and had various dens, libraries, and other rooms that were being used as guest gathering places. If your inn is one of these, you will have several options.

Whether your inn does or does not have a bunch of extra rooms lying around, I would strongly urge you not to bring your guests into an "office" environment, especially a side door office environment. We have been to inns with this arrangement and right away they had a motel feel to them. It seemed more like a business than a home away from home. Also, these offices were usually quite small and messy which made them unattractive and the whole luggage thing rather clumsy. Even worse is the problem of having to crowd into a small office when it's raining or snowing. Which guest gets to wait in the rain or in their car if more than one arrives at the same time?

We asked our guests to place their luggage in the front hall - assuming, of course, that they brought their luggage in with them - and, in either case, asked them to come in to the sitting room and relax on the couch or in a chair for a minute. It gave us a chance to say hello, round up the registration form from our little office area in the kitchen, which they couldn't see, and introduce them to our inn. It gave them a chance to have an oatmeal and chocolate chip cookie or two and simply take a deep breath from their travels. We always had a dish of cookies sitting on the antique trunk that served as a coffee table in the sitting room. If pressed, we would even make them some coffee.

To accomplish all of this guest greeting business meant that we needed enough room for a couple of guests - or many guests during high season - and one or both of the innkeepers sitting in a chair or chairs. We also needed space for a couch, other chairs, an antique trunk, luggage, and a plate of cookies.

So let's get into the purpose of the sitting room and its set up.

Inns should have what are known in this industry as common areas. These are areas that can be used by the guests (in addition to their guest room) in common with the other guests - hence the name. The dining room serves this purpose during breakfast, but what about check in time, before dinner, and after dinner? These are all perfect times for you to get to know your guests and for them to get to know each other or for them to simply relax. There is, of course, a leap of faith here - that being that you will want to get to know your guests and that they will want to get to know each other. Assuming that everybody does, in fact, want to get to know each other, the sitting room serves this purpose and to achieve this goal, it should be comfortable and relatively large. Be careful here. Remember that one man's comfort is another man's pigsty. Stay away from clutter.

Your sitting room certainly doesn't have to have enough seating capacity for all of your guests. The day never came that all of our guests were in the sitting room at the same time. And, if, by chance, that does happen to you, rest assured that they all won't be looking to sit down

- some will be on the move from their room to a place of interest or vice versa.

It would be wise not to have your fine porcelain tea service on display on the coffee table next to the cookies or your treasured Royal Doulton figurines on the end table next to the wing chair. Nothing says this is going to be a most uncomfortable stay like a smashed family heirloom. Remember that your guests will be carrying luggage, camera bags, purses, recently purchased bottles of wine, and anything else you can imagine. They will be excited and will be moving quite rapidly. They will, in short, be accidents waiting to happen. So decorate your sitting room to your heart's content, but keep it somewhat sparse of breakables.

For most of the reasons I just enumerated, I would suggest that you avoid light colored fabric on your furniture and, most assuredly, avoid light colored floor covering. Our inn, being in Vermont, catered to a substantial winter crowd and in with them came salt, sand, pine needles, and parking lot stones. And, of course, all of the other seasons brought forth their own assortment of filth that was destined to end up in our sitting room. If we had thought about it soon enough, we would have begun to shoot those guests who never even took a stab at wiping their feet. Our hope would have been that the word would have gone forth to the rest of the great unwashed. But, alas, we didn't. So it is up to you to be prepared for smudges and stains and footprints. Many smudges and many stains and many footprints.

The sitting room also contained a modest collection of antique items that could be described as "conversation pieces" - although someone once said "If

all you have to talk about are the things you own..."
Primarily these were things that folks used to use to do
household chores that have been replaced by things that
folks use to do the same chores except now they plug
them in. These were excellent icebreakers. As was the
collection of light reading material and assorted parlor
games that everybody looked at and talked about with
keen interest and never touched throughout the rest of
their stay.

For the pleasure of our guests, the sitting room had
a large rack of maps and flyers of area attractions right by
the door. This served two purposes. First of all, we used
them as our supply of material that we sent in the
envelope with our brochure to those potential guests who
requested our brochure and information on things to do.
The purpose was to further entice them to visit our neck
of the woods. Second of all, it helped the guests who had
absolutely no idea what to do between breakfast and
bedtime decide what to do during the day. These were
some of the tools that I used to help me play tour
director. As an aside, I was told by innkeeper guests who
saw me in action that I would succumb to innkeeper's
fatigue or burnout faster than I otherwise would - it being
a foregone that I would indeed eventually suffer from
burnout - if I kept spending so much time helping my
guests plan their day and evening. We'll go into this
fatigue factor in some depth later as well as my approach
to it and ways to avoid it.

Needless to say, but I will anyway, the sitting room
has to be kept immaculate. We dusted and vacuumed daily
and straightened up throughout the day as needed. The
guests who just came back from their day's traveling

about, or the guests who just came back from dinner, or the guests who were just checking in will probably not give you the benefit of the doubt. If the place is dirty, they will assume that it is always dirty. What kept our clean up juices flowing was the possibility that the AAA inspector who had our three-diamond rating in his hands and who always arrived unannounced was just about to walk in the door. A powerful motivator.

More than one innkeeper whose establishment we visited, thought it would be a good idea to have their guests spend part of their day working on a jigsaw puzzle at least we assumed that that's why they had one on a table in their sitting room or one of their other common rooms. Just what I wanted to do while I was on vacation - spend three hours placing six pieces in a thousand-piece puzzle that I would never see completed. What an atrocious waste of common area space, a card table, and vacation time. As you set up your inn and specifically its common areas, think about what you did or always wanted to do on your vacation. Did you ever say to each other, "Let's spend several hundred dollars of our hard earned money on a vacation in Vermont during their spectacular Fall foliage season and let's do it up right by staying in a lovely country inn and while we're there, honey, let's work on their jigsaw puzzle?" I can only hope not.

Also in our sitting room was a small antique trunk, which held menus of all of the area restaurants. Most of the time we spent with our guests - other than introducing them to the inn and their room and feeding them - was discussing dinner plans and options. Another reason to have enough comfortable places to sit to accommodate you and some of your guests. We'll go into the details of what was in the trunk and how we handled this part of our duty to our guests in the section on actually running your inn.

So that's really it for the sitting room. In a nutshell, it should be warm, inviting, spacious, uncluttered, and very clean. Not amazing revelations you may say, but we have seen many sitting rooms that looked like gone-to-the-dogs antique shops or used book shops - did they really think that we were going to take a musty book off a filthy shelf and read it during the two days of our stay? So be mindful of what you expected in your travels and provide your guests with nothing less and, hopefully, a good deal more.

E. The other rooms in your inn...

The other rooms in your inn that might on occasion, or very often for that matter, be seen or visited by your guests should be given the same attention to comfort and detail and cleanliness. If your inn is blessed with other common area rooms besides a dining room and sitting room - dens, reading rooms, music rooms, etc. you probably paid too much for the place - but they all have to be kept clean and they should be decorated with the same level of guest-satisfaction care.

Your hallways and stairways should also be kept clear of clutter - don't put your collection of baskets or doorstops or crocks on the steps leading to the second floor. Think of the poor guest who is trying to navigate your stairway with a suitcase in each hand and other pieces of luggage draped over each shoulder along with some packages his wife made him carry in from the car. That doesn't mean that these areas shouldn't be decorated with the same charm as the rest of your inn - they just need to be as spacious as your inn will allow and certainly uncluttered.

We stayed in an inn in New Hampshire that redefined Victorian frufru. Angels, pillows, lace, flowers, more pillows everywhere and I mean everywhere. It would have been laughable if we had been able to find the bed under all of the pillows after banging our way down the hallway, which was filled with more crap than you can imagine. We did, finally, find the bed. But, once we had removed all of the stuffed pillows and animals and placed them around the room, there was no room for us and our luggage.

Remember the recommendation that you should sleep in each of your guest rooms periodically. Don't just sleep in the room - take along a piece of luggage or three and try to figure out where to put them. By the way, when you do this, your luggage can actually be empty. This exercise is to determine if you have left sufficient room for your guests to navigate through your inn and be comfortable, not whether you can carry heavy suitcases.

And, while we're on the topic of keeping everything clean and tidy, you will also be amazed by the frequency with which some of your guests will wander into your kitchen like they own the joint and - at least in our case - then have full view of your personal living space. Besides your guests, these unannounced kitchen travelers, could be the aforementioned AAA inspectors and the Mobil Guide inspectors who don't announce their visits, but actually stay in your inn as regular guests. That's right, the Mobil inspectors make a reservation and stay overnight and eat breakfast the next morning and leave and you never knew that they were there. Well, you knew that someone was there, but you didn't know that they were inspecting the place or, at least, that was their approach when I was an innkeeper. Inns can also be visited - unannounced - by some of those inn book editors or their surrogates. The point is that one never knows what evil lurks just outside or just inside your kitchen door.

So if you're the type who lets your cat walk around on your counter tops or lets your dog drink out of the kitchen sink - and as an innkeeper I would suggest that you seriously consider discontinuing these practices - you could be in for a rather shocked and, perhaps, distraught guest not to mention a rather nasty write up from the occasional inspector or editor. "A charming inn," the editor may conclude his report, "but don't eat the breakfast because the kitchen is a pigsty." How would that ringing endorsement in the latest edition of Country Inns and Bed & Breakfasts affect your business?

Oh, and don't forget the occasional state inspector if you happen to be in a state that cares enough to send its very best to hassle you annually. We'll deal more with this issue later, but in Vermont we had two licenses - one for Lodging and one for Restaurant. And, needless to say, we had to pay the state for the privilege of being inspected in addition to fixing whatever they found broken, chipped, dented, dusty, musty, rusty, smudged, or unpainted.

So, in addition to all of your other chores, it is incumbent upon you to keep your entire place immaculate all of the time.

One more thing to be on guard about regarding your common rooms. If your owner's quarters consist of little more than a bedroom and bathroom off of the kitchen and you intend to use your inn's dining room and sitting room and other common areas as your own personal space as well as common space for your guests or if you have plenty of personal space, but think of the common areas of your inn as more personal space for you, be careful. You might have a tendency to have a lot of family photographs - like those of your grandchildren - lying around in addition to other items of personal interest. One can go overboard in making the place look too much like your home and less like an inn.

By far, most of our guests were veteran inn guests, but many weren't. Those who weren't arrived somewhat confused about what really was supposed to happen in an inn. Do I have to ring the doorbell each time I come back during my stay? Should we make the bed each morning? What should we wear to breakfast? What time do we have to be back at the inn each evening? Can I sit in your sitting room and read your travel-related books, or do I have to take them back to my room?

Some of these folks and even some of the veterans, I presume, might be uncomfortable if they thought they were in your home instead of being in your inn. Make your place friendly from a traveler's perspective, but not so friendly that your guests think they have to share family photos and family secrets.

Your guests, especially those who are not seasoned inn folk, might find it a bit too much like Aunt Ethel's for their taste. Sorry, Aunt Ethel.

If you don't think that everything outlined in this section is a serious matter deserving of your careful attention, you're wrong.

F. How about your grounds...

How about your grounds, not your coffee grounds, but your front, side, and rear yards and, of course, your parking area? Earlier I mentioned curb appeal - the look and feel of your inn as your guests first arrive - what it looks like from the curb (assuming that your street has curbs). They probably already know what your place looks like from your website or from your brochure if you use real live photographs rather than pencil drawings of your inn or some cutesy flower arrangement or fruit bowl or wine bottle to depict your inn. More on this later in the section on creating your inn's marketing pieces. But, the first impression your guests have when they actually drive up to your inn and pull into your parking lot can go a long way toward making their stay a thoroughly enjoyable experience.

If your inn has some natural or even man-made curb appeal - it's set way back from the street up a winding country lane or it has a lovely stone wall with things growing over it (over the wall, not over your inn) - you've got a leg up on having your arriving guests feel good about the decision they made to stay with you assuming that you're not so tucked back up a country lane that they had a hard time finding you. Even if your inn is blessed with some or all of these nice features, you should still pay careful attention to most of the following suggestions.

However, if your inn is lacking in curb appeal and needs all of the help it can get to have your guests arrive in a joyous frame of mind, you should pay careful attention to all of the following suggestions.

146

G. Signs...

Signs are rarely given the attention they deserve, so I'm going to correct that right here and now. Once again, you should put yourself in the shoes, or actually in the car, of an arriving guest when you think about your inn's sign and the story it tells.

The first things your arriving guests will see or, let me put it this way, the first thing your arriving guests *should* see is your sign - not your astrological sign, your inn's sign. It should be as large as your local zoning ordinance will allow, but if there is no limit in your local code or the limit is really excessive, the size should be reasonable - it should "fit" your inn. And the fit should be in both size as well as style. A country inn or a village Victorian inn, for example, shouldn't have a neon sign. As a matter of fact, I can't picture any inn that would have its curb appeal enhanced by a neon sign. And stay away from plastic or other man-made materials. Wood is the best bet and make sure it's very high quality and always kept clean and in perfect repair. Finally, it should only say what it has to say - it shouldn't be used as an advertising billboard. The name of the inn and, perhaps, if there are any vacancies. More on this vacancy thing in a bit. Your address and phone number aren't necessary on your sign since your guests or potential guests are already there by the time they see it.

Oh, and please have your sign professionally done. Unless you are very good at sign making, DO NOT have a homemade sign. Nothing says tacky like a sloppy, homemade sign.

And keep in mind that virtually all of your guests will be arriving for the first time. They shouldn't have to guess which drive to take if there is more than one, where they are supposed to park or which door to use. If these things are not absolutely and completely obvious to your guests, a separate sign or two would be appropriate. It should go without saying, but I feel compelled to say it, that these directional signs should also be of very high quality and should always be kept clean and in excellent repair and large enough to be seen for heaven's sake.

But, please don't over sign your inn. Nothing ruins your sought after curb appeal like having your arriving guests assaulted by a bevy of signs. No, I don't know how many signs it takes to make a bevy, but you know, or should know, what I mean. Keep them sparse and keep them simple. If, for the lack of an extra sign, a guest happens to park in the wrong place or walks to the wrong door, big deal. It is better to have them move their car or, with honey dripping from your lips, have you direct them to the proper door, than having one too many signs. By the way, "honey dripping from your lips" is just an expression for being extra nice. Please don't ever come to your door to greet your guests with anything dripping from your lips - even honey.

Remember that your arriving guests may come at dusk or actually at night. So your signs should be well lit. Much like my previous suggestion that you should sleep in each of your guest rooms every now and then to make sure that all is well, you should also drive slowly up to your inn every now and then pretending that you are an arriving first time guest and do it at night some of the time. Don't assume anything. Make sure your signs do what they are supposed to do - greet your guests and make them feel welcome. And make sure that they don't need any repairs or repainting. Also make sure that your signs' lights are lit. You will probably want to do this on one of your night practice runs. Keep spare floodlight bulbs around and replace burned out bulbs the minute they burn out - or the minute that you are aware that they are burned out. The next arriving guest will need the same help finding your parking lot and your front door as the last arriving guest. And they won't want to hear and probably won't believe you that the bulb just burned out.

All of this also applies to your front door light or your side door light, if that's where your guests are supposed to enter your inn. And if you don't have a front door light or a side door light, install them. And make sure that they fit your inn's decor. Spend an extra buck or two. Outside lighting, properly done, adds immeasurably to your arriving guests feeling of warmth, comfort, and safety.

One last thought on the lighting of your signs. If your inn is in a northern clime where it snows a lot, mount your lights above your signs facing down rather than at ground level facing up for two reasons. First of all, a floodlight buried in snow probably won't do a very good job in lighting up your sign. Secondly, if your floodlights are at ground level, you'll probably smash them with your snowplow or snow shovel trying to clear away the ice and snow.

Back to the issue of whether your main inn sign should indicate that you do or do not have vacancies. I would suggest that there are two schools of thought regarding this, however, 'schools of thought' might be

149

considered a rather high-powered term to apply to a discussion of vacancy signs. It really boils down to whether or not you want anybody who drives by your inn to know that you have vacancies. An arriving guest with a reservation could care less unless, of course, it's during high season and the guest might wonder why you have vacancies. Other innkeepers in your area might see your vacancy sign and gloat a bit - if they don't have any vacancies - or commiserate with your plight if they aren't full either. The flip side of other innkeepers knowing that you have availability is that they might be in a position to refer someone to you. This could be a good thing, but don't expect it to happen unless they are full or simply can't or don't want to accommodate the couple with the kids, the dog, and the mother-in-law who dropped by their place.

Another point on having a vacancy or no vacancy sign as part of your inn sign is whether you want to take "drop ins." As the name implies, a drop in is a guest who arrives at your door without a reservation and this could happen at virtually any hour of the day or night. Some innkeepers steadfastly refuse to take drop ins. Drop ins are, or certainly can be, a major disruption to you as well as to your other guests - assuming that you have other guests. You may have already set the dining room table and prepared the next morning's breakfast casserole. Your other guests could already be asleep or doing whatever guests do in their rooms after they get back from dinner and they probably would rather not be disturbed by arriving guests banging their way to their rooms. On the plus side, of course, is the fact that a drop in can end up being a guest for at least one night and potentially for several nights and could become a return guest with a whole bunch of traveling friends. And, after all, you are in the lodging business aren't you?

The last point on having a vacancy or no vacancy sign as part of your inn sign is the requirement that you have to change the sign when your vacancy situation changes. As I mentioned earlier, we had a small sign hanging below our inn sign that read 'No Vacancy' and there were little hooks above the word 'No' so it could be covered with little blank flaps that fit on the little hooks. And to add to the workload, we were on a main road with a two-sided sign so we had two flaps to hang up and remove. Not a lot of hard work, but something else to remember especially if you want to take drop ins or if you are full and don't want drop ins to pull up to your place only to be turned away.

If you remember anything I've told you in this section, remember to check with your local zoning or design review board or both or whoever else rules on things like the size, shape, color, height, material, lighting, etc. of signs in your neck of the woods. And, until you have every single permit signed by the appropriate signer of such things and have waited the appropriate amount of time for your neighbors to file appeals - if your local code gives them appeal rights - don't spend a dime with a sign maker or sign any contracts with a sign maker or make any commitments to a sign maker. Got it?

H. Parking lots...

Parking lots require more attention than you might think. I was actually going to begin this section by reminding you that every single one of your guests will arrive at your inn in some sort of motor vehicle. I was going to do that in order to stress the importance of your parking lots. However, I spent a brief and enjoyable post-innkeeping couple of months working in the local chamber of commerce's information booth helping visitors maximize the time they would spend in and around our village. One late afternoon during this stint, a somewhat bewildered young man, dragging a small wheeled suitcase behind him, who had arrived by bus - up to that moment, I didn't even know that a bus came to our town - walked up to the booth and asked directions to an inn at which he had a reservation. Unfortunately, the inn was almost three miles down an extremely busy road with no sidewalks and the afternoon sunlight was rapidly disappearing. Whereas, one of several closer inns would have served him better, who was I to suggest that he cancel his reservation at inn A and book into inn B? I did offer him a ride, which he rejected. The other sad part of this story is that he pulled a folded up page from a magazine out of his jacket pocket and proceeded to show me a picture of a classic Vermont farm scene - barn, rolled hay in the fields, maple trees in glorious fall colors, etc. - and asked me where he might find that barn. It was one of a thousand such scenes in Vermont and here he was with no means of transportation save his feet. He certainly wasn't going to find that barn on his way to the inn and I didn't quite know how to tell him that without a car - or at least a bicycle - he wasn't going to find it at all. So off he went dragging his suitcase behind him.

So, because of him, I need to start this section by reminding you that *virtually* all of your guests will arrive at your inn in some sort of motor vehicle. And, of course, they will all arrive with luggage - even the befuddled young tourist had a suitcase. So, on to the things you need to think about regarding your parking lot. And, once again, these are not presented in any sort of order. Oh sure, I could have gone back and prioritized them after I finished writing the section, but if you think that the order is really that important, prioritize away.

If your parking lot or parking area is some distance from your inn's guest entrance, you should try to have some sort of load and drop off area closer to the entrance and it should be signed as such so anyone using it will know right away that they have to move their vehicle rather soon after loading or unloading their luggage and their mother-in-law. Not a parking lot issue, but a guest-friendly issue is the suggestion that you have more than one large, sturdy umbrella just inside your guest entrance. Most folks don't travel with umbrellas and those who do, don't usually travel with large, sturdy ones that will protect them and their luggage from the elements.

I would suggest that you not designate your parking spaces with the names of your guest rooms (if you have chosen to name your guest rooms) or their room numbers (if you've taken that approach). Arriving guests with reservations probably won't remember the name or number of their room and drop in guests, of course, won't know where to park. Besides, why would you want to subject yourself to having to explain to the guest who has to park in the space furthest from the inn, why that space is the furthest from the inn? First come, first served would seem to win the day here.

If the size of your parking area is somewhat of a problem - that being that it will barely hold all of the cars it needs to in order to service you and your guests - you may want to consider designating each separate space with lines if your lot is paved or designating each separate space with little car window height signs that say something pleasant like Guest Parking. Even if your lot is paved, the little signs are still a good idea since the lines may not be visible at night and certainly won't be when they are covered with snow. Keep in mind that some of your guests will arrive in very large vehicles. So that your other guests don't begin their stay looking for the inconsiderate New Yorker who is taking up two spaces in your lot, make sure that your spaces are large enough for these oversize vehicles. No offense New York. Or take offense if you deserve it.

As proof that these things really do happen, we had a guest who traveled all the way from Arizona with a car carrier in tow. He was coming east to exhibit his prized antique car in several New England shows. There was no way that it would fit in our lot, but in anticipation of the arrival of oversized vehicles, we had made arrangements with a church across the way to let us use their very wide driveway overnight every now and then. You simply have to anticipate this kind of thing happening. Of course, it would have been nice - and could have avoided a potentially awkward situation - if the guest had let is know in advance that his vehicle was just this side of a semi.

We also had a situation where the folks in the tour bus were staying at the big inn in the village and we were blessed with the driver - and his bus - as our guests. Space for the driver was no problem. The bus was another story. Again, however, in anticipation of these oddball situations, we made arrangements to park bus-sized vehicles in the regional school parking lot way behind us. We followed the bus to the lot and drove the driver and his luggage back to the inn. Just one of those little courtesies that folks remember. Yes, we took him back to his bus the following morning.

As with everything else about your inn, your parking lot should be kept in excellent repair and very, very clean. If it's made of concrete and there are cracks and you can't afford to have it redone right away, fill in the cracks. If it's made of asphalt and there are cracks and you can't afford to have it redone right away, fill in the cracks. If it's made of crushed stone, make sure that there are no depressions that are deep enough to retain water which, when it gets cold, will become little skating rinks. Remove the weeds and sweep the lot almost every day and police it for trash every day. Remember, even if you don't have any advance reservations, the various inn inspectors we mentioned earlier and the dreaded drop ins are lurking out there somewhere.

And, while we're on the subject of keeping things very clean, make sure that the walkway from your parking lot to your guest entrance is kept that way. It probably won't take you ten minutes a day to do all of this policing, but it's time well spent. Pick up the cigarette butts, candy or gum wrappers and anything else that your guests might have inadvertently dropped - I'm giving them the benefit of the doubt here.

I. Entranceways...

Entranceways deserve as much attention as any other part of your inn. Having finally made their way to your inn's entranceway and having found everything along the way to be in perfect order so far because you have paid attention to everything I have told you to pay attention to, your arriving guests deserve nothing less than the perfect entranceway.

What is the perfect entranceway, you ask? Read on.

First of all, and this should come as no surprise, your guest entrance must be immaculate at all times. If some paint was chipped by an arriving guest wielding an over-sized piece of luggage, repaint it. If this happens every day, and it might, repaint it every day. A little sign that says "Wet Paint" is far better than a paint chip to an arriving guest. It sends the right message. But if you paint in the morning, it should be dry before your next guest arrives - no sign will be needed.

Much like the earlier comments on the signage leading to your inn, your arriving guests shouldn't have to guess what they are supposed to do when they arrive at your inn's door. Tasteful signs should tell them what to do. "Please ring the bell," "Please come in," etc.

Make sure your door bell works. And, if your inn doesn't have a doorbell, install one and make sure it has a light so your evening arrivals can find it. We had ours set up so that it only rang in our personal space. This way, we heard it, but sleeping or resting guests who had arrived on time didn't.

An alternative to a doorbell is a tasteful, but large enough to see, sign that tells your guests to come right in. This gets them out of potential inclement weather and makes them feel at home, but it still doesn't alert you to their presence unless you just happen to be standing in the front hall when they arrive. And, I would suggest that if all you have to do is hang around in your front entrance hall waiting for your guests to arrive, you're doing something very wrong - or, perhaps, very right. So how will you know that they have arrived?

Simple solution. A little electric eye that your guests trip when they enter your inn. It should ring a bell in your personal space and in your garage and in your basement and anywhere else that you might be - other than in town grocery shopping. If you show up to greet them a little grubby, that's okay. It tells them either that you have a life besides engaging in innkeeping - like you have a hobby - or that you are busy doing innkeeper stuff like baking something or weeding something or painting something. Noble tasks all and totally expected by your guests.

Finally, and this is really more about running your inn than just guest entrance stuff, what if you have to be away from the inn for a while - like on the aforementioned grocery shopping expedition? Here again, a neat, perhaps even typed, sign should do the trick and not make your arriving guests feel that they have come at a bad or wrong time. If more than one guest was expected, each guest found a note addressed to them taped to the door. The notes told them when we would be back, what room they were in and where it was, how to get settled in, where the menus for the area restaurants were located, etc. The notes were as welcoming as a note can be. But, having done all of that, we made sure that we greeted the guests as soon as we arrived back at the inn.

So, having loaded you down with all of this stuff about the various rooms and common areas and parking lots and signs in and around your inn, how big should your inn be, what type of inn fits your goals, where should your inn be located, how much income and what lifestyle expectations should be on your personal radar screen, how long should you expect to own your inn, how much should you spend and have left over, and a bunch of really neat things you should look for or include in your inn both inside and out - it's now time to get down to the basics of finding and buying one.

V. Warnings

#1

Starting pretty soon, I will be hanging around the edges of a lot of legal stuff - Listing Agreements, Dual Agency Agreements, Disclosure Statements, Confidentiality Agreements, Letters of Intent, Purchase and Sale Agreements, and all manner of things contractual and all manner of things financial.

Whereas, I come into this area with a lot of personal experience both from my innkeeping days as well as from my corporate life and I also have a ton of both common sense and business sense, I am not an attorney, I am not a CPA, I am not a real estate broker, and I am not a banker. I will be telling you how to create your own dream team to help you find, purchase, and then sell the inn of your dreams. If you don't take that advice seriously and if you think that you will be very wise and save yourself some money in the process, you deserve what happens to you. You will most likely do some pretty stupid things as you travel from where you are now to where you think you want to be, but don't shortstop the dream team process. Simply factor in the few thousand dollars in various fees and commissions you will pay your experts to help you reach your goal. Spend the money and don't look back.

To this end, I will not go into great detail on all of the legal forms, procedures, and other nuances. That way, you won't be able to shortstop the process and you won't be able to blame me for your mistakes. What the heck, as long as you're going to pay an attorney and a financial wizard and a broker and perhaps even a consultant, let them earn their keep.

2

Before you actually start your search and the creation of your dream team, be ready to buy an inn and move. Why, you may be asking yourself is he telling me that? Of course, I'm ready. But, are you really? Have you actually sat back and mentally prepared yourself for the unbelievably dramatic changes that your life will undergo? Have you actually pictured yourself quitting your day job, selling your home, leaving your family and friends, packing up all of your belongings and moving on to the next phase of your life? Have you actually come to grips with the fact that you may be investing a large chunk of your assets to make your dream come true? Have you?

Because it is just possible that the first inn (or almost the first inn) you find and visit will be the inn of your dreams. And, what a shame it would be if you have gone that far only to end up with cold feet because you're not really ready. So, get ready. Get mentally, physically, and financially ready. And, by the way, where does the expression "get cold feet" come from in the context of backing away from something or other?

VI. Finding Inns for Sale...

Finding inns for sale is much easier than it used to be. Twenty years ago, when there were only 2,000 - 3,000 inns in existence (at least in this country so I read) and the world wide web hadn't been invented by Al Gore yet and there weren't any real estate brokers who specialized in the field, it was a Herculean task to do a major, perhaps even a nationwide, search. Now the job is relatively easy.

And, in addition to the Internet and inn brokers there are always the local residential real estate brokers, and, of course, innkeepers themselves.

But, the first thing you need to do is develop the parameters of your search, which we dealt with earlier, and stick with them. Oh, you may want to broaden them just a bit since you probably know that you will never find exactly what you are looking for. But don't stray too far. Don't just chase after inns in every part of the country because they look good on a broker's website and seem to be the right size and you figure that you could learn to live anywhere. If you don't develop some serious criteria, you are heading for a lot of grief and you will waste a lot of time and spend a lot of money in your search and you just may end up buying the inn of your nightmares.

A. The Internet...

The Internet is far and away the easiest, virtual one-stop-shopping way to find inns anywhere in the world - literally the world. But, let's concentrate on the good 'ol U.S. of A. Following is some of the information that took about .3 seconds to find from a Google search using the words "inns for sale" in quotes. The five websites listed below are out of 183,000 entries - that's right, 183,000 - on the Google search. In the 30 or 40 that I looked at, there were already many duplicates - the same site under slightly different listings - but you get the idea. It is all out there and it is not hard to find. Keep in mind, however, that even as I write this, changes are undoubtedly in the works. It is the classic moving target. So don't blame me if some of these sites are long gone by the time this book gets into print and you get to this chapter. Others will have undoubtedly taken their place. And, by the way, these sites will often have listings for homes that would - at least in the minds of the broker or the seller - make ideal inns even if they aren't inns at the moment.

http://www.bedandbreakfast.com/
http://www.bbonline.com/
http://innkeepers.com/
http://bedandbreakfastforsale.com/
http://innsforsale.com/

Some of these are single real estate broker sites with that broker's own listings. Others are comprised of listings from several different brokers with links to the individual brokers' own sites for more details and possibly more properties for sale. Farther down the Google list are individual innkeepers who have listed their own properties and apparently haven't figured out how to get their listing to the top of the search engine's list.

So all you have to do is block out an hour or two, have plenty of paper in your printer, and go online. Stick very close to your criteria. There are literally hundreds of inns for sale in every corner of the land. If you don't stay focused, you will be in big trouble.

At the end of your Internet search, you will probably be very pleased with the variety of properties that seem to meet your criteria and, in the process, you will have obtained the names of the real estate brokers or innkeepers who have these properties listed for sale. More on what to do with this wealth of information later.

By the way, it occurred to me that some of you have absolutely no idea what a Google search is and how to do one. It does sound rather odd now doesn't it? So here is a very brief run through.

The first thing you have to do is log onto the Internet. If you don't know how to do that ask your seven-year-old nephew or your eight-year-old granddaughter. Somewhere on the screen will be a blank space with the word "search" next to it - in that space type in www.google.com.

When the Google home page comes up, there will be another blank space with the words "Google search" below it. In that space type the words "inns for sale" (including the quotes) and click on the words Google search. Bingo. In milliseconds you will have before you every one of the 183,000 entries or some such number the day you do your search with a brief description about each one. Well, actually, you will have to scroll down and change pages to see all 183,000 of them, but they're all there. All you have to do is keep reading and keep scrolling until you find one that looks promising and click on it. You will then be on that parties website and if they've done their job right - or, if their web master has done his job right - the rest should be obvious and, therefore, easy. By the way, under "B&Bs for sale" there are 80,800 entries. Several of them are duplicates of the "inns for sale" list, but some of them may not be. We'll get to contacting these sellers in a moment. A way to fine-tune your Google search is to fine-tune what you type on the Google search line. Try "Inns for Sale in Virginia" if you're looking for inns for sale in Virginia.

Or, rather than using Google, you can enter the actual website from the previous list and you'll end up directly on their sites. If none of that web search made any sense, good luck in designing your inns website and taking reservations through the site or through e-mail. We will deal with this later in the section on marketing and advertising.

B. Local newspapers...

Local newspapers are not usually a good source, but let's talk about them for a moment. If your geographical criteria have narrowed your search all the way down to specific towns, you might find inns for sale in those towns' local newspapers, but don't count on it. Innkeepers rarely advertise locally or allow their brokers to advertise locally because they want to keep the knowledge that their inn is for sale away from their own townsfolk, their fellow area innkeepers (it might hurt referrals), and especially their guests. Think about it. How would you feel as an arriving guest to see a For Sale sign on the lawn as you pull up to an inn with your reservations in hand? Of course, an inn can be advertised locally without having a sign on the lawn. But the reality is that the odds of finding a buyer in a small town are very small so why waste the money on local advertising. So the local, small town newspapers are rarely good sources so subscribing to them would be the classic search for the needle in the haystack. And, in most cases, small town brokers don't specialize in inn sales. There simply isn't enough business in that arena to allow them to do it full time or to do it well, for that matter. Having said that, a local real estate broker - even one which doesn't specialize in inns - could be aware of one for sale in the area they service and might actually have a listing or they could be aware of a private home that is just waiting to be converted into an inn. So, if all else fails and you really want to live in a specific town, check out the local paper and contact a broker or two and find out if there are inns for sale or possibly old homes waiting to be converted. It couldn't hurt.

C. Trade journals...

Trade journals can be a very good source. Throughout the years they have come and gone as many trade journals do, but as of this writing there is a very good one still publishing. It's called Arrington's B&B Journal at www.BNBJournal.com. Each issue is usually filled with excellent articles on how to run an inn, clean an inn, tidy up your website, and things like that, but like most trade journals, they survive on their advertising and Arrington's is loaded with advertising. You can buy everything from little bars of soap with your inn's name on them to really fluffy towels to inns themselves.

The last several pages are usually devoted to inns for sale and homes that could be converted into inns listed by area of the country and a bunch of ads by inn brokers who would just love to sell you an inn that they have listed or represent you in your search.

As an aside, you might want to subscribe to Arrington's because your search will probably take several months if not longer and in the process of seeing all of these inns for sale, you will be able to clip and save articles that will make your innkeeping life a lot easier. Why, you might want to continue your subscription on into your innkeeping days. Trust me, there is always a better way to make a bed and another breakfast recipe worth trying.

D. Innkeepers...

Innkeepers who have decided to sell their inns themselves, will, of course be an excellent source. Those who are actively trying to sell their property should have ads in all the right places - the inn website search engines and the trade journals. Also, as I related earlier, most of the inns you have stayed in have been for sale. You just didn't know it. Now that you are actively in the market, you have almost nothing to lose by thinking back over your inn visits when you were merely a guest and contacting the innkeepers whose inns you think you would like to own.

If one or more of the inns you call are, in fact, actively on the market and are listed with a real estate broker, the innkeepers are legally bound to simply give you their brokers' name and phone number. No problem there. Just add the properties to your list of possibles. If a property is on the market and not listed with a broker, again, add it to your list. And, if a property you call is not on the market, your call just might spur the innkeeper into action.

At this stage in your search, don't make too many calls to innkeepers, brokers, or send any e-mails, just make notes and make copies of any ads that interest you. What you are trying to do at this stage is scope out the market and it won't take very long so don't worry about losing out on a property that is really exciting. You are simply looking for inns that meet your criteria.

E. The real estate broker...

The real estate broker for better or for worse, is the key player in the inns for sale marketplace. Except for the innkeepers who try to sell their own properties, the real estate brokers are the characters who bag the listings, run the ads, and facilitate the sales. So the broker who has the listing for an inn and advertises it, is probably going to be your first contact on the long and winding road that will lead to your eventual purchase.

In addition to dealing with the brokers who have the listings on inns that interest you, you might opt to hire your own broker to assist you in your search and be a key member of your dream team. In fact, you might hire several brokers if your search is going to cover several states. So now may be as good a time as any to begin to demystify the terminology, nuances, and legalities of broker/seller/buyer relationships and to spend some time in dealing with who they are, what they do, how much they get paid, who pays them, and how to tell the good ones from the bums.

Listing Agreement

When you contact a broker who advertises a property, remember that no matter how nice and perhaps even qualified the broker is he was actually hired by and will be paid by the seller of the property. And since the Listing Agreement that the broker has in place with the seller has a bunch of fine print and legal requirements, there is only so much that the broker can legally reveal to you. Things that you *probably won't learn* from the broker that could be of extreme value are things like why the property is really for sale, how much the seller is really willing to accept, what offers have been refused and why, are there really any other buyers who are about to strike, etc.

It is also possible, but unlikely, that the broker whose ad you saw isn't the only broker with a listing on that property. The seller might have engaged more than one broker which would result in what is known as an open listing - more than one broker could be working the property. The only effect that this situation should have on you is that while you are doing everything possible to see and perhaps buy the property, another broker could be about to close the sale with another buyer. Boy, would that make you mad. Remember that in the open listing scenario, all brokers working the property will only know what the innkeeper has told them because only the innkeeper will know everything that is going on.

Even if the broker, whose ad you saw, has the only listing on the property, other brokers might still be working on a sale of that property. In this case, however, the broker with the listing will be aware of those situations because he will, of necessity, be involved in those transactions.

So just to keep everything straight and up front, what you need to do when you contact the broker whose ad you saw, is simply ask him if he has an exclusive listing. If the answer is yes, forge ahead. If the answer is no, there's an open listing on the property, forge ahead anyway, but make sure that when you find out who the innkeeper is, you make him aware of the fact that you know what is going on - it's all perfectly legal - and that you expect to be kept up to date on the status of other interested parties. This way you won't spend a lot of time, money, nervous energy, and wishful thinking on a property that could be sold out from under you. This should not be a contentious issue between you and the broker and the innkeeper. It boils down to a matter of common courtesy and fair play.

If this section isn't clear to you, read it again, because I just did and it's clear to me.

Dual Agency Agreement

So that he doesn't have to split his commission with another broker that you might bring into the picture, the listing broker, with permission from the seller, *might* ask you to sign a Dual Agency Agreement. This agreement states that the broker is actually representing both the seller and the buyer, but his commission is coming from the seller.

Ever since the dual agency concept came into existence a few years ago, I've had a lot of trouble with it conceptually. How, in heaven's name can a broker fairly represent both the buyer and the seller? How can he discuss the strategy of an offer with you and at the same time discus the strategy of your offer with the seller? How can he share with you how anxious the seller is to sell - a bit of information that would, obviously, be quite helpful in your negotiations - without betraying the seller's confidence? What if he tells the seller how anxious you are to buy the property? Think what that would do to your negotiations. At the end of the day - there's that phrase again - in my opinion - the listing or selling broker is in reality working for the seller. If the listing broker tries to get you to sign a dual agency agreement right out of the box, tell him, "No thank you." He is still duty bound to represent the seller and you can still bring your own broker into the picture.

Confidentiality Agreement

The only thing you should sign at this stage of the buying game is a Confidentiality Agreement, but only if you are asked to do so. This is an agreement that allows the broker to send you the details of the property - things like income and expense statements, occupancy figures, owner's tax returns, the seller's Disclosure Statement (see below), etc. Stuff you absolutely have to have to begin to make an informed decision to continue exploring the property. The Confidentiality Agreement states that you must keep this information confidential - hence its name. But, for you to make the best use of the information, you must be able to share it with all of the members of your dream team - usually this is your broker if you have one, your attorney, and your accountant. The agreement must give you that right.

Remember that you have been warned not to sign anything until your attorney has given you the okay. So this is the time to round up an attorney. In this case, however, your attorney can really be any old real estate attorney. He doesn't have to be licensed in the state that the inn is in and he doesn't have to really be an expert regarding the sale of inns. There is nothing special about a Confidentiality Agreement except that it *must allow* you to share the information with your attorney, your accountant, your consultant, and your own real estate broker - even if you don't have an attorney, an accountant, a consultant, or your own real estate broker yet. If the listing or selling broker or the seller if there is no broker won't allow you - in writing - to share the information with your entire dream team, walk away. Are you paying attention? I said, walk away. If you cave in on this point, there is virtually no hope for you to get through this whole ordeal in one piece.

STRATEGY NUMBER 1 IN THE ART OF NEGOTIATING IS THE ABILITY TO WALK AWAY FROM THE DEAL.

Disclosure Statement

In case you are not familiar with a Disclosure Statement, which may not be named exactly that from state to state, many states now require the seller of a property to disclose to the buyer - to the best of his knowledge - the problems with the property. The seller must disclose things like does the basement leak, is there asbestos around the pipes or around the insulation, is there a vermin problem, are the water pipes made of lead, etc. This document does not give you a whole lot of protection because all the seller can disclose is what he knows. To this end, I have somewhat sarcastically renamed the Disclosure Statement the I Know Nothing Statement. You still need to do your own inspection and we'll get into this in more detail later.

F. Getting your own broker...

Getting your own broker might make a lot of sense. If, for whatever reason, and there could be a host of them, you and your attorney think that it would be in your best interest to have your own real estate broker to conduct your inn search and be on your side of the table during the ensuing negotiations, here's how to find and qualify one.

Oh, heck, before we get into that, let's take a minute and highlight some of those reasons - once again, not in order of importance:

It won't cost you anything. Your broker will be compensated for his efforts on your behalf by being paid one half of the commission paid by the seller. The commission is a percentage of the sales price and is usually around 6% - the actual commission varies somewhat from place to place and deal to deal. So, if the final sales price of the inn is $500,000, the commission should be around $30,000. If there are two brokers involved - the seller's broker and your broker - they will split this amount and it will all come from the seller.

Note: If the inn owner is selling the property himself - without a broker - forget what I just wrote. In this scenario, you will pay your broker if you have one from your own funds. His fee or commission will be an item that you two negotiate before he begins representing you.

Another note: In some unique circumstances, there could be three brokers involved in a sale, which would mean that the commission will be divided up three ways. How would this happen, you ask? Well, there could be a listing broker, a selling broker, and your broker. Not to worry. The money will still all come from the seller.

A good broker who is experienced in this field will make sure that you - and your attorney - get all of the information that you need to make a decision and to close a sale. He will ask all of the right questions at the right time in the process.

A good broker who is experienced in this field will know who to call for the appropriate inspections - structural, mechanical, environmental, health agencies, surveyors, etc.

A good broker who is experienced in this field will know which local financial institutions might consider your deal and he might even know the name of the key person at the bank or at the savings and loan or at the mortgage broker.

A good broker who is experienced in this field will simply make your life easier.

So, how do you find one?

Interestingly, the best place to look is the same place you will look to find inns for sale - the Internet, local newspapers, and trade journals.

It might come to pass that you will engage the broker who has a listing on a property that you are interested in to be your broker as your search continues beyond that initial property.

Whether you retain this broker or go into the market place to find another one, there are things you must do to qualify him.

Look at the quality of the broker's advertisements and then check out the number of inns the broker has listed on his website. Try to ascertain the geographical area that the broker services and whether the broker specializes in inns. It would ease the pain of your search if one broker who specializes in inn sales could handle all of Virginia for example. However, if a broker's ad also mentions the fact that he will handle your insurance and heating oil needs as well as arrange to have your lawn mowed, and cater your daughter's wedding, keep looking.

So when you have honed in on a broker or two in each of the areas that are on top of your list geographically, the next step is to phone interview them. Please don't shortstop this step. You are going to rely on this person to lead you to your personal promise land. You should be extremely comfortable and confident with your choice.

When you call, you might as well give him your real name and the purpose of your call - no need for subtlety here. "I'm John Smith (if that is your real name) and I'm thinking about purchasing an inn. I saw your ad in the _____ (name where you saw the ad - brokers love this because it tells them they their advertising dollars are working) and I have a few questions." Try these - and take notes:

- ✓ Are you licensed as a real estate broker in _____? (here would be a nice place to name the state that will be part of your search). Brokers are licensed by state real estate boards. They are required to take courses, pass tests, and pay for licenses. They are also required to take continuing education courses so that they keep up to date with changes in the law and other things that brokers do that might change from time to time.

✓ Do you specialize in the sale of inns?
✓ If not, what else do you do for a living?
✓ What percentage of your time are you a real estate broker?
✓ How long have you been a real estate broker?
✓ How long have you handled the sale of inns?
✓ How many properties do you have listed at the moment? Are these exclusive listings?
✓ How many inns have you sold in the past three years where you have been the selling broker?
✓ How many inns have you sold in the past five years where you have been the selling broker?
✓ **Note**: What you're after here is to learn whether the broker you are interviewing is lucky or even good enough to get listings, but can't sell them without other brokers involved. This isn't necessarily a bad thing, but it is a bit of interesting information you should have in your evaluation of the broker.
✓ What is the price range of the inns that you have sold?
  o **Note:** The point here is to ascertain if the broker is working in your price ballpark or is he at least in the parking lot of your ballpark.
✓ How many associates do you have with complete knowledge of your listings?
  o **Note:** If the broker is a one-man shop, you may not get the attention you deserve and need. He could be off working another deal on the only day that you can arrange your

schedule to see the inn that generated your call. Or, he could get hit in the ass by a bus and nobody will be able to step up and complete the deal.

✓ Have you ever had any lawsuits filed against you for screwing up a deal? You may choose to use a word besides "screwing" but you know where I'm going.

One last, but very important step in the process of evaluating a broker is to contact the state real estate board and ask if the broker is in good standing. They are usually unable to provide commentary on whether the broker you are asking after is any good and they probably can't recommend one broker over another, but they can tell you if the guy plays by the rules, pays his dues on time, and is current in his continuing education courses. Just one more piece to the puzzle.

All of this information is most valuable if it can be compared with similar information obtained from a competing broker or two. Then you get to pick the broker you would prefer to be part of your team. But, there might not be a competing broker in a small market. Therefore, if the broker you have interviewed meets all of your criteria, has no serious competition, but also happens to be a real jerk - someone you are having a hard time communicating with - you have three choices. You can still deal with him and make the best of it, you can go on without a broker on your team, or you can see if each broker with a listing in that geographical area with the sellers' permission and signature will entertain the infamous Dual Agency Agreement. Sometimes you won't be able to round up the perfect dream team. In that case, of course, your dream team won't be a dream team.

If luck is on your side and you find a broker to be a member of your team, what do you do next? Well, how about signing him up. I will leave this agreement to you and your attorney and, once again, this is not a major legal issue and doesn't require an attorney with much if any inn-sale experience and, therefore, could be handled by your "regular" attorney from back home.

The agreement must include a non-performance escape clause - a way for you to get out of the agreement, without a legal battle, if the guy doesn't perform to your satisfaction. The decision should be entirely yours and should be quite subjective. Don't get locked into performance criteria like he has to bring a certain number of properties to your attention in a certain length of time, because to meet this objective the broker might send you information on properties way outside your range - at either end of the range. To avoid this sham attempt to be in agreement, you could always strangle your broker contractually by spelling out exactly what is an acceptable property, but you should really leave this relatively wide open. A property that may seem at first blush to be out of your range - again at either end of the range - might actually be one that you might consider. For example it might be smaller than you are looking for, but is in the perfect community with really neat part time job opportunities or expansion possibilities. Just make sure that you can crash the agreement virtually at any time that suits you. (By the way, what does "at first blush" really mean anyway?)

The only other things the agreement *must* spell out is how, how much, and when your broker will be paid for his services. You should not pay a dime up front and you should pay nothing in fees or costs for the broker to conduct his search. The broker should only get paid when he actually ends up being part of a sale. The best of all worlds here, of course, is if he gets involved in a co-broke situation wherein he gets half of the commission, which is paid by the seller. When your broker contacts the broker with the listing, he will ascertain what the commission arrangement is and he will know how much he will get paid at closing depending, of course, on the final price.

If the broker finds a property that is not listed with another broker and he can't convince the seller to list the property with him - and thereby have the seller end up paying the commission - your agreement should include a fee for this situation. And the fee should be related to what one half of a normal commission would be. One half because that's all he would receive if the sale was a co-broke situation. Get it?

Likewise, if you bring a property to your broker's attention that you found in your own search - like a property on the Internet that a seller is selling on his own, or a property that you once stayed in and found out was for sale after you contacted the owner - your agreement should include a similar fee for this situation.

It probably goes without saying that your attorney will think up about a dozen other clauses, but I'll leave that up to the two of you.

G. Filling out the rest of your team...

Filling out the rest of your team should be done with the same level of intensity as you heroically displayed in the selection of your broker. I really don't think it is necessary to provide you with separate list of questions for you to ask your potential attorney and your potential financial advisor/accountant because it would look a whole lot like the list of questions you asked your potential broker. Things like: Are you properly licensed by the appropriate licensing authority? Are you experienced in the buying and selling of inns? Do you have sufficient staff to back yourself up in the event of a work overload or emergency? And so on. And, please don't shortstop this process either. Ask the questions and write down the answers.

The question you are or should be asking yourself at this point is how do I find attorneys and accountants to interview? This really isn't a difficult process. You might and probably should ask your broker to provide you with the names of attorneys and accountants that he has dealt with in past, successful inn negotiations. Don't worry about this becoming a "Good 'Ol Boys Club." You will be conducting your own interviews and, hopefully, face-to-face meetings to make sure that you are comfortable with the quality and style of your team members.

A real positive outcome of this approach - that being obtaining the names of your attorney and accountant from your already-screened broker - is that this team, having already worked together, will know each other and be familiar with each other's approaches to things. This will reduce, if not completely eliminate, the learning curve - the time it would take for them to get familiar with each other. And, this will reduce your expenses for those team members who are paid by the hour.

Actually, the only learning curve will be the time they will all take in figuring out how the heck to deal with you.

Just a note of caution: While you are creating your dream team please don't sign anything - let me repeat that - please don't sign anything, no, let's make that *don't sign anything* until you have engaged competent legal counsel to review all documents before you sign them.

I have mentioned elsewhere that your dream team could include a consultant. There are folks out there who will, for a fee, assist you in the inn buying process. Those who do this are not licensed and can only provide sage advice such as that included in this book. But, in the real world, they can actually apply it to specific inns rather than in the abstract. They certainly can be invaluable. Look for their ads in trade journals and on inn-related websites.

Some real estate brokers also act as consultants and actually conduct property inspections and issue reports in very pretty binders. Their ads in the same places (journals and websites) will mention the fact that they do this for a living.

Just another note of caution: If, given the circumstances of your search and your desire to have both a belt and suspenders holding up your pants, you do chose to have your own broker and a consultant, be cautious. It is strongly recommended that you engage separate individuals or firms to perform these tasks to

184

avoid a conflict if interest. If your broker is also your consultant, he just might "overlook" something important in his consulting capacity in order to keep the deal alive so he can bag his commission from the seller as well as his consulting fee from you. He may actually do this unwittingly, but the damage could still be irreparable. As long as you are paying someone to assist you, that person might as well look at the property with a fresh pair of eyes.

One last note of caution: Screen your consultant just as carefully as you have screened the other members of your team and ask for samples of actual reports that they have prepared for other clients and an approximate cost of the report which will, most likely, depend on the size of the property. You should compare the report to what you have learned in this book and try to determine if you would be getting your money's worth.

You might be better off finding your attorney first - before you find your real estate broker and your financial wizard and your consultant. Your attorney back home - the one who may not be an experienced inn purchase and sale attorney - might be able to provide you with the name of an associate in the area of your search. That attorney then could be an excellent source to help you find a broker, an accountant, and a consultant. Regardless of where you begin the process - begin the process and follow all of the steps outlined above. You will need all of the help you can get.

So now that your team is in place and you have begun your search for an inn to buy, what do you do next? What documents and other material should you expect to obtain from the seller or broker at the beginning of the process? When do you make arrangements to actually visit an inn and what should you do when you get there? When and how do you prepare and submit an offer? What special clauses should your offer include? And things like that. Well, read on.

VII. How to Actually Buy an Inn...

How to actually buy an inn should be thought of as part art, part science, part business, part legal, and part financial, not to mention part emotional. And speaking of parts, for the most part, I will remove the emotional aspect from my discussion for I can hardly be expected to factor into the mix the range of emotions that all potential innkeepers will bring to the table in the inn buying process. Suffice it to say that emotions will have a lot to do with your buying decision, much as they will in even getting you to decide to really start looking for an inn in the first place. The only caveat that I can give you here is that, to the greatest extent possible, you should keep your emotions in check. In fact, that's why I strongly recommend that you have a top notch attorney and a top notch accountant and a top notch real estate broker and, perhaps a top notch consultant - your own personal dream team - all of whom have extensive experience in buying and selling inns and who you should expect to individually and collectively both figuratively and literally slap you around when your emotions begin to win the battle with your common sense and your pocketbook. Perhaps a really good psychiatrist should also be on your dream team.

If you didn't get the picture in the last section, here are some reminders. Please, please, please don't hire your brother-in-law the lawyer and your spouse's uncle the accountant (even if he's the guy who is lending you some or all of the funds you will need to get into this business) and your third cousin on your mother's side, the real estate broker, unless they are really good at what they do and have been involved in several inn transactions and just happen to reside in and are licensed in the state or states where you are conducting your search. This is a specialized field that requires specialized skills and don't let anybody tell you otherwise.

And don't create your dream team from experts in your current backyard. If you intend to conduct a multi-state search say in Vermont and New Hampshire, you may get away with dealing with one real estate broker/consultant and perhaps one financial wizard and perhaps one attorney if you find one of each licensed and experienced in both states. However, even in searching relatively small neighboring states, you may still need an expert from each discipline from each state. And certainly if your search will cover Vermont and Virginia - this, of course, assumes that one of you likes it hot and the other doesn't, which means that you could already be in trouble - you will need two complete sets of experts.

But, let's go back to buying an inn. Here are the steps to follow at this stage of the process:

✓ Develop a list of the information that you must have in your possession to enable you to determine if the property is worth a visit. You could create this list from the information presented here. It could include input from your broker and it could also include input from your consultant. But, regardless of where it comes from, at the very least it should include the following:

o At least three years of income and expense statements - this of course assumes that the place has been in business for at least three years or that the current owners have owned it for that long. These need not be audited financial statements. We'll talk about how to prove the accuracy of the information later on.

o A batch of photographs of the exterior, the interior, the innkeepers personal space, and the grounds. These will enable you to determine if the inn meets at least some of your visual criteria.

o A plot plan or site plan that will enable you to see how the inn sits on the property and where it is in relation to the road, the parking lot, the neighbors, etc. The plan should also indicate who all of the neighbors are - not just their names, but what they are, i.e. a farm, a motel, a McDonald's restaurant, a fireworks factory, etc. and what they are zoned for. And don't forget to have included on the site plan what's across the street. But remember that what's happening on those neighboring sites now could change in the proverbial heartbeat. Hence the need for zoning information.

o A floor plan of the inn - all floors including the innkeeper's personal space - with measurements shown on the plan.

o A really comprehensive list of all personal property - guest room furniture, common area furniture, innkeeper's furniture, window coverings, dishes, linens, appliances, you name it - indicating what is and what is not included in the sale. The list should include seasonal equipment as well since the seller may be retiring or moving to a different clime - things like roof rakes - and if you don't know what a roof rake is call an immediate halt to the Vermont portion of your search. An inn sold with everything included - so, in theory, you don't have to bring or buy anything except furniture for your personal space - is called a *turnkey sale*. I don't know this for sure, but I'm pretty sure that the phrase came from the fact that all you have to do to take over an inn sold on a turnkey basis is have the seller turn the key - presumably to the front door - over to you. If the inn is being sold on other than a turnkey basis, you need to know what you're up against - what is and is not included - to make the place fit to run the day of the close.

o The inn's current marketing material, which should include its brochure, its website, the list of websites and publications in which the inn is listed - not listed for sale, but listed as a place to stay - and any designations the property has received, such as its AAA, Mobil Guide, and Fodor's ratings.

o Information on the area so you can begin to determine the strength of the community, its ability to continue to attract tourists, whether it has a Chinese restaurant, and whether you want to live there. This should include the website of the town or the local chamber of commerce or both.

- o A general description of the physical condition of the property. How old are the mechanical systems - the heating, plumbing, electrical - and the roof? And what condition they are in.

- o Are there any environmental conditions that you should be aware of?

The way you get this information amazingly enough is to simply ask the broker or seller for it - depending on whether the property is listed with a broker or being sold directly by the innkeeper. If the innkeeper or the broker doesn't have all of the information that you are asking for, tell them to round it up. A good marketing package whether prepared by the seller or his real estate broker should include most if not all of this stuff anyway.

The marketing packages prepared by some real estate brokers and innkeepers are extremely comprehensive and include all of these items and more. The thinking in creating this type of comprehensive marketing package is why waste everybody's time by dribbling out the necessary information.

Other brokers and innkeepers take the position that the marketing package should be a bit of a tease - tell the potential buyer just enough to pique his interest. The thinking here is that despite a well-defined set of criteria, most buyers will be flexible on some of their demands so show them just enough at this stage to get them to see the property.

There is merit in both approaches, but obviously, the more information you have up front, the easier it will be for you to determine if a visit is worthwhile. And, even if you stumble into the tease-type marketing package, other information can still be had at this stage of the game by demanding it. Remember that you are the customer and the customer is (almost) always right. Be polite, but be firm.

An ideal situation will be if you are able to round up the necessary information on more than one inn in a chosen area. This will enable you to make the most out of your inn-visiting trip. You might actually make arrangements to see a second inn in a given area even if it isn't exactly what you are looking for. The more inns you visit, the more experienced you will become in making the process worthwhile.

If you intend to build your own inn or buy a really neat old home and convert it into an inn, your search will take the same approach, pretty much. Everything to do with location and zoning and floor plans - if it's an existing building - and environmental issues and plot plans, etc. The only thing you won't have - and it could be a very big "thing" - are income and expense figures and perhaps things like furniture linens, dishes, etc. We'll deal with this issue later.

So, lets go into what you should say and do in the inn-visiting process. That is after all the next step.

A. Visiting an inn...

Visiting an inn should be both educational and enjoyable. Educational because the purpose of the visit is to learn as much as you can as fast as you can. Enjoyable because, if at all possible, you should stay at the inn overnight and, why not treat the stay as a mini vacation. After all, when you end up buying an inn, as we said before, you will never be able to take a vacation again.

But, seriously folks, there is much to do when you make an inn visit and the more preplanning you do with all of the information that you've obtained, the more worthwhile the visit will be. So here is what your visit should include and what you should expect to accomplish.

How ever many brokers are involved - you may have hired one and the seller may have listed the property with one and there could be a third one involved in the process as we said before - they should all be there during your initial visit. If the seller doesn't have a broker, but you do, you should advise the seller that you have engaged a broker and that you require that he be with you during your initial visit. If you have retained the services of a consultant, you may or may not want to have him along on this initial visit. If the property appears to be everything you have hoped for, bring your consultant in now. If the property is in the close, but maybe not quite category, you may choose to save yourself some consultant fees until you have scoped it out. Finally, if you don't have a broker or a consultant at this point, forge ahead with your visit. You can always have your broker and/or consultant visit the property with you on your second visit - if it comes to that - or have them visit it without you.

It is critically important that you are able to see the entire inn on this initial visit - the entire inn. Every room. So make sure that the innkeeper and his broker, if there is one, know that this is an absolute requirement. It may mean that you will have to see a room or two with guest's stuff in them. Big deal. It will be up to the innkeeper to come up with a plausible story for his guests. One that always worked for us was to have him tell the guests that a couple will be visiting the inn to make arrangements to rent the entire inn for a family gathering. The broker(s) and or the consultant could be passed off as family members. Of course, the innkeeper could always tell his other guests that the inn is for sale and that it will be shown to a prospective buyer during their stay. How novel would that be? The reality is that none of that should matter to you. You simply have to be able to see everything.

Take along your camera and don't forget to use it. Photograph absolutely everything. Stand in every corner of every room - guest rooms as well as common area rooms as well as innkeeper's personal space as well as the basement as well as the attic. Well, don't just stand in every corner - take a picture while you are there. Photograph the exterior from every angle. Photograph the neighboring properties. Photograph the inn from the neighboring properties. You should think about keeping a log of every shot especially if you are going to be visiting more than one property. These pictures can certainly get confusing. "Which room was that, Ethel?" As I recall, this is where the a-picture-is-worth-a-thousand-words phrase actually came from. Later, when you are back home you can spend time at your leisure revisiting the inn through these photographs and making appropriate notes.

Taking the outside pictures could cause the seller some concern - the neighbors might wonder what's going on. A good story here is that you are having new brochures made up and you are having a bunch of pictures taken as part of that process.

Take along a large tape measure and measure everything even if the floor plan that you received in advance of your visit contained measurements. If, after a few measurements it becomes obvious that the measurements you were given are accurate, you have my permission to stop measuring.

If you happen to know about things structural and/or mechanical plan to spend some time looking into these things. Again, take pictures and take notes. If you don't know about things structural and/or mechanical, don't waste your time and everybody else's time by pretending that you do. Leave this up to your inspector. We'll deal with the requirement to have an independent inspection a little later.

When you check in, use the inn as though you are a guest - which you probably will be because, most likely, the innkeeper will charge you for your stay. As an aside, don't expect to use your search as a means to stay for free in a bunch of inns. Some sellers might comp your room, but most won't. So, get your money's worth. Move into your room with all of your luggage. Hang your clothes in the closet - if there is a closet. Put all of your toiletries in the bathroom. In short, begin the process of determining if the inn meets the objectives outlined in the earlier part of this book.

Make arrangements in advance of your visit to spend some quality time with the innkeeper after the brokers and/or consultants have left - perhaps during or after dinner. Make this meeting a requirement of your visit. I can't think of one good reason why the request should be denied. In preparation for this session, make up a list of questions, ask them in a conversational style, and write down the answers. The purpose of this session is to just talk when everybody is pretty much off guard. Talk about the life of the innkeeper. Talk about life in the town. Talk about what the innkeeper would do over if he had the chance to do things over. You should weave your questions into this conversation like Columbo weaved questions into his conversations with suspected bad guys. "Oh, and by the way, why are you really selling the inn?" Act like you know but it skipped your mind. If you don't remember or you never heard of Peter Falk's portrayal of Detective Columbo, ask your mother. In most real estate transactions brokers fight tooth and nail to keep the buyer and seller from meeting each other without the brokers present. Heaven forbid the seller should say something that his broker doesn't think he should. But buying an inn is quite different from most other real estate transactions. Because you are buying a business as well as a home as well as a life style, there is much that the broker doesn't know. These one-on-one or probably two-on-two sessions - two innkeepers and two of you - can be the most valuable time spent in the inn buying process. Of course, you may feign illness or cut this meeting short if the inn isn't really what you are looking for once you have seen it live. Come to think of it, you could actually be honest with the seller and tell him that the inn isn't exactly what you are looking for and then go to your room.

Visit the town hall and the local chamber of commerce and get a hold of a new resident's package. You do this by telling the clerk that you are thinking about moving to wherever you are. Yes, you could have made arrangements to round up this package in advance of your visit. Don't tell anybody that you are thinking about buying the XYZ Inn unless the seller has told you that the fact that his inn is for sale is common knowledge. Remember that you may have already signed a Confidentiality Agreement, which makes you legally bound to keep your mouth shut. Also, at the town hall or the chamber office or perhaps at the local visitor's center or information booth, pick up copies of all the flyers and brochures of the area attractions including all of the areas inns and restaurants. Oh, and buy a copy of the local newspaper especially if the town has one of those Thursday local papers the kind with all of the local gossip and other local happenings. They sure tell you a lot about where a town is and where it's going. And, there just might be an ad for an inn that's for sale. If the town is high on your list, you might purchase a subscription and pay extra for having them mail you your weekly issue. Do this even if the inn you are there to see doesn't measure up. Another one might come along.

If there are other inns in the area that you found perhaps on the chamber's website or elsewhere that either weren't for sale or, if they were, weren't of particular interest, drive by all of them anyway and take pictures and make notes. These could end up being both your competition as well as your new neighbors so you might as well begin to scope them out now.

You should find a few moments in what has obviously become a very busy schedule to drop in on a local real estate broker or two. You cannot tell them that you are in town to see the XYZ Inn, but you can tell them that you are very interested in buying an inn and you were wondering if there are any for sale in the area. If they mention the XYZ Inn you can tell them that you are aware of that one. You can even tell them that you are staying there and that you are possibly interested in it. This will let them know that you are serious. Since it is highly unlikely that any local broker is in the inn business as we discussed before, don't expect any of their ads to mention that they sell inns for a living. In fact, the first broker you drop in on just might end up referring you to another broker who might be more familiar with the inn market. If one of the local brokers happens to have a listing or knows of an inn for sale simply gather the information as you would have from any other source and make arrangements, if appropriate, to see the property either on this trip or on the next one. Once again, don't sign anything - like a representation letter - that hasn't been blessed by your attorney.

If religion is an important consideration in your life and/or you think it will be an important consideration to your guests, you might want to spend some time going through the phone book as well as driving around town to see which religious denominations are nearby. Remember if your search is taking you to a small town, you or your guests might have to drive to a neighboring town to attend religious services. If you happen to be into some far out California sect and your search is in New England or, perhaps, Kansas, forget it. But, here's a thought. You can always start your own church in your spare time.

If membership in groups like Rotary or the Elks or the Masons or the Royal Order of Something Or Other are important to you and if you think they will be important to your guests, go through the same drill as you went through in finding churches and temples. And, just like you can always start your own church, you can always start your own lodge or brotherhood or whatever your organization calls its local pockets if there isn't one within a reasonable driving distance of your inn.

Finally, drive around the area. Spend a fair amount of time doing this and do it with a fresh pair of eyes. Often when we go to a tourist or resort area we are wearing traveler's blinders. We want everything to be lovely so all we see is lovely. We go from the lovely inn to the lovely restaurant driving past the lovely town green past the lovely homes alongside the lovely little churches. But every town has its dumpsters, a home or three in need of extensive repairs, the grubbier end of town, and so forth. Find these and make sure that they don't change your mind about becoming a resident of the community.

Having done all of that during your visit, the inn will either still be on your list of possibles or it won't. If it isn't, take some time to think through the visit and how you might improve the process. Did you learn things during the visit that, had you known them in advance, would have had you scrap your plans for a visit? If so, make sure that you add them to your list of pre-visit information that you will require of the next seller or broker. If the whole experience worked, but the inn just didn't measure up, so be it. Keep looking. If the whole experience worked and the inn did measure up, it's time to take the next steps in the inn buying process.

One last thought on the inn visit strategy. If the inn is everything you have dreamed of, if it fits all of your criteria, if you would buy it on the spot and move in that afternoon if only you had all of your clothes and furniture with you, don't let anybody know it. Remember how I told you to keep your emotions out of the equation? Well, I meant it. There will be much to negotiate as the process continues and, needless to say, but I'll say it anyway, you will have seriously damaged your bargaining position if the seller and his broker observe you hugging each other and whispering things to each other like, "Honey, isn't this just perfect?" Please try to remain stoic - pleasant, observant, but stoic. And, if you have to whisper to each other, don't be smiling while you are whispering.

Actually, there is one more thing to add to the inn visit strategy - the second visit. Despite the previous commentary about not looking at everything through the proverbial rose-colored glasses, you will have done exactly that. Trust me. So it is critically important to see the property and the town again and leave the rose colored glasses on the dresser at home.

Obviously when you make arrangements for a second visit, you are tipping your hand that the inn meets most, if not all, of your criteria and expectations. Done right, however, you still can retain some bargaining power if you remember that:

STRATEGY NUMBER 1 IN THE ART OF NEGOTIATING, IS THE ABILITY TO WALK AWAY FROM THE DEAL.

B. Visiting an inn the second time...

Visiting an inn the second time without the rose colored glasses should be the real test. And a strong recommendation is to try to stay at least two nights and stay in a different room than you stayed in the last time and a different room each night. If the seller balks at this request, tell him to jump in the lake - but tell him nicely. Remind him that you could be two different guests - one each night - whom he would gladly accept, so you are not adding to his workload. You can also remind him that you just might end up purchasing his inn - the inn that he obviously wants to sell - and that he should do everything in his power to accommodate all of your reasonable requests and most of your not so reasonable requests. If you feel the need to give him a reason for your room-changing request, tell him the truth - you simply want to "experience" as many of the rooms as your time allows.

When you get back to the inn, plan to take the entire tour again and do it even more slowly than you did the first time. Having digested your photographs and studied your measurements - well not your measurements, but the measurements of the inn - and having mentally thrown out some of the seller's furniture and replaced it with your own and having realized that virtually every surface needs to be redecorated, you will definitely see the place with a fresh pair of eyes. Make more notes and, if necessary, take even more photographs.

You should also use this second visit to scope out the town even more. Visit as many of the shops, restaurants, and tourist attractions as you can. Drive around the entire area early in the morning and in the evening. Picture yourself as a visitor to the town - which you are - and as a resident. Where is the drug store? Where is the hardware store? Where is the grocery store? How are their prices? How large are their inventories?

And, here is a key stop to make on your second visit. If the inn requires some extensive remodeling - I'm talking about some serious remodeling not just cosmetic redecorating, you know, the kind of stuff that might require permits - you should find out if what you want to do is legal and doable according to current local codes. Can you add that dormer to Room 3? Can you extend the front porch ten feet to the right? Can you build a garage in the rear left corner of the property or will it be too close to the property line? That kind of stuff. And, of course, all of these issues apply to converting an old home into an inn.

This means that you will have to visit the local planning and zoning administrators - or in some cases the local planning and zoning administrator since it could be one position. And this means that he will then know that the inn is for sale and that cat will be out of the bag. I could ask here how and why the cat got into the bag in the first place, but I won't.

This visit to the local authorities will require the approval of the seller and, once again, if the approval isn't forthcoming you can either walk away from the deal or tell the seller that the things you want to change will be included in the offer to purchase as necessary conditions to the agreement so you need to know now if they can be done. This should make the seller stand up - assuming he was sitting down - and take notice that you are serious and that sooner or later these issues are going to be addressed so they may as well be addressed now. A solution to the problem of the local officials knowing that the inn is for sale is to have the owner go to these folks with your plans as though they were his. I'm not a fan of this approach for several reasons including the fact that the innkeeper might take "no" for an answer and you might be able to discuss your way into a "yes."

Oh, and make sure that the appropriate town functionaries will be in town and available to see you during your visit - or the owner if that's how you're going to approach this issue.. If you are looking to build an inn or convert an old home into an inn, find out what the current zoning requirements are for either of these two ventures. Some towns, fearing that all of their old homes will become inns, have enacted laws limiting the number of guest rooms or not allowing any more inns at all. I think it would be wise to find out about these limitations quite early on in your search.

When you get to see these administrators you might stumble into small town bureaucracy at its finest - fill out these seventeen forms, attend these eight meetings, present eleven copies of your request including life size drawings from your architect five weeks in advance of the meeting, things like that. But best you should find out now what you are or will be up against if the upgrades that you are contemplating are, in your opinion, "must haves" rather than "nice to haves." There is always the possibility that the administrator will say something like "sure, no problem," but don't count on it. In most towns - large and small - these functionaries make their living shoveling papers and charging fees. Some of them like to be obstreperous just for the sake of being obstreperous.

So, even if you don't leave his office with a permit in hand - which you couldn't because you don't own the place yet - or even a good feeling that you may someday end up with one, you will have determined what the steps are in the process and how much time and money and aggravation you will have to devote to the process. You may learn that for various reasons having to do with deed restrictions, town fathers' wishes, historical district dos and don'ts, and so forth, that some or all of what you want to do just ain't going to happen.

We had an idea that turning a small barn on our property into an antique shop would be really slick. When we approached the local planning and zoning guy on our second visit to what would eventually be the inn of our dreams, he said something like, "Don't bother filling out and submitting the forms because in our collective lifetimes there will never be an antique shop in that barn. Am I making myself clear?" He was, indeed, making himself clear. So we had to decide up front if this was going to be a deal breaker for us. It wasn't. But if it was and we had waited until we were the proud owners of the place to approach the town - well, you get the picture.

And, as long as you're in the zoning office, you should find out what the zoning is for the property you are looking at and every neighboring property. In this process, don't be satisfied with the standard lexicon of the world of zoning people - things like C-1 or R-3 (C for commercial and R for residential). Get a copy of the local code - buy one if you have to - so you can find out what those letters and numbers mean. Because what they mean in one town could be a far cry from what they mean in another town. That nice farmstead to the east of your property could be a really crappy housing development in three years because of a wrinkle in the code. Of course, a developer could apply to have the code changed two years after you buy your inn, but at least you would be able to fight that change. However, if no change in the current code is necessary, you could be screwed.

And while we're on the subject of zoning, there is an old adage in real estate that goes something like "Anybody who buys a house next to a vacant lot deserves what happens to him." I recently attended a Village Trustee's meeting in our town at which the issue of a permit to build a house came up. Seems as though a local builder was applying for a permit to build a house on - you guessed it - a vacant lot at the end of a street. The lot was big enough to build on and his plans met all of the zoning requirements for setbacks - how far any building on the lot has to be from its property lines - how tall the house can be and things like that. Two of the neighbors were concerned about the impact of the house on their view, additional traffic on the street, and a host of lesser issues. Too bad said the trustees as they voted to grant the permit - although they said it nicely. If these neighbors thought that the lot would be vacant forever or that they would have input into what could be built on it, shame on them. That's exactly why there are zoning rules - so that each application for a building permit doesn't become a pissing contest. These folks should have found out what could be built on this vacant lot before they bought their homes.

Depending upon how serious you are about the property and you are probably pretty serious since you are making your second visit, you might want to begin the process of meeting and, hopefully, befriending local bankers. Some if not all of them will have been burned or at least challenged by an inn deal or three and suffice to say that you will never meet a banker who wants his bank to own an inn because of a foreclosure. As a result, their financing requirements might be a bit onerous. So the earlier you start the financing process the better off you will be - maybe. Just like your visit to the town planning and zoning folks or folk, your visit to the bankers should be arranged in advance and with the permission of the seller. First of all, you shouldn't just drop in on a banker and begin talking about a major deal and second of all the fact that the XYZ Inn is for sale should be handled tactfully - especially if the bank you are visiting holds the mortgage on the inn. By the way, the bank that does hold the mortgage on the inn you are contemplating buying is probably a good bank for you to visit. They know the property - which could be a good thing - and the whole financing process could be sped up considerably.

If you are planning to build your own inn or convert an old home into one, remember that you will have no income with which to pay your mortgage until the inn is built or the conversion is complete. And remember that even when your inn's doors are open for business you will not have the level of guests you will have eventually - most likely. If you haven't factored this into your economic situation, your bank certainly will. You won't be paying the seller for the "business" he has created, because he hadn't created one, but you will need a substantial sum to do the conversion or build the new inn, furnish it, and eat in the process.

To give you a feel for the challenges in the finding a bank process, I will relate a story about friends of mine who were looking to purchase the inn of their dreams. They found an inn that met all of their criteria. They made an offer, which was accepted - subject, of course, to obtaining financing and other things we'll deal with later. They paid a lot of money for an independent inspection, which didn't bring to light any major problems. Then they started to look for someone to hold the mortgage.

Unfortunately the lady who had been running the place for the past 17 years - the last 7 on her own after her husband passed on - didn't run it very professionally. She discounted the room rates in a rather random fashion. She comped rooms on busy weekends for reasons that make absolutely no sense. She rented the entire inn for events at ridiculously low rates. She didn't charge nearly as much as she should have during busy seasons, etc.

Even though my friends were accomplished business people and prepared a very professional, but rather conservative pro forma - a business plan showing what the income and expense picture will be if the place was run properly - all the banks would look at was the inn's history. As a result, their deal crashed. Banks simply do not want to own inns. Which means that it might take a while and more of a down payment that you might have thought to make the deal.

During your second visit, drive around the town and the surrounding area some more. Drive around a lot and drive around slowly. The place won't be perfect, but just make sure that there is nothing at this juncture that would have you change your mind about investing a small fortune in the town and becoming a resident of it.

Finally, arrange to spend some more quality time with the innkeeper in order to ask the 23 questions you forgot to ask during your first visit and to ask the 47 additional questions that popped into your head after your first visit.

C. When and how to make an offer...

When and how to make an offer is, obviously the next step in the process and what is included in the offer will go a long way in determining if there will even be a next step with that particular seller or his broker.

Here again, there are a lot of legal nuances and even some local customs to consider and I will leave most of them up to you and your attorney to ferret out. I will, however, provide some important items for you and your attorney to consider.

But let's go back to making an offer. And, to do that, let's assume that the property that interests you is already in your economic ballpark. How much should you offer for the place? And here we are talking only about the price - we'll deal with the non-financial parts of the offer a bit later. The following rule of thumb may sound rather simplistic, but don't offer more than you can afford and even if you can afford the asking price, don't offer it. You must know at this stage of your life that the seller has included at least some bargaining room in his asking price especially if there is a broker involved. Brokers invariably talk a property owner into adding a few thou to what might be considered an appropriate asking price - it helps them bag the listing over competing brokers and if some damn fool comes along and buys the property at the inflated price it adds to their commission.

So, how do you determine how much to offer? It really isn't rocket science, but here is where your accountant and your common sense should both come in to play.

We talked before about how much an inn is worth if there is any validity to the "times the number of rooms" approach or the "times the annual income" approach formulae for evaluating inns. So start by using both of those approaches and see what you come up with. If the numbers are not the same - and they probably won't be - blend them together as in add them together and divide by two. Use this number as a theoretical offering price - a starting point.

Then figure how much you are going to comfortably be able to put down having factored in all of the extra expense items we also talked about before such as redecorating, doing some extensive remodeling - if the inn needs it - buying some new furniture and appliances and linens, etc.

Finally, determine if the inn's historic income less its historic expenses - remember you should have at least three year's of income and expense figures at this point - can support the mortgage that you and your banker friend talked about. Please don't assume that you will be a better innkeeper than the seller was. Don't assume that you will book more rooms and run the place more efficiently. The main reason for not making these assumptions is that the bank won't make these assumptions. The bank will rely on the inn's existing track record. And besides, what the heck do you know? You've never run an inn before.

If your plan is to build a new inn or convert an old home into one, you will have to go through the design process with a builder or an architect and then obtain bids for the work. These costs plus the cost of the land or the old home, the sheets and pillow cases, the beds, the dressers, the dishes, the forks, the knives, the outside sign

- well you get the idea - will determine what you will be up against financially. Think about furnishing an entire inn - not just the cost, but the time and the decorating skill required. A huge undertaking and a huge expense.

If all of this comes together, you will have determined your offer. And, hopefully this number is somewhat below the asking price. If it's appropriately below the asking price, it can be your offer. If it isn't quite far enough below the asking price, drop a little lower. If it's above the asking price then the seller isn't asking enough and you're in luck.

Here's another approach. You already know how much you can afford as a down payment. You have a general idea of what your mortgage terms will be. You know what the inn's income and expenses are. So, as they say, do the math or as some others say, run the numbers. Figure out - or have your accountant figure out - how much of a mortgage the property can support.

The number that you and your accountant come up with, plus your down payment should be your offer. And, if you think about it and you should, you really can't go above that number. Because if you go above that number, where is the money going to come from to make your mortgage payment?

Just a point on negotiating strategy: Circumstances may justify you making a low-ball offer even if the numbers you came up with above would support something higher than a low-ball offer. And no I don't know where the expression "low-ball offer" came from. What type of circumstances you ask? Well let's say that in your discussions with the seller he let it "slip" that the purchase of his retirement home in the Bahamas is about

211

to close or that his divorce is about to finalize or he is so fried that if he makes one more bed or cooks one more breakfast he is going to go stark raving mad. In other words, his situation is desperate.

Otherwise, a low-ball offer is an insult and can seriously jeopardize the possibility of a deal. And, remember that you are chasing after your dream and the inn you are negotiating to buy is the one you want to buy. Don't screw yourself.

Having said that, at the other end of the economic spectrum, don't offer more than you can afford or you will be hung with a mortgage that the inn and you can't support. Remember that

STRATEGY NUMBER 1 IN THE ART OF NEGOTIATING IS THE ABILITY TO WALK AWAY FROM THE DEAL.

So now that you have come up with your offer, what do you do with it?

Letter of Intent

There is a strategy in real estate known as a Letter of Intent that we should discuss for a moment. Don't you just love this stuff? The definition of a Letter of Intent should not come as a surprise. It is an expression of the buyer's intent to enter into an agreement to purchase a property and it comes in the form of a letter. How about that? A legal thing that is exactly what is says it is. A Letter of Intent is not an offer to purchase a property. It is a way to determine if the buyer and seller are on the same page -

in agreement on most of the key elements of a deal - before they go through the slings and arrows and the expense and the heartache of negotiating an actual Purchase and Sale Contract. A Letter of Intent to purchase a property is usually non-binding and it says so right in the letter.

This shouldn't come as a surprise either, but a Letter of Intent that is non-binding is called a Non-binding Letter of Intent. If you don't know what non-binding means ask your attorney and then seriously consider keeping your day job - unless you happen to be an attorney in which case change day jobs. It isn't necessary to begin the purchase through a Letter of Intent - you can go directly to a Purchase and Sale Contract - but you should consider the use of a Letter of Intent especially if there are several issues that might be challenging. Following are some things that you might want to include in a Letter of Intent which will also be included in the Purchase and Sale Contract should the deal get that far:

✓ The purchase price. Assuming that you are not dumb enough to pay what the seller is asking, you will have to come to agreement on the price. The Letter (which is what I will call the Letter of Intent from this point on) is the perfect vehicle to use to "make an offer."

✓ As part of the purchase price issue, the Letter should include how much of a deposit you will put down as part of the deal. Usually you will pay a modest amount with the Letter in "good faith" with the stated agreement that you will put down a larger chuck of cash with the execution of the

Purchase and Sale Contract (which is what I will call the Contract from this point on). You, of course, will want to put down as little cash as possible and have all of it be refundable if the deal doesn't come to fruition. The seller, however, will want you to put down a whole bunch of money with the Letter and another whole bunch with the Contract and have all of it at risk if the deal doesn't come to fruition. "At risk" means that the seller gets to keep it. These amounts and the at risk issue will be the subject of some modest negotiations, but shouldn't be stumbling blocks. And what pray tell is a stumbling block anyway?

✓ The requirement that you must obtain a financing commitment on terms and with conditions acceptable to you. This financing requirement and many of the items that follow are known as contingencies because the deal is contingent on them being done. Even if you're going to pay cash - which you probably won't - or make an enormous down payment which you think will make obtaining financing a piece of cake - which it might or might not - your Letter and Contract should still include a financing contingency. And don't lock into a set interest rate and a set number of years for the term of the mortgage. Things can change in a hurry in the mysterious world of mortgages and the general information that you got from your meeting with a banker or two during one of your visits to the inn might not hold when your deal comes before the infamous loan committee.

✓ The conduct of a physical examination of the property by someone you choose - and pay for - and the receipt of an inspection report satisfactory to you.

✓ The performance of an examination of the business, financial, and tax records, which will establish to your satisfaction that everything is as presented by the seller and/or the seller's broker. Your accountant can perform this task if you're not up to the challenge.

✓ The determination to your satisfaction that the business conforms with all applicable zoning, land use, building, fire prevention, and related codes and regulations.

✓ The determination to your satisfaction that pertinent deeds, surveys, plans, and land records properly address all rights-of-way, easements, boundaries, and other rights appurtenant to the property. If you don't know what a right-of-way and an easement are not to mention appurtenant talk to your attorney or your broker - that's what you are paying them to know and do something about.

✓ If you own a home and the sale of the home is an important matter in your inn purchase - as in you need the proceeds from the sale to buy the inn or you just don't want to own an inn in one town and a home in another town - you should make the sale of your home a contingency in the deal. This will be the chance for the seller to tell you to jump in the lake, but asking for a sale of your home contingency is worth a try. And, if you can't get this in the deal, think about what it means to your overall financial situation. Do you have sufficient funds to pay both mortgages and other expenses if need be? Will you be able to effectively work on the sale of your home while you are beginning your new innkeeping career? Things like that. If these matters are too challenging for you and your personal budget - not to mention too challenging for your banker - you might consider selling your home in advance of starting your inn search. This somewhat draconian measure will, however, increase your agility. Find the inn, buy the inn, move into the inn. Keep in mind, however, that living with your sister-in-law or, heaven forbid, your mother-in-law or in an apartment might have you rush into an inn deal just to change your living conditions. Not a good thing.

✓ The execution of a Covenant Not to Compete must be included in the Contract and should be included in the Letter. If you're not familiar with a Covenant Not to Compete you will be in a minute. This is a clause that prevents the seller from opening up or buying or managing or working for an inn within a certain distance from the inn you are buying for a certain period of time. This means that he will not be able to compete with you within that distance and for that period. How far and how long you ask? When I bought my inn, the non-compete clause was for a 20-mile radius and for 2 years. When I sold my inn the buyers asked for 50 miles and 5 years. Little did they know that I would have given them the *universe* for distance and *eternity* for the time period. So it really depends on whether you perceive the seller to be a potential threat to your business if he opened up an inn next door or down the block or went to work for another inn next door or down the block and contacted all of his former guests who loved him so dearly that they would rather stay with him than with you. It also depends on what the seller's plans are - is there any chance that he would go back into the inn business. Even if there appears to be no chance, you should still require a non-compete clause. People do change their minds and, even if he doesn't end up buying an inn, he could end up working for an inn for a while and steal guests in the process or consulting with an inn and steal guests in the process. It's in your best interest not to allow him any of these options.

✓ Since the seller will still be trying to sell the property during the time between the execution of the Letter and the execution of the Contract, you should cover your butt by including a Right of First Refusal in the Letter. This clause gives you the right to match any offer that the seller receives during the 30 days or so that it will take to, hopefully, negotiate and sign a Contract. Keep in mind that this clause wouldn't *require* you to match another offer. It would just give you the *right* to do so.

✓ Any other important deal-breaker matters should also be included in the Letter. Things like the necessity to obtain a permit to add an addition or expand the parking area or even change the color of the place if things like that are controlled by local codes and are extremely important to you. And, if you're converting an existing old home into an inn, you will need a clause that addresses the time and permits necessary to pull that off.

✓ And, finally, the Letter should mention that the Contract itself will contain other provisions - terms and conditions if you will - lest the seller think that the stuff in the Letter is all there is.

✓ All of the matters in the Letter, which have a time element to them, like getting permits or obtaining inspections should have a specific number of days included in the Letter. Something like 45 days to get this done and 30 days to get that done. You will, of course, want a lot of time to do all of this stuff and the seller will want it all done by next Tuesday. Once again, you should be able to negotiate your way past this, but don't put yourself in a contractual corner for things that are beyond your control. For example, don't commit to obtaining an inspection report in 30 days until you know that that is doable. Just as a point of clarification, the meter doesn't start running on these time element issues until the Contract is signed. The Letter merely states that these things will be included in the Contract. All that happens contractually after the Letter is signed is the preparation of the Contract. You may want to make arrangements for a garage sale back home in preparation for your move and you may want to get into the production schedule of the inn inspector, but don't do anything rash - like spend money - until you are under contract.

If you do use a Letter as the means to begin the purchase process it must have occurred to you, but I'll bring it to your attention anyway, that just because you included it in your Letter, doesn't mean you're going to get it. So there will be a round or two of negotiations between you and your broker and your attorney and the seller and his broker and his attorney before everything settles down into a Letter that you and the seller will sign.

It also must have occurred to you that once a Letter has been signed, it is virtually all over but the shouting unless, of course, once a Contract is in place you or the seller cannot perform - as in you can't obtain financing or the inspection report unearths some ungodly problem that can't be resolved at all or in time or you can't get a permit to do some really important thing or the seller can't produce the required financial or deed information. So be aware of the fact that the signing of a Letter is a really big deal.

Purchase and Sale Contract

Whether you begin with a Letter of Intent or move directly to a Purchase and Sale Contract, at some point you will indeed present a Contract to the seller. The Contract will contain everything that was in your Letter if you used one and some other stuff that your attorney and the seller's attorney want to include in order to justify their fees. They will both come up with a lot of legal nits that are time-tested. Some of them are referred to as Representations and Warranties and some of them are quite important. They are clauses wherein (since this is a paragraph about legal things I thought it was appropriate

219

to use the word wherein) the Seller and the Buyer represent or warrant that certain things are true - to the best of their knowledge. Things like the seller warranting that he really owns the furniture. I won't go into those here since I have to leave some things for your attorney to do. What I will go into are some of the major things that the attorneys might not have thought about, things like:

- ✓ How much additional money you will put down when all of your contingencies have been satisfied - this sum doesn't increase your down payment, it merely moves some more of your eventual down payment from your pocket into the escrow account as an expression of your continued good faith to close on the deal. Of course, if good faith was the order of the day we wouldn't need all of these legal documents now would we? For your edification and enlightenment, an escrow account is an account set up usually at a bank (known here as an escrow agent) to hold all funds and documents until the moment of truth - that being the close of the sale - at which time everything that you're entitled to ends up in your hands and everything that the seller is entitled to ends up in his hands and everything that the brokers are entitled to ends up in their hands and everything that the attorneys are entitled to ends up in their hands and everything that the taxing authorities are entitled to ends up in their hands and so forth.
- ✓ When and where the close will take place. This is usually at the bank or at one of the attorney's offices. If you've never gone through a "close" you are in for a treat. A blizzard of documents will

come flying at you and the seller from every angle. Papers are signed or initialed at a furious pace. Checks are cut and handed about. Hands are shaken. The attorneys and brokers go home paid and happy, the seller goes home paid and happy and you stagger out of the room broke and bewildered. More about the close later.

✓ The final list of what is and isn't included in the sale. To avoid confusion, the more detailed this list is the better.

✓ A requirement that the real and personal property - that being the inn itself and the stuff in it that you are buying - shall be maintained in the condition they were in when you first saw them. Think about it for a minute. You visited the inn, you loved the inn, you are purchasing the inn. Wouldn't it be a bit of a tragedy if sometime later when you and your moving van arrive on the scene, the place was all beat up because the seller let it go to hell? Well this clause would give you some legal recourse if that happened. This clause should also give you time just a bit before the close - maybe just minutes before the close - to conduct a "walk through" and make sure that everything you're buying is there and in the same condition it was in when you last saw it. Don't pass up conducting a walk through. It will only take a few minutes and they could be extremely important minutes.

✓ A requirement that between the time of signing the Contract and the close of the sale the seller must use his "best efforts" to continue to run the inn with the same care and professionalism that he always did - this might be referred to as maintaining the good will. Taking the seller's responsibilities during this interim period a step further, he should also be required to keep the existing insurance coverage in place, notify you immediately of any event that has a material adverse effect on the business - like the town burned down or the folks next door finally got permission to open up the used car lot of their dreams in their front yard - and he should be precluded from entering into any contract or agreement that would extend beyond the close of the sale without your prior written consent - like hiring a contractor to paint the place or running an ad every month in some journal for the next two years. And what would you do with and how would you pay for that truckload of toilet paper that arrived each month for the next year that he bought from his brother-in-law the toilet paper supplier?

✓ A clause that spells out how the total amount that you will pay for the inn will be divided up among the real property (the building and the land), the personal property (the stuff inside it), the non-compete provision, and the good will. Yes, they actually assign a dollar value to each of these things. How the total purchase price is allocated will be the subject of some negotiations because the allocation will have tax consequences for the seller and you now and for you when you sell the inn to the next idiot. I will leave this allocation in the capable hands of your attorney and your accountant.

✓ How about this? A requirement that the seller provide you with consultation and training on how to run the business and maintain it. "Honey, that boiler alarm thing is going off. Where did the guy say the shutoff switch was?" Something like two days before and two days after the close would probably suffice. And maybe the seller should be required to graciously respond to phone calls from you for a month or so.

✓ A requirement that the "risk of loss" is assumed by the seller until the close. This means that if a fire or some other disaster befalls the place between the signing of the Contract and the close - it ain't your financial problem. This clause should also give you the right, but not the obligation, to terminate the Contract and, if you do decide to terminate the contract because, for example, the time it will take to repair the damage is longer than you want to wait, to get your deposit back.

✓ A requirement that if any of the examinations that you have requested - the inspection of the property, the inspection of the books, the determination of the property's compliance with zoning, land use, building, fire prevention and related regulations and things like that - bring to light some problems that you just don't want to fuss with, you can either crash the deal and get your deposit back or require the seller to fix them before the close - a period of time to "cure the defect." This might mean that the close would have to be delayed. Please don't accept the property with problems that the seller promises to fix after the close. Talk about a lawsuit waiting to happen. Get this stuff taken care of now. You will have enough to worry about when you own the place. By the way, it's possible that the seller will require that there be a dollar figure included in this clause. It could be something like if all of the identified problems can be fixed for under $2,500 they're your problem and if the problems exceed $2,500 then the seller has to fix them or you can walk. The specific dollar figure isn't important here, what is important is the element of reasonableness. Why would you crash the deal if your inspection revealed that the toilet in Room #5 is running when the cost to fix it is a $13.95 ball cock? The assumption here is that you know what a ball cock is and how to install one.

✓ You might want to include a clause that gives you the right to enter the property to conduct a site survey - an actual survey of the land - so you know exactly where its boundaries are. This doesn't mean that you have to actually do the surveying unless of course you happen to be a surveyor. It means that you can hire a surveyor to do the surveying and he can go where he needs to go on the property to do what surveyors do. Whether or not you do a survey may be a function of whether there are or would appear to be property line issues or what local custom is regarding the need for surveys. There's an anecdote coming up that deals with this matter.

✓ A good faith clause that requires both you and the seller to use your best efforts to do all of the things you are required to do in a timely manner. The simple phrase "time is of the essence" captures this. It means that wherever a certain matter has a time factor to it, like you must do something within 45 days or you must do something by March 31, you will do all that you can to do it or have it done in that time frame. Staying on this time element thing for another moment, the Contract should require you to notify the seller usually in writing within a certain period of time - like 7 or 10 days - after you obtain the property inspection report or the survey or the review of the books or any of those kind of things that something is wrong. The Contract should also give the seller a specific amount of time to cure the identified defects or problems.

✓ This next one is a bit touchy, but could be really important. The seller should warrant (one of those representations and warranties we spoke of earlier) that there are no lawsuits or threatened lawsuits or liens or claims or anything like that which could become your responsibility or may have some sort of adverse effect on the property or on the value of the property after the close. Or, if there are any, that you are advised about them and given time to judge their importance and whether they are of sufficient concern that you might crash the deal. Touchy or not, demand that the clause be included.

✓ If there is a local or state requirement - or maybe they both have requirements - that permits be in place to run an inn, there should be a clause that addresses this issue. The seller must produce his current permits and you have to be able to transfer them into your name or be able to get your own without a break in the action. For example, the property might have to satisfactorily pass a health department inspection, which could result in the issuance of a permit for lodging and, perhaps another permit for serving food. We were actually docked a point in the annual State of Vermont inspection because the free standing thermometer that registered the temperature in the refrigerator was cracked - it worked perfectly, but it was cracked. With a score of 99 out of a possible 100 there was really no need to spend the $6.95 on a new thermometer since we would have been able to stay in operation with a score of 70, but we did it anyway.

✓ Somewhere along the way, you and your financial wizard, perhaps in conjunction with your legal wizard, are going to have to determine how you will take title to the property and the business. Are you going to set up a partnership with your partner and your investors - assuming you have investors? Are you going to set up a corporation, perhaps a Sub-Chapter S corporation or perhaps a limited liability corporation, known as an LLC? Who will be the officers - or in the case of an LLC - the members of your corporate entity? Are you going to have the property in one name and the business in another name? Is one entity going to lease the property from the other entity? Are you going to try to actually pay yourself a salary? Will you have a staff who will have to receive actual paychecks? If so, which entity will be their employer? All of these questions and a host of others that your dream team will come up with have to be answered and the proper forms and applications have to be obtained and completed and submitted - probably with the appropriate filing fees - in a timely manner so the closing documents can be properly prepared and so the insurance policies and bank accounts can be in the appropriate names. There is no doubt that an entire book could be written on this topic alone, but remember that I told you that I wasn't an attorney or a CPA. And whereas there are many options, only a few of them will be the right ones for your particular situation and any competent accountant and attorney can get you to where you should be pretty quickly and relatively inexpensively.

Remember that all of these items are in addition to those that would have been included in a Letter of Intent. If you and your attorney decide not to begin the purchase process with a Letter, make sure that all of the items in the Letter of Intent section are included in the Contract.

Let me give you three real live examples of how some of these things that might not seem really important are, in fact, really important.

The Tale of the Parking Lot Easement

The guest and innkeeper parking for the inn we were buying was on the left side of the inn head in to the building. The neighbor on that side was a barn, which had been converted into a residence and bike shop. Actually the barn was formerly the barn for the farm when the inn we were buying was a farmhouse, but that's another story and not relevant to this story. The neighbor's entire front yard was a parking area, which blended into the inn's parking area. There really was a property line there somewhere, but where? And did it really matter? Well, it mattered to me and here's why. Existing documents showed that the inn's property only extended 30 feet from the inn itself on that side, hardly enough to pull into and back out of a parking space. You need 38 feet and 40 feet is better. Or at least that's what parking lot designers told me. And, yes, there are people who make a living designing parking lots.

This meant that the inn's guests and the innkeepers had to drive over part of the neighbor's front yard in order to park facing the side of the inn. "No problem" the seller told us. "We and our guests have been driving over the neighbor's yard for twelve years and the neighbors are really nice people and they aren't going anywhere."

"Not good enough," I said.

This actually led to a really unique phone conversation. The seller arranged a phone call between the neighbors and me. The purpose of the call was for the neighbors to convince me that they were really nice people and that they weren't going anywhere - just like the seller had told us. At the end of the conversation I told the neighbors that they had convinced me that they were really nice people and that I wasn't worried about them putting up a fence or a brick wall on the property line which would have blown away my inn's parking lot. But, I was worried about the person they might end up selling their place to. I really was worried about them as well, but I didn't tell them so in the conversation.

The end result was the structuring of a thing known as a permanent easement, which I required be executed between the seller and the neighbor before the close. With this easement in place, forever more the owner of the inn property and the inn's guests would be able to drive over 10 feet of the neighbor's property. This was an absolute deal breaker issue. After all, what would an inn be without a parking lot? It would be a very large house with a bunch of bathrooms and a very large mortgage with no income from which to pay it because there would be no guests because there would be no place for them to park.

The neighbors, who up to this point had been good friends with the seller, realized pretty quickly that the existence of an easement might make it difficult, if not impossible, for them to sell their property. So, the good neighbors ended up extracting a few thousand dollars from the seller as payment for their signatures on the easement. I didn't blame the neighbors. Why should they potentially suffer a financial loss as a result of a deal that they weren't even a party to? And, (are you ready for this?) the husband half of the neighbor couple died of a heart attack one and one-half years later at the age of 53. And, (are you ready for this?) they had already been in negotiations to sell their place. Remember this was the neighbor who wasn't going anywhere.

Fortunately there was no need to have a surveyor survey the site to determine where the property line was or how to describe it in the easement. Existing documents described things in enough detail to craft the agreement.

The Tale of the Gasoline Pump

Even my own attorney thought I was way over the top when I demanded that the Contract include a clause that gave me permission to have an environmental inspection conducted on the property. This was Vermont he told me. What kind of environmental problem could there be on an old farmstead? Well, I told him about the vacant parcel in an industrial park that the corporation I had toiled for had purchased fortunately before I got there. This purchase took place back in the late 60's or early 70's when things environmental weren't on the radar screens of most corporate real estate guys and most real estate attorneys for that matter.

And, besides, the land had been an apple orchard. What could possibly be wrong with an apple orchard? Well it seems as though apple seeds contain something called arsenic. Yes, that arsenic. And it turns out that when we went to build an addition to the distribution facility - the original building was built before anybody knew or cared about environmental stuff - the environmental impact study discovered that the top two feet of the soil was laced with arsenic. No pun intended.

How we resolved that matter is another story, but suffice it to say that the memory of that event and others like it stayed with me and hence the environmental inspection requirement. What is an environmental inspection you ask and what do the inspectors look for?

Without going into extensive detail, what is known as a Phase I Environmental Impact Study is primarily a search of the written records of the property as well as a visual inspection of the site. The inspectors look at the property's history. Who owned it since the beginning of available records and what was it used for? What type of equipment was kept on the property? What type of hazardous material might have been stored or used on the property? Is there any stained soil or other evidence of contamination? Is there asbestos insulation around the heating pipes which is damaged or in the parlance of the environmental inspection industry is "friable?" Are there lead waterline pipes, which may be sufficiently corroded to allow lead to be in the water? And of course, is there radon present. Things like that which could cause you and your guests serious bodily harm, not to mention serious harm to the value of your investment.

By the way, if a Phase I Environmental Impact Study finds any of this stuff, for an additional and substantial fee, the inspectors will conduct a Phase II Environmental Impact Study. In a Phase II, they take samples of the suspected soil or insulation or take radon readings to determine if the stuff or the readings are of such magnitude that something must be done about it - like, perhaps, remove it. Of course, you don't have to go to a Phase II unless you want to. If you are uncomfortable with the results of the Phase I, your environmental inspection clause should allow you to crash the deal. But, if you do take it forward and the results of the testing require any clean up or repair, that should be the responsibility of the seller. This can be a tough clause to negotiate and administer.

Think about it. You are asking for permission to have a piece of property that you don't own inspected and the results of the inspection could end up with you backing out of the deal and the seller being in possession of a report showing that his property is environmentally flawed. So be it. He could also end up with an inspection report showing his boiler is shot. We'll talk about this possibility shortly.

What did the Phase I find in the property that I was considering? It found some friable asbestos wrapped around some heating pipes by the boiler, which we required the seller to repair. It found radon just a hair below actionable levels so there was nothing to be done at the moment, but there was a strong recommendation to retest every now and again. And it found a mention of a gasoline pump and fuel oil tank in the deed that covered the sale of the barn years ago. The assumption was that the pump and tank were involved in gassing up the farm equipment and since it was most likely an above ground tank which had since been removed and there was no evidence of a leak - there were no dead cows or dead chickens lying around - and since the tank would have been at a lower grade than the inn - so any spill would have gone in the other direction - everybody was happy.

But here's the real reason we required the environmental inspection clause. There was an inn a very few miles away that we had some interest in until we learned that it was down grade from a former gas station which had a leaking underground tank which had resulted in the installation of monitoring wells along the inn's property line to trace the direction and amount of the flow of the leak which actually made the property unsaleable. Unsaleable as in nobody would buy it. At least nobody in their right mind. So one never knows, does one?

Make sure that your Phase I inspection is conducted by an appropriately licensed firm with a verifiable track record which you have taken the time to verify. No sense in throwing your retirement savings down the same hole as the oil leak now is there?

The Tale of the Temporary Floor Jack

Different from the Environmental Inspection is the regular inspection of the property looking for structural, mechanical, and electrical problems. Once again, make sure that the inspector you retain for this effort does these inspections for a living and comes highly recommended by people like your banker. And make sure that the inspector is independent as in he isn't a contractor who could end up making the repairs that he finds are needed in his inspection. However, if circumstances do require that the inspector is also a contractor because there isn't anybody else who does these inspections in your inn's neck of the woods, make sure that he knows up front that there is no way in hell that he will end up doing any of the work unless he is asked to do so by the seller.

By the way, if for some reason you choose to ignore this very important recommendation that you have an independent inspection conducted before you purchase your inn, I mean if you are really that stupid, have no fear because most likely you will be rescued from your own stupidity by your banker. Your banker will require this type of inspection - and an environmental inspection as well if he has reason to believe that there might be an environmental problem or two - before he puts his bank's funds on the line. Since the bank just may end up owning the joint after they are forced to foreclose on your loan, they will want to be the proud owners of a reasonably well-repaired and environmentally tidy inn.

So on to the inspection of the inn we were looking to buy. The good news is that one particular inspector came highly recommended by every banker, broker, and attorney we talked to. The bad news is that because he was so well regarded, it was hard to get into his production schedule. However, we persevered and the arrangements were made and they fit into the time allowed in our Contract with the seller. The report was several pages long and it not only included recommendations to repair things that were currently broken or were about to break, but equally as important, it included an aging schedule so we knew what we were likely to run into as the years went on. How long will the hot water heater continue to heat water? How long will the boiler continue to heat air? How long will the exterior paint job last before the inn looked very bad? How long will the roof continue to keep the elements where they belonged?

This was very helpful for two reasons. Not only did we know what to expect and approximately when to expect it, but it also helped us to figure out how much we needed to put into a "reserve for replacement" fund to be ready for these relatively major expenditures. Unless you will have a pot of money that you will be able to dip into when these things come up - and they will come up - you might want to seriously consider setting up a reserve. Things are going to break and leak and you are going to have to fix or replace them. You might as well be prepared financially to take them on.

And, if some major stuff is about to go bad sooner than later, you might be able to re-negotiate your offer. We actually did this in a small way and here's how we did it.

After we received the inspection report, we reviewed it quite thoroughly and selected the items that, in our opinion, given what we were paying for the inn, should rightfully be fixed by the seller. There were about a dozen of them including the replacement of the metal jack posts in the basement that were literally holding up the inn. In the inspector's opinion, metal jack posts are only to be used as temporary supports and should have been replaced some time ago or perhaps never should have been used in the first place. With some reluctance, the seller agreed to make all of the repairs on our list including replacing the jack posts with treated wood posts before the close. In essence this didn't reduce the price we were paying for the inn, but we were avoiding some additional post-ownership expenses. And, we were getting a little better place in the process. We also made it our business to verify that these repairs were done and done well in our final, pre-close inspection.

Once again, if you are buying an old home, which you plan to convert into an inn, the seller will have to be willing to put up with all of this inspection business. If not, if he just wants to sell his home and take the position that all of these inn-related matters are your problem, not his, I would strongly suggest that you keep looking. If you think you can simply buy an old home and then go about the business of doing all of these inn-related things later, you could end up owning a big old home that will never become an inn. There could be planning and zoning issues and construction issues - maybe the water and sewer lines cannot be rerouted like they would have to be to have all those pesky bathrooms added. Then what will you do? Perhaps you will have to offer the seller some sort of financial incentive to make all of these inspections and other things worthwhile. A very small price to pay - an insurance policy if you will - to protect your investment.

D. The close of the sale...

The close of the sale is the next step in the process of getting you from being a regular working stiff in your comfortable corporate job, to unblocking toilets on New Year's Day.

But getting from being under contract to the close of the sale is not your proverbial stroll in the park. All of those things that you, your attorney, and this book stuffed into your contract have to be addressed under the pressure of tight time frames and with your head on straight. This is indeed a time when your desire to get to the finish line could play havoc with your common sense and business sense. But remember if circumstances beyond your control or even circumstances within your control make the completion of certain requirements impossible to achieve within the time limits imposed by your contract, there is a really neat thing you can do. Are you ready for this? You can request more time.

The seller will be getting as anxious as you are to close the deal, but you are actually in the driver's seat. If the seller says no to a reasonable request for an extension of time and as a result the deal crashes, he has to start all over again looking for another buyer, negotiating another Letter of Intent, negotiating another Purchase and Sale Contract and, quite possibly, being asked for an extension of time by the new buyer to complete some term or condition. But don't wait for the last day of a time requirement to ask for the extension. Assuming your negotiations and your relationship with the seller have made it to this point with some degree of pleasantness and professionalism, you should continue in that posture since there just might be other favors that you will need to ask down the road like "Where did you say the reset button was for the sump pump?"

The key point is to refrain from shortcutting any of the steps or speeding them up to the point of being dumb. You are nearing the end of a major expenditure and a major life-changing event. Don't screw it up now. Remember the axiom that goes something like "if you do things in a hurry, you deserve what happens to you."

Often, Purchase and Sale Contracts will have at least one addendum and maybe two or three, before the deal officially crashes or moves on to a close. Your attorney will surely guide you through this part of the process, but just make sure that every change - however minor - brought about by the need for more time or the uncovering of some sort of hidden condition that has to be addressed is properly reduced to writing and signed by both parties. However nice and cordial your relationship has been with the seller, it will be hard to activate him from his Florida retirement home to finalize the replacement of the faulty water softener system which your eagle-eyed inspector realized was about to pass away and which the seller promised he would take care of - but didn't - before he took a lot of your money and left town.

And remember to build into your last minute schedule the final property inspection. You may want to have your inspector and/or your broker and/or your consultant tag along for the ride. What you are looking for is verification that the seller did all of the things he was supposed to do - make the repairs he was supposed to make, the furniture and fixtures he was supposed to leave behind because you bought them are left behind, the property that was supposed to be left in the same condition as it was the day you first saw it is in the same condition, etc. Actually, it will or should be in better condition because you wisely required him to make a bunch of repairs.

Somewhere between the signing of the Contract and the close you will have to address four areas of ownership that historically fall off the radar screen if, in fact, they ever made the radar screen in the first place - insurance, utilities, the staff, and the maintenance team.

Insurance

Most likely, the seller didn't have enough insurance on the property and its contents and its exposure to liabilities - because most folks don't. So, before you become the owner and the risk of loss of the property and the risk of liability to guests and other visitors falls on your pocketbook, make sure that you have purchased proper coverages and have binders - if not actual policies - in place before the close.

You are now in the hospitality business. Guests will be staying and eating in your inn and all manner of things can and will happen to them in the process. You actually had these same exposures to loss when you were a homeowner and your former college roommate and his new trophy wife spent that weekend with you last summer, but he probably wouldn't have sued you if something had gone wrong. Not so your guests.

What types and levels of coverage are proper, you ask? Well I'm going to give you some suggestions. But you should be aware of the fact that some areas of insurance are quite subjective. It can really depend on whether you want to hold up your pants with just a belt or if you want to hold up your pants with a belt and suspenders. But there are some absolutes and here they are:

✓ The contents (the furniture and everything else in the inn) should be insured for their replacement value - the amount it would cost you to replace everything in the inn if it burned down or was felled or at least severely damaged by some disaster. You could, of course save a few bucks and insure everything for its depreciated value - the amount it's worth on the books - but then where will the money come from to make up the difference when you're standing at the cash register at the appliance store. It certainly won't come from the insurance premium you saved by purchasing the cheaper coverage. For example, the stove that was included in the sale might have cost $700 when it was bought new by the seller six years ago, but now it is only worth $300. If a new stove just like it will cost $1,000 and you only insured it for its $300 depreciated value, where are you going to get the $700 to buy a new one after the fire turns the old one into a molten hunk of metal? The premium savings will be woefully insufficient. Multiply that situation by everything in the inn including the items you brought with you and you see the problem you will run into if you don't insure to replacement value.

✓ The insurance on the building itself should also be sufficient to rebuild it now. This figure may have no relation to what it cost you and no relation to what the bank had it appraised for. What you paid and what the bank appraised it for are a function of its market value - the old willing buyer, willing seller, and willing lender story. But your insurance coverage should be enough to replace it *in kind* the day after it burns down. In kind means with like material and workmanship. An appraisal done by your insurance company - which should not cost you anything - is the best way to arrive at this number. And when you are thinking about the ultimate loss, don't forget the clothing and jewelry and luggage and all that other stuff that your guests have in your rooms and those gas-guzzling SUVs that are in your parking lot and which can be destroyed or at least severely damaged by the fire. The liability for all of those losses and damages could actually be your responsibility depending on what or who caused the loss.

✓ If the inn happens to be in a flood plain, you should ask the local insurance broker or agent about flood coverage because it surely isn't included in the standard property insurance policy. By the way, an insurance *broker* can represent many insurance companies, but an *agent* can only represent the insurance company that has hired him as an agent. Just thought you'd like to know the difference.

✓ Whereas the building and the stuff in it are worth a certain number of dollars and if you are paying attention you will buy that amount of insurance, the proper level of liability coverage is really subjective. How much will the guest in Room #2 sue you for when he is scalded by a surge of hot water while showering? How much will that lovely couple in Room #4 expect from you to compensate them for their fiasco of a honeymoon - mental anguish - because your boiler decided to stop working and you couldn't get it fixed for two days while they were guests in the inn and freezing their butts off? How about the case of food poisoning suffered by that charming middle-aged couple in Room #7. Things like that. Is a $1,000,000 policy enough? $2,000,000? $3,000,000? The more coverage you buy, the less it costs per million so ask your broker or agent to give you several quotes. You may end up buying $5,000,000 because it is so cheap and it will let you sleep more comfortably. Come to think of it, that's probably why the extra $2,000,000 or $3,000,000 of coverage is called "sleep insurance" by those who know about such things.

✓ Do the same with your automobile insurance policy. Buy as much property damage and liability coverage as you can reasonably afford. There is no reason that I can think of to have somebody place a lien on your inn and eventually force its sale for the amount the jury awarded him over and above the limit of your insurance policy, but that could happen if you under insure your exposure to loss.

✓ You should also consider buying some *loss of income* insurance because during the time that your property is being rebuilt after the fire, most of your expenses will continue - at least the big ones like your mortgage - but you will have little or no income with which to pay those expenses. Loss of income insurance will pay you the amount of income you normally would have received if your inn had remained open and you actually had guests.

✓ A good broker or agent should be able to provide you with quotes from insurance carriers that have special innkeeper packages - a batch of coverages designed specifically for innkeepers, which will include all of this stuff. The key point is to have the coverage in place the moment you become the owner. And, with all due respect to your broker or agent, you should insist on having the actual policy in your hands at the time of the close or at the very least a binder. Since it can take an insurance company some time to actually issue a policy, they often issue a binder as evidence of coverage. A binder is a listing of all of the coverages that are in place, the amounts, the dates, the address of the inn, etc. - in short, all of the particulars of an insurance policy without all of the clauses and related verbiage that you will never read anyway. And, the binder must be signed by the insurance company to be valid. Please don't settle for anything less. Once, in my corporate days, we had just changed insurance companies - I mean we had JUST changed insurance companies - when one of our warehouses burned to the ground. All we had was a binder as evidence of our coverage, but it was enough to win the day.

Utilities

Those who provide heating oil, propane, natural gas, water, sewer, electricity, cable, Internet access, and telephone and whatever else powers and heats your inn, enables you to wash and flush things, and enables you to communicate with the rest of the world must know of your existence before you become the owner. Some will require applications. Some will require deposits. Final readings will have to be taken at the time of the close. Some bills will have to be prorated between you and the seller. So before the close, you should obtain all of the appropriate names and addresses and phone numbers and account numbers from the seller and spend an afternoon making all of the necessary arrangements.

The Staff

If you were foolish enough to buy an inn that requires a staff - see my previous comments on the slings and arrows of being an employer - you should make sure that the seller's current staff intends to stay on at least long enough for you to figure out how to run the inn with or without them. Don't assume that they will want to remain in your employ. There is always a fear of new ownership and if you wait too long in the process to approach them, they might have made plans to jump ship by the time you are the owner. If that happens, you won't have the necessary team to run the place, you won't really know what each of them did for a living, you won't know how or where to place an ad for new troops, you won't know if there is a local job bank to help you out of your fix - in short, you'll be in a lot of trouble.

Way before the close, you should have a meeting with the seller devoted entirely to staffing issues. Hopefully the seller is organized enough to actually have personnel files on each of his employees in which there should be things like job descriptions, pay history, annual reviews, benefits, commendations - maybe complimentary letters from guests - and, at the other end, documented misdeeds which brought along some type of warning or disciplinary action. If none or not all of this is available, get as much as you can from the seller's memory so that you can begin to create your own files and so that you will be in a position to have a meaningful meeting with each of the staff members.

As soon as you are under contract, you should make arrangements to meet the entire staff as a group. Tell them you're a nice guy and that, besides a recipe or two, you do not plan to make any changes. Even if that is a pack of lies, they will like to hear it. Then you should interview each of them individually having already found out from the seller which ones are the bums and which ones are the keepers. How you handle the staff from this point on will be up to you and your management skills. The key thing at this juncture is to at least have a staff.

Just before we leave the topic of your staff, you should contact your state's Bureau of Labor and Industry or whatever it may be called and find out what rules you are required to follow. Minimum wage, minimum age, hours of work, safety rules, reporting requirements, taxes (state, county, city, town, village, etc.) - things like that. There is absolutely no doubt that they will be able to send you at least one booklet and probably a whole packet of booklets to lead you down this path. Oh, and don't forget to have in place - either through an insurance policy or through a state agency depending on the state you're in - a Workers' Compensation Policy to cover the medical bills and wages of your employees who get hurt or become ill on the job. Oh, and don't forget to have in place - through a state agency - Unemployment Compensation Coverage in order to compensate the employees you decide to fire for being incompetent while they look for a new employer to screw. See, I told you that being an employer can be a real pain in the ass.

The Maintenance Team

If there is one thing that you can take to the bank besides a lot of money at the close, it is the fact that something will break that you will be unable to fix - and it will happen just as your first guest is arriving. Count on it and be ready for it.

Don't just get the names of the plumber, the heating guy, the carpenter, the electrician, and so on from the seller. Call each of them. Tell them that if all goes well you will be the new owner soon and that you want to keep them on as part of your outside team. Be subtle here, but also let them know that you have talked to the seller about the marvelous work that they have done and that you have reviewed the files just to get comfortable with the whole operation. This will let them know that you know what they charge and how often they have appeared on the scene.

If you do have some trade skills and plan to do some, if not all, of your own maintenance, find out where the local building supplier and hardware store are and scope them out. This way you will know what they carry and what their hours are. If the seller doesn't have a modest inventory of replacement parts and light bulbs and things like that, get some during the breathing room you will learn about in a few moments. Just be ready for things to go wrong.

Now, back to the close

The close itself is a rather anticlimactic event. As I mentioned previously, everybody meets at the bank that will handle the mortgage or maybe at one of the attorney's offices - the seller and his broker and his attorney along with you and your broker and your attorney and at least one banker with an assistant or two. Papers are taken out of brief cases and folders, they are read by the attorneys and the banker, they are passed around the room for signature and everybody, but you, leaves the room with a lot of money - mostly your money. But you leave with something much more important than money - you leave with the keys to your dream inn.

The main thing to remember here is that as of the close you are an innkeeper. The next guest to arrive at the inn is your guest, the next electric bill to arrive is your bill, the next phone call from a prospective guest must be answered professionally and politely by you, the brochure and website are now yours, the next breakfast to be prepared has to be prepared by you, the next blocked toilet has to be unblocked by you, the next bed that has to be made has to be made by you, and on and on. You are now the proud owner of a bed and breakfast.

So what's left? Being an innkeeper, that's what's left.

VIII. Running the Joint...

Running the joint should be fun, relaxing, and otherwise the perfect beginning to your new way of life. Well, it might be after a while, but at the beginning you'll have your work cut out for you. So let's first deal with the take over and then move on to being an innkeeper on a day-to-day-to-day basis. This section assumes that you have purchased an existing inn. If you're establishing a new inn, you will have to go about the process of finding your guests, but what you do with them when they arrive will be the same for those buying an existing inn so read on and on.

A. The takeover...

The takeover, the day you actually become an innkeeper, just might be the most exhilarating and frightening day of your life so you should prepare for it accordingly. You should build some slop time into the time between the close of the sale and the arrival of your first guest because you are going to need it.

This is a major suggestion. Give yourself some breathing room. We knew an innkeeper who had guests arriving at the same time as their moving van was arriving at the inn with their furniture. Yes, they were nuts. We were scheduled to have our close and move in on a Monday so we told the seller months before not to rent any rooms until the following Friday. Whereas, we suffered a small loss of income, so what. By the way, we also knew in advance of the close that we were going to have a full house both Friday and Saturday nights on our first weekend as innkeepers. Wow!! Here's what we did with some of the time we gave ourselves.

We set up our quarters just enough to make them livable - they were in fact left a bit chaotic - while we slowly and methodically made sure that every room in the inn that would be used by our guests was immaculate.

Whereas we didn't have time to redecorate, we made sure that every chip in the woodwork and every suitcase-smudged wall was sanded and repainted. The seller had left over paint from previous redecorating jobs and we made sure before the close that it was still good and properly labeled - Room #5 trim, Room #3 bathroom walls, etc.

I mentioned previously that we had reduced to writing - something else to occupy your time between the signing of the contract and the close - the rules we wanted our guests to live by. It was going to be our inn and they were going to be our guests and we wanted to have them do things our way from the get go. All we had to do now was find something to put the rules in and place them strategically in each guest room. I'm sure you're saying to yourself, why did they wait until they owned the place to find something to put their rules in? Well, we simply forgot we'd have to do that. So go ahead and learn from our little mistake.

We once stayed in a lovely fieldstone farmhouse in rural Pennsylvania incorrectly furnished in very heavy Victorian - what were these guys thinking? But, that's not the point of the story. The point of the story is that everywhere we looked - and I mean everywhere we looked - was a sign telling us to do or, more specifically, not to do something. They were little carved wooden signs which I'm sure in the minds of the innkeepers made them less obtrusive, but at the end of the day, they were obtrusive and, in some cases, downright insulting. "Don't smoke. If you have to smoke, smoke over here." "Take off your shoes and put them over there." "If it's after 10 p.m. be quiet." You get the idea. Not wanting to tromp on our guest's freedoms, but wanting to get some very important points across, we wrote a one page set of "rules" that we placed in a hard plastic, standup sleeve in each guest room. Notice, please, that the list is lighthearted and that we pretty much stayed away from the word Don't and other such negatives. We didn't even call them rules. We called them "stuff." When we were checking in a guest and showing them how everything worked - more on that later - we made sure that they saw and hopefully read the rules by placing the plastic sleeve on the bed. I actually said to the guests, "Sooner or later, you're going to go to bed and hopefully you will remove this before you do and, hopefully, you will read it as you are placing it on the dresser." Here is what we came up with:

The Winslow House
Just some stuff to help you get comfortable and make your stay more enjoyable

- **CHECKING IN** - After you have arrived and taken your luggage to your room, please see one of us to finalize the payment of your room charges. Our mornings are very busy. We appreciate your cooperation.
- **CHECKING OUT** - So we have time to get your room ready for the next guests, we request that you check out by 11:00 a.m. on your departure date. If you stay later, you may have to help us make the bed and clean the room.
- **SMOKING** - The inn is smoke-free. Not only do we, therefore, comply with the Vermont Clean Air Act, but it also makes the place smell better. You can smoke in your car or in the parking lot or in the back yard. Please leave the grounds butt free. Thanks for your cooperation.
- **ROOM KEY** - For your convenience, each room is equipped with a dead bolt lock and key. Even though you are in a small town in Vermont, you should lock your room door and take your key with you whenever you leave the inn during your stay. PLEASE LEAVE THE KEY IN THE LOCK BEFORE YOU CHECK OUT.
- **PARKING** - Please park facing the side of the inn relatively close to, but not too close to, the other guest cars.
- **THE FRONT DOOR** - We leave the front door unlocked. You don't have to ring the doorbell once you've

---

checked in. Just come and go as you please and enjoy the place.

- **BREAKFAST** - A full breakfast is included in your room rate and we serve it between 8 a.m. and 9:30 a.m. If everyone comes down at once, you may have to wait a couple of minutes, but we'll make sure your wait is enjoyable with a cup of coffee or tea and some reading material. Or, if there is space at the table, you can sit and chat with the other guests. UPON CHECKING IN, PLEASE LET US KNOW IF YOU HAVE ANY DIETARY RESTRICTIONS.
- **LUNCH & DINNER** - This is a bed & breakfast inn. For your dining pleasure, there are many fine restaurants in the Woodstock area. We have menus on hand and we can give you our recommendations and those of other guests.
- **CHILDREN** - If you are here with children, PLEASE remind them that there are other guests and they should act accordingly.
- **TELEVISION AND RADIO** - The television and radio in your room are for your viewing and listening pleasure. Even though this is a well-insulated house, it was built in 1790 or so and sound does travel. Please respect the other guests, not to mention the innkeepers, by keeping the sound at a relatively low level. And unless there is something really good on, please turn them off by 11:00 p.m.
- **FRESHENING YOUR ROOM** - If you are staying more than one night, we will freshen your room each morning - after you have left for the day. We will change the pillow slips and the towels as well as re-make the bed and gently clean the bathroom. Let us know if you don't want to avail yourselves of this service.
- **TRAVEL PLANS** - We have a lot of experience in traveling about Vermont and even New Hampshire and we enjoy giving suggestions and directions to some of their obvious and some of their "hidden" treasures. Don't hesitate to ask.

- **EXERCISE ROOM** - If you find it necessary to work up a good sweat during your stay, the small barn contains exercise equipment which you are welcome to use as long as you are already in reasonably good condition and promise not to have any sort of an attack while you are using it. Please see one of us to gain entrance. The barn is well lit, heated, paneled, carpeted, and has cable color TV - not your average barn.
- **RUNNING AND WALKING ROUTES** - We have developed 2, 3.2, 3.8 and 5-mile routes from the inn. They are scenic, challenging and copies are available upon request.

Thank you for choosing *The Winslow House*. We hope your stay will be enjoyable and relaxing.

Some innkeepers put things like these "rules" in some sort of binder in each guest room along with other information like area attractions, the location, dress codes, and phone numbers of area restaurants, etc. We chose to do it the way we did it so that we would be sure that they would be read. I mean what makes you think that just because there is a binder in the room that a guest is going to open it?

Speaking of rules and amenities, there are many things you will need to think about - are you going to be pet friendly and, if so, will you have restrictions on the number and size of pets in each room; are you going to accept children and, if so, will you have restrictions on the number and size of children in each room; are you going to allow your guests to have food and drink in their rooms (you'd better); are you going to allow your guests to smoke in the inn or in their rooms (you'd better not); will each room have an ironing board and iron or will you have one your guests can borrow (you'd better have one or the other); will each room have a hair dryer for your guests to use and steal when they leave; will you have computer hookups in each room or will there be one in a common area for all of your guests to fight over, or will you have WiFi. Think about these things in advance, prepare for them, and fold them into your "rules" if appropriate.

We made sure that the outside signs were crisp and clean and that the parking lot was likewise crisp and clean. In short, we did as much of the things we had time to do from the room-by-room and area by area lists from earlier in the book.

We went about the business of getting ready to make our first breakfast - like buying food. And speaking of buying food, pay attention to this little tale. As a result of our many visits to the area, we were aware that there was a small, but full service grocery store right in the middle of the village. We were even aware that when it was built a few years before, it caused quite a dust up from the purists who didn't want a grocery store with its sizable parking lot right in the middle of the village. They were also concerned for the plight of some of the relatively historic structures that had to be demolished or moved in the process. But that's another story. The important thing is that we knew we had a very convenient grocery store just a mile or so away. So, with grocery list in hand we went into the village on Tuesday afternoon - the day after we moved in. We became suspicious that all was not well when it became obvious that ours was the only car in the parking lot. Our suspicions turned into fear when we read the sign on the front door that said something like. "Closed." It turned out that a new grocery store operator had just bought the place and had closed it to make some renovations and restock it. The sign went on to say that it would be opening soon - as in two weeks or so. Not quite soon enough for us, however. As far as we knew, the nearest grocery store besides a couple of country stores and convenience stores in the area was some 30 miles away over the Green Mountains. What to do? We arrived back at our inn bewildered and confused and fortunately the bike shop owner neighbor living in the converted barn next door was out front doing something that he must have thought was important at the time. We explained our plight and learned that about 15 miles away across the Connecticut River in West Lebanon, New Hampshire was every store then known to man - Sears, Penney's, Burger King, Mac Donald's, Pizza Hut, Taco Bell, and too many grocery stores to count and each one bigger than the last. A veritable shopper's Mecca. Crisis averted.

We scouted out the area printers who would be able to rapidly print the brochure and reservation form that we had also designed during the period between the Contract signing and the close. Nothing looks worse to a potential guest - well almost nothing - than a brochure with the previous owner's name crossed out and the new owner's name written in. And even though we were pretty sure that the deal was going to close in time for us to have our brochure printed "back home," we were just hesitant enough that we decided not to spend the money and then figure out what to do with a couple thousand brochures if the deal crashed. There was a highly recommended printer in a small town about 20 miles north that was able to take on our project and finish it in a hurry. The project, however, was slightly delayed by us, because we wanted pictures of the inn and some of the rooms in the brochure. And we wanted them to be as we had just redecorated, furnished and rearranged them. This of course required us to find a film developer - this being in the pre-digital era - who could also give us fast and quality service. A funny thing happens when you live in a small town - everything you need is available, you just have to drive farther to get it.

As an aside, make sure that any photographs that you take for your brochure and your website - more on these marketing tools later - are professionally done. The right size wide angle lens, the right lighting, the wine bottle and wine glasses on a tray on the dresser in the corner of the photograph, live flowers in the room, etc. really make a difference. Please don't take out your Brownie Hawkeye or one of those disposable jobs and take a bunch of snapshots. Does Brownie still make the Hawkeye? Is Brownie still in business?

We had every reason to believe that our first guests and all of our guests to follow would need our tender loving care - Where's a good place to grab a light bite to eat? Which restaurant is the best in town? Can you get us reservations and do they have a dress code? What's the best route to take to get to (wherever) so we can see a lot of covered bridges along the way? My wife forgot to bring her hair dryer - she might tell you that I forgot to pack it - but it's really her fault. Where can we get one first thing tomorrow morning or do you have one we can borrow? We heard about (some sort of tourist attraction). Is it worth seeing and how long will it take us to get there?

It never ceased to amaze me how far some of our guests traveled and how much time and money they spent to get to little Woodstock, Vermont and they had absolutely no idea why they came. So, I would ask them - in a light-hearted manner - Why did you come here? And the response was invariably something like, my sister and her husband were here a few years ago and they had a wonderful time or this guy I work with comes up here every year and said that we'd really enjoy the area. But they were clueless about what they wanted to see and do. So if you didn't think that part of your job as an innkeeper was to be a tour guide and concierge, think again. Even though we knew a lot about the town and the area, we spent part of the few days we had between the close and the arrival of our first guests rounding up current menus from all of the area restaurants - from all ends of the price scale. We knew from our traveling days that even guests with a lot of money don't necessarily want to have a major league meal every night. Sometimes all they wanted was a place to pick up a pizza or a sandwich and maybe even bring it back to the room. All of the menus went into a small antique wooden box, which we placed in the Sitting Room. I'm now going to start another paragraph because this one is getting very long, but the subject is still the same.

Since guests also want to know what to see and how to get there, you will need to round up information on area attractions. In our case, the seller had hooked up with a company that supplied inns and restaurants - and I suppose anybody else who wanted them - with brochures of almost every attraction worth seeing in Vermont and travel maps of Vermont and New Hampshire since we were only 15 miles from the border and there was much to see and do just across the Connecticut River. We were told that a representative would come to the inn - often unannounced, which was okay with us - and restock the bins in the brochure rack that we kept in the Sitting Room. We were already aware of most of these places of interest, but we read about those that were new to us so we could at least be somewhat knowledgeable when confronted by a guest. As the days and weeks went by, we made it our business to get to most of them so we knew even more. Of course you could simply send your guests to the local chamber of commerce information booth or otherwise let them fend for themselves, but if you don't want to help your guests enjoy their stay why did you buy an inn in the first place? Surely not to make money.

If you haven't already done so, you will have to set up the appropriate bank accounts and if you will have a staff and are afraid to be your own payroll clerk or your own bookkeeper for that matter, you will have to find a firm or person to do these things for you. It might be convenient to use the team that has been performing these tasks for the seller or perhaps your own accountant can do them or recommend someone who can. And, of course, the bank that holds your mortgage, assuming it is a local bank and not an out-of-town bank or mortgage company, would be an ideal place to establish your business and personal accounts.

Finally, we made sure that we had all of the necessary cleaning supplies for the guest rooms and the common areas. We also thought about a cleaning regimen even though we knew that it would be adjusted over time. When - as in what time of day - would we start to clean the rooms? Who would do which tasks? By the way, to this end, we made sure that we had portable phones so as we went about the innkeeper's daily cleaning chores, we were also able to take reservations. And speaking of taking reservations, let's begin with that task as we move further into the job of being an innkeeper.

So, with food in the cupboard, furniture in the rooms, brochures in the rack, menus in the small trunk, etc., we were really ready to go - or so we thought.

B. Taking reservations...

Taking reservations really begins the innkeeping process, so it seems like a good place to start. I remember the excitement the first time the phone rang after we were officially innkeepers and fielding the myriad questions that the potential guest was asking. There is much to be ready for besides the obvious rates and availability - things like do you take children (to answer with a smart-ass "Where do you want me to take them?" is probably not a good idea); do you accept pets; can we walk to the village; is the room quiet; do any of your rooms have king size beds; do any of your rooms have fire places (you can assume that you will only be asked this question in fall and winter); do your bathrooms have Jacuzzis; I see by your advertising that you are pet friendly, but my wife has severe allergies so I need to know if you have a room that has never had a pet in it; and of course the infamous, my husband has sleep apnea so we need an electrical outlet by the bed to plug in the unit that will, hopefully, barring a power failure, keep him alive through the night; not to mention can you make scrambled eggs with just the egg whites?

In addition to these questions there are about 614 that I haven't included here. All of the answers have to be at your fingertips and if your answer is not a positive one - like no, we don't have any rooms with king size beds - you have to be enough of a salesperson to try to bag the booking anyway. Never ever tell a lie, but pitch your positives like a madman. "What do you need a king size bed for? You'll be so tired when you get back to the inn what with everything there is to do around here that you could fall asleep on a pile of bricks. The good news is, however, that we threw away the bricks when we took over the inn and we now have extremely comfortable queen size beds." Things like that.

As you have seen from the style of this book and the list of "rules" from the previous section, I took a rather light-hearted approach to the whole innkeeping experience. I was serious when I had to be, I always gave the guest or the potential guest everything they needed to know, but I had fun doing it. That approach made the process of handing out bad news – "No, we don't have any Jacuzzis in our bathrooms, we keep them in the health and fitness center down the road apiece" - more palatable. The idea was to deflect them away from what they thought was important and convince them that staying here even without a fireplace in the room will be a thoroughly enjoyable experience. "When we converted this magnificent old house into an inn, we had a choice of fireplaces or bathrooms and we thought, what the heck, let's go with the bathrooms."

Whether you choose to use humor or some other type of salesmanship, just be prepared to sell what you have to offer - assuming that you're not offering everything - and making light of what you don't have.

When it came time to actually take a booking, we thought it would be appropriate to write everything down. Following is the reservation form that we used. It was a three-part form in three different colors. We mailed the pink copy to the guest with the charge slip - more about that in a moment - and we kept the white and yellow copies clipped together with our copy of the charge slip. We gave the yellow copy to the guest when they arrived at our door and paid their balance - again, more about that in a moment.

The Winslow House
xxx Woodstock Road
Woodstock, Vermont 05091
(xxx) xxx-xxxx

Name_____

Street Address _____

City _____ State _____ Zip Code

_____
Phone Number

_____
Date Reservation Taken _____ Room(s)

_____
Extra Person _____ Child(ren) _____ Age(s) _____
Dog(s) _____ Cat(s) _____
How Referred

_____
Number of Nights _____ @ $ _____ per night $_____
Vermont Rooms Tax .... _____
Total .... $_____
Less Deposit .... _____
BALANCE DUE UPON ARRIVAL .... $_____
MC/VISA_____-_____-_____-_____ Exp.

_____
Check _____ Check Number _____ To be received by _____
Cancellation date to receive a refund _____
Check in time is after 3:00 p.m. Please call for special arrangements or late arrival. Check out is by 11:00 a.m.
The Winslow House is a non-smoking inn. Thank you for your cooperation.

We could have added a few more things to the form. Things like dietary restrictions, morning beverage choices (regular or decaf coffee, regular or decaf tea, milk, etc.), reason for coming to Woodstock (vacation, anniversary, birthday, tryst, etc.), e-mail address, but we wanted to keep the form small and manageable and, as you can see, we were running out of room. We did ask some of those questions during the reservation process - not the one about the tryst because, you see, that was a joke - and we wrote the information on our copy of the form.

Two critical things to point out in the reservation process are the deposit and the refund. We required one half of the total stay in advance and the entire amount in advance if the stay was only for one night. No negotiating. No questions asked. I felt that to do any less was foolhardy and since I had already done enough foolhardy things, like getting into the innkeeping business in the first place, I didn't want to make things worse. If the guest wanted to pay the deposit by check, they needed to get the check into my hands within five days of making the reservation. Perhaps as a result of this policy, we never had a "no-show." Everybody who made a reservation, which wasn't subsequently canceled, appeared at our door. I also don't recall anybody not making a reservation because of the deposit policy. I know the last sentence contains a double negative, but live with it.

The normal refund policy was 14 days in advance of the reservation. Outside of 14 days, the deposit was refunded. Within 14 days, the deposit was refunded if the room was re-rented. Again, no negotiating. No questions asked. Even following the horrific events of September 11, 2001, which was just before the incredibly important fall foliage season in Vermont. This was a topic of discussion among area innkeepers. Some decided to give refunds to anybody who asked for them. Others decided to stick to the relatively uniform policy of requiring some sort of notice period - 10 days, 14 days, etc.

Remember that you are in business and your bank isn't going to waive or reduce your mortgage payment because your income is down some. It was a tough call, but we hung tough with our regular policy and it ended up being a record foliage season for our inn. When things calmed down a bit after the initial shock - the shock of 9/11, not the shock of making a deposit - folks needed to get away. Unfortunately, not all of our local innkeeping brethren faired as well, which points out that even an inn in a small town in Vermont is subject to the slings and arrows of international happenings.

After that event, I actually decided to increase the fall foliage cancellation period to 30 days. And, lo and behold, no one balked at the 30-day cancellation rule. Of course, that statement begs the question, what does lo and behold mean?

Finally, to show you how you have to face reality even as a small innkeeper - or should that be "the keeper of a small inn" - having been burned by a relatively last minute cancellation the year before, I imposed a 6-month cancellation policy for the Dartmouth College graduation weekend. Even though Woodstock, Vermont is actually 20 miles away from Hanover, New Hampshire (the home of Dartmouth College), the entire area books up over a year in advance for that weekend and you're not going to get a reservation within 30 days or so of the event. If someone doesn't have a room booked at that late date, they aren't coming. Again, no one balked at that policy either. When we sold the inn, the entire graduation weekend was booked one-year in advance with 50% deposits in place and a three-day minimum stay required.

The point is that you have to adjust your policies to local practices and conditions and, for heaven's sake, enforce them.

Since we weren't set up to take reservations online, I won't address how that might work. The one thing I do know about that process is that you need some sort of disclaimer about the reservation because two people could be reserving the same room for the same dates at the same time and you could be one of the two. The guest booking a room online must be informed during the reservation process that the booking is not confirmed until you either phone, mail, or e-mail a confirmation. That's one of the main reasons why we didn't go that route. Besides, I wanted to actually talk to my potential guests. I know that many unpleasant surprises were avoided in this process. "Why didn't you say on your website that your inn was 9 feet from a major highway?" "Your website said that each room had cable color television, but you didn't say they were only 13" models."

Our inn was many more than 9 feet from the road, but you get the idea. Our TVs were, in fact, only 13" models, but they were plenty big enough considering the size of the private sitting rooms they were in, but you get the idea.

By the way, if guests calling to make a reservation failed to ask about everything that was important to them, there was nothing I could do about it and they wouldn't or shouldn't expect me to upon their arrival.

There are several excellent software packages on the market designed specifically for innkeepers. You can find them on line or in the advertising section of innkeeping journals. And the inn you are buying might just have one that you can take over. These packages will lead you down the reservations path and will also help you and your accountant establish the appropriate records for keeping track of your income and expenditures so that at the end of the year or when it is time to pay your rooms and meals tax - if you happen to buy an inn in a state that has such things - you will be in position to just push a button. Well, I mean, you're going to have to write a check, but the amount of the check should come from the button pushing process.

Another approach is to develop your own booking forms and procedures if you come with some level of skill in that area. I developed my own record keeping forms and my accountant was dazzled by how thorough they were. Better to have too much data than too little data. The size of your inn will also dictate how far you need to go in this process.

Whether you have a software package to track your bookings or you only have a calendar on which you enter your bookings, make sure that you enter your bookings immediately. And make sure that everybody else who takes reservations for your inn does the same. What we are trying to avoid here is the dreaded double booking - two different guests, same room, same night. And just to be on the safe side, I spent a few minutes every month manually matching the reservation slips with the entries in the booking calendar. Every now and then, I caught a little whoops and always in time to fix it.

I suppose that this is as good a time as any to show you the list of booking related "rules" that we included both on our website as well as on an insert that was part of our brochure. What you are about to read was actually one side of the insert, the other side was a list of rooms along with their features and seasonally adjusted rates.

The Fine Print

Our rates are based on double occupancy – that means two people in each room. If you bring your mother-in-law and she stays in your room, we are going to charge you an extra $30 per night – after all we have to make her bed and feed her. This, of course, assumes that there's an extra bed in the room. Actually, that extra charge applies to any third traveling companion, not just your mother-in-law. And, we have to charge you the Vermont Rooms Tax. As we go to press it's 9%, but don't hold us to that because they change it every now and then.

More Fine Print

To reserve your room, we ask you for a deposit equal to half of your total stay within one week of receiving your reservation. We will, with great sorrow, send all of your money back if you change your mind more than two weeks before your scheduled arrival date. After that, your deposit is non-refundable unless another guest takes the room you reserved. We will gladly charge your deposit to your MasterCard or Visa. The balance will be due upon arrival after we help you take your luggage to your room and get you settled in.

If you lose the key to your room, you're in really big trouble. Actually, we'll only charge you $10 – just enough to cover our cost of going out and getting another one made.

Even More Fine Print

We do require a minimum two-night stay during Fall Foliage and on Holidays, but you'd probably want to stay here at least two nights anyway, so what's the big deal?

We kindly ask that children under 8 be left home, but not alone.

268

Believe it or not, we welcome pets under certain conditions. Please ask us about them if you just can't leave the little critters at home when you travel.

So that we have time to do all of the things we have to do, check-in is after 3:00 p.m. and so that we have time to do all of the things we have to do, check-out time is by 11:00 a.m.

We request that you refrain from smoking anywhere on the premises with the possible exception of your car.

Finally, please inquire about our extended stay discounts and the availability of gift certificates.

So our potential guests knew what they were getting into even before they booked a room whether they learned about us the old fashioned way - through a brochure they received in the mail - or the high-tech way - from our website. Some of these rules were even included in our listing in the AAA Tour Book. More about that later.

C. Checking in your guests...

Checking in your guests is one of the most important steps in the process of being a successful innkeeper. It can determine how enjoyable the guest's stay will be and whether they will return and whether they will spread the good word. So you should plan to spend as much time as possible with each guest and don't cut the process short. Each guest deserves your best shot at this critical moment. Remember also that some of your guests will never have stayed in an inn before and they could be apprehensive about the experience. Calm them down. Show them around. Be gracious. Be informative. And if two guests arrive at the same time, offer coffee or tea to one of them while they await your return to the sitting room to take them through the checking in process.

Note that the only thing in all capital letters on the reservation form we used was BALANCE DUE UPON ARRIVAL. Remember that this was also the first thing on the list of Stuff in the plastic sleeve in each guest room and it was in the fine print in the brochure and on the website. And we meant it. With extremely rare exceptions we followed through on that requirement. What we didn't want to run into was any sort of hassle about the bed being uncomfortable, the room being too noisy, or the scrambled eggs made from just the egg whites being a bit runny. And we figured that if luxury hotels require payment up front, why shouldn't we?

As an aside, we did have one guest - a mother and father and teenage daughter and their dog - who booked in for a two-night stay (which was our minimum) during fall foliage. They seemed nice enough as they checked in except for the fact that the teenage daughter was acting like a teenage daughter who would rather have been hanging at the mall with her friends. After they put their luggage in the room, he came downstairs and said that "it" wasn't what they expected and they would only be staying one night. He didn't volunteer what "it" was and I chose not to get involved in a discussion defending my inn. He had obviously made up his mind. I said that I didn't want an unhappy guest for any reason, but I would have to charge them for the second night unless I could bag a guest to take their place. Since it was foliage, I had no trouble doing that and the next morning at breakfast we all took the high road, exchanged pleasantries and they left. I'm not sure where they ended up since they had their dog with them, but neither did I care. But you see the value in receiving full payment at check in time or a 50% deposit in advance.

Take your guests to their room and show them how everything works - the TV, the ceiling fan, the A/C unit, etc. And take your time in doing it.

An anecdote on this matter may help drive home the point. Once. A long time ago, we stayed in the luxury cabin of a lovely inn with all manner of gadgets. The charming, but harried, innkeeper ran through what all of the remote control devices were for. All seemed well until - sometime in the middle of the night - the fake logs in the fireplace came "on." Try as we may - pushing button after button - we couldn't shut the damn thing off. We were able, however, to open the remote controlled skylight even though I'm not sure how we did that and the balance of hot and cold air made for a fairly pleasant night's sleep. Take your time or have VERY CLEAR instructions on or near the remote controls.

One last comment on the check in process. Make sure that your guests know what services they can expect from you. Remember that some of your guests will never have stayed in an inn before, so chances are they won't know what to expect. And because of the personal nature of the guest and innkeeper relationship - they know you own it, they know you live there, they know that you are going to be cooking and serving them breakfast, they know that you're going to be cleaning their room - they might feel awkward in asking for something that you are ready, willing, and able to give them or lend them.

Your guests who are veteran inn stayers will know that all inns are not the same. They will have experienced different service levels and they have the right to know where you fall in the continuum of "Ethel, why did you pick this place?" to "Ethel, aren't you glad I picked this place?"

You might actually ask your guests during the check in process if they have ever stayed in an inn before - I did. This enabled me direct my comments specifically to that fact and to try to convert them to disciples of the inn staying fraternity.

D. Checking out your guests...

Checking out your guests as in saying goodbye - might be just as important as checking them in. Try to be there when they are leaving, but don't be obnoxious about it - just kind of be there. Often, when I was in the middle of some early morning chore or when guests were leaving the breakfast table on their last morning, I would say to them, "Please try to find me to say goodbye when you're ready to leave." How clever a line was that? But it told them that I cared and that I wanted to say a proper goodbye and thank you.

And that's exactly what I did. I said goodbye, I thanked them for staying with us, and I asked them if I could help them with their travel plans. I only hugged the guests who had become huggable type friends during their stay - and sometimes these were guests who only stayed one night. You'll know - or you'd better know - when a hug is appropriate or when a simple handshake is the proper physical contact. Some people are warm and friendly from the get go, others cherish their space. Some inn guests still think they are staying in a motel-type arrangement and, as such, would never consider hugging - or perhaps even kissing - the guy at the counter in the Marriott much less the lady who cleaned their room.

I also asked departing guests to think about us if their travel plans brought them back to our neck of the woods and asked them to tell their friends about us.

Some inns we stayed in mailed us a thank you note within a few days of our stay. Others included us on the mailing list of their periodic newsletter, which often contained information about the innkeepers and their family - usually much more than I cared to know. I didn't do either of these things, but done right, they can be nice reminders of your existence. Your choice.

E. The day-to-day activities...

The day-to-day activities of being an innkeeper, will fall into some kind of pattern that you and your partner and/or your staff are comfortable with, but after you think about the day in the life of an innkeeper - all of the tasks that need be done - you may want to consider the following:

Try not to do two or three things at the same time while you have guests in the inn - don't do the laundry when you are in the middle of breakfast, don't start cutting the grass when guests are scheduled to arrive, don't start repairing that dripping faucet in Room 4 while your guests are finishing breakfast and will be either checking out or looking to you for travel-related help - of course this last one assumes that Room 4 was vacant. You owe it to yourself and to your guests to concentrate on them. If you want to multitask do it on your own time.

When the last guest has left the dining room, you should attack the dining room and the kitchen. I could spend some time telling you how to bus your dining room table and how to clean your dishes, but I'm not. If you don't know how to do things like that, you should not even think about being an innkeeper. The one tip I will give you is don't rush things. If some of your guests are finished eating, but are sitting around the table chatting with other guests, remove their dishes slowly - no sense pouring food scraps or coffee onto a guest's lap, now is there? And, there is no reason to have them feel that you want them to leave the table.

If you are fortunate or really good in your timing, when the kitchen is clean enough to pass the occasional surprise inspection, your guests will have left for the day - or for the rest of their vacation. Now you can attack the guest rooms.

Once again, I won't go into the details of how to make a bed or how to clean a bathroom, but clean them you must. Please reread the earlier section on how unbelievably clean everything must be. To drive this point home to your guests, you might want to consider some type of disinfectant that has a clean and refreshing, but not overpowering, scent. This way, those coming back for their second or third night's stay and those just arriving will know that someone cared enough to really clean the place. And if you keep the entire inn clean all of the time, it will be easier to keep it clean.

You should have pillow covers under your pillowslips and mattress covers under your sheets. And, please don't forget to clean them periodically - something like every 30 days should do it, barring some sort of spill.

Clean and sanitize every part of every fixture in the bathrooms every day including things like the underside of the faucet that you will only be able to see when you are sitting on the commode - or rather when one of your guests is sitting on the commode. And remember that most of your male guests will miss the toilet bowl - hey, you're the one who wanted to be an innkeeper.

Dust everything all of the time.

Don't ever allow yourself to get lazy. Clean every groove and dust catcher all of the time - places like the top of the curtain rods and the lower cross bar on the headboard just down from where the pillows are and just below your guests' heads when they are sleeping.

Even if you don't have a guest scheduled to arrive for one or more of your rooms, clean them anyway and get them ready for a last minute guest or that dreaded drop in. All of your rooms should always be ready all of the time. You also don't want your guests to see an unclean room as they make their way to their room - or at least you shouldn't.

Now hit the common areas - the sitting room, the hallways, the yard, the parking lot. If you happen to be interrupted in the middle of cleaning these areas that's okay. At least the guest rooms are ready for the early arrival or the guest who decides to stop back after lunch to pick up their sunglasses and needs directions to someplace or other or perhaps just wants to take a nap. If I was in the middle of a relatively noisy task like vacuuming or mowing, I kept at it even if it might delay the onset of that nap. No one ever complained. There was simply an understanding that these things have to get done. By the way, someone once told me to "cut the grass when the good Lord lets you." If you plan to cut the grass on Tuesday and it's raining on Tuesday the grass won't get cut. And if happens to rain again on Wednesday and the lawn is too wet on Thursday now it's Friday and your place looks like hell. Do the outside chores when weather permits.

Now comes all of the other stuff you have to do - grocery shopping, plumbing repairs, bill paying, taking reservations, touching up those paint chips and smudged walls, meeting with the zoning administrator about that overhang you want to construct above your side porch, trying to find a heating contractor who won't build his retirement plan around finding out what is causing that pipe knocking in Room 1 when the heat comes on, going on line to see if anybody has made a reservation (or thinks they have), reordering supplies like toilet paper and laundry soap, and kicking the cat out of frustration for ever having become an innkeeper. This last activity might end up with a trip to the vet and good luck finding the time for that trip. When you have not quite finished all of these tasks, your stay-over guests will be arriving back at the inn to freshen up before dinner and, of course, they will ask you to recommend a good place to eat and to make reservations for them and your new guests will be arriving to check in. Wow! The day in the life of an innkeeper.

Speaking of buying room and cleaning supplies, you should do yourself a favor and find a distributor who will deliver this stuff to your door either by their own truck if they are local or by UPS or some other common carrier if they are not.

Oh, I forgot to mention that somewhere during your day, you will probably want to eat breakfast, lunch, and dinner. Ah, but when?

Oh, I also forgot to mention that you should always have a phone hooked to your belt so you can always be in a position to answer it. Remember that if a caller gets your answering machine, he probably won't leave a message and the next inn on his list will end up with the booking.

As with so many things that appear obvious, I feel duty bound to bring to your attention that you should spend part of your day planning your breakfasts so that the guests in Room 3 who have booked in for four nights won't eat the same entrée twice during their stay. Then think about the guests in Room 2 and Room 1 who are staying for three or four or five nights and whose stays overlap each other. Our longest stay was a seven-nighter. They were all the way from the State of Washington and used our inn as home base for their travels all over Vermont and New Hampshire. When they booked in we joked with them about the fact that we didn't have seven entrees and we did, in fact, end up repeating two of their favorites.

Speaking of breakfasts, it occurred to us early on that there was no good reason to wait until morning to set the table - so we set it in the evening. Just one less noisy task to do in the morning.

And whatever you can prepare the night before you should prepare the night before. Please don't cook it and reheat it in the morning, just prepare it.

I wasn't quite sure where to put this next tidbit so I put it here. Be wary of serving tea and crumpets - or some other beverage and snack - in the afternoons. You will have enough to do during your day and most of your guests will not take advantage of the offer. For the same reason, be wary of serving an early evening desert. And keep in mind that once you start either or both of these, it's very hard to stop especially if the fact that you do either or both is plastered all over your website (although this is relatively easy to change) and brochure (this isn't). We began to place a dish of very tasty chocolate chip and oatmeal cookies in the sitting room every afternoon and on into the evenings. The guests loved them. So when we took new photographs for our website, the plate of cookies appeared in the picture and the existence of the cookies made it into the caption under that photo.

1,723,536 cookies later we were not so sure that it was such a good idea.

And somewhere during the day you had better find a few moments to sit quietly and listen to your favorite music or read a book or go for a jog or sit quietly by the brook at the rear of your property - hopefully, it's a babbling brook - and just do nothing.

Finally, that famous quote from Samuel Pepys diary, "And so to bed."

F. How good an innkeeper are you...

How good an innkeeper are you is quite difficult to measure. Are you doing all of the things you should and are you doing them well? One measure of how well you're doing, of course, is your bookings. But they could merely be a measure of how good your advertising is and where your inn is located. Are you really satisfying your guests lodging needs? Are they really telling their friends and neighbors about your inn? Are they saying nice things? You may think you have the whole innkeeping thing down pat - I'm sure that the couple who let their grandson peddle his tricycle into our room did as well - but by the time you find out that your inn and your innkeeping skills need work, it could be too late.

We began to ask ourselves questions like: Were the rooms as clean as we thought they were? Were we being too attentive? Were we not being attentive enough? Were we providing the proper level of guest services? Were our breakfasts tasty and filling?

So we took a relatively bold step. At least we thought it was. For a period of time, we gave each of our guests who stayed for more than one night a questionnaire. Here it is:

The Winslow House

We really would like to find out how you think we're doing as innkeepers, so please take a moment and lend us a hand.

On a scale of 1 to 5 (1 meaning we should find another line of work and 5 meaning we should write a book about innkeeping), please answer the following questions

1.   Did everything work? 1 2 3 4 5
        If not, what was broken or jiggly?

_____

_____

2.   Was the room clean enough for you?1 2 3 4 5
        If not, what was dirty or messy?

_____

_____

3.   Was breakfast tasty, filling and well presented? 1 2 3 4 5
        If not, what was wrong with it?

_____

_____

4.   Were you warm enough or cool enough, depending on
whether you wanted to be warm or cool? 1 2 3 4 5

_____

_____

5.   Was the bed (mattress & pillows) comfortable? 1 2 3 4 5
        If not, what was the problem?

_____

_____

6.   We're your innkeepers attentive and charming? 1 2 3 4 5
        If not, what could we have done to make your stay more
enjoyable?

_____

_____

7.　　　In general, how would you rate your stay (keeping in mind that this is a 200 year old farmhouse on a very busy road)? 1 2 3 4 5

Since questionnaires typically have a space for comments, this is the space for comments

_____

_____

_____

_____

If you have nice things to say, you can fill this out and leave it in your room, otherwise, fill it out and take it with you (just kidding - we really value your feedback).

　　　We gave this to the guests on the last evening of their stay so if they had mean and nasty things to say, we wouldn't know it until they were gone. We left them on the bed with a pen attached. As you might expect, we didn't always get our pen back, but we thought that was a small price to pay for valuable feedback.

　　　Most of the guests took us seriously and we received some very good suggestions - like having a second wastebasket in the bedroom, not just the obvious one in the bathroom. One guest commented on the noise from the street, but went on to say that by the second night - of a three-night stay - they had become used to it and actually had slept very well. Another guest actually wrote that we served too much food at breakfast and that it was a shame to waste so much. The suggestion was that we ask our guests how much of everything they wanted rather than serve set portions. We began to do this with the number of pancakes.

　　　Some of the guests had fun with the questionnaire - like the woman who wrote that the only thing in the room that was jiggly was her underarms, but went on to say that she knew that there was nothing we could do about that. We took those comments as a compliment - they were obviously enjoying us and their stay.

The overall point is that you shouldn't think that everything is as it should be. You will be amazed at what some guests expect - how difficult it is to please some people and how easy it is to please others. Be willing to learn and to adjust.

G. Innkeeper associations...

Innkeeper associations probably don't belong in this section of the book, but I had to put it somewhere. So here it is. A brief section on innkeeper associations and what they can do for you coupled with some caveats - proceed with some level of caution and do your homework.

The apparent granddaddy of innkeeper associations or the thousand pound gorilla, if you will, is the Professional Association of Innkeepers International known as PAII. They hold conferences, trade shows, training programs and the like. Check them out at www.innkeeping.org. They've been around since 1988 and appear to have a good following.

There are also several state and more local associations that you might want to consider. Some of these local organizations might also offer consolidated purchasing for things like fuel oil. To find them, just Google or Bing innkeeper associations.

The good news is that these organizations exist. The bad news is that it usually costs money to join them or to attend their meetings and you might not have any extra time or money once you're an innkeeper.

In the interest of full disclosure, I never joined PAII or any other innkeeper association for that matter. I could afford to do so, however, there really wasn't any time. I was too busy being an innkeeper. Here's an idea. Do everything in this book and then spend some time being an innkeeper. Then consider joining something if you think it might help.

IX. Preventive Maintenance...

Preventive maintenance is the art of replacing things just before they break. Practice this art form until you have perfected it. On a regularly scheduled basis, tug on everything that can be tugged, flick everything that can be flicked, raise and lower everything that can be raised and lowered, open and close everything that can be opened and closed, slide everything that can be slid, flush everything that can be flushed, and turn on and off everything that can be turned on and off.

If something isn't working right, fix it or replace it. If something looks a little worn or frayed, replace it.

It's axiomatic that these tasks are easier and much less stressful to perform on a Tuesday afternoon, than they are on Saturday evening when the place is packed and a bunch of guests are coming and going. It might also be cheaper because your outside contractors will undoubtedly charge less when the project isn't being done on an emergency, after hours basis.

X. Marketing and advertising...

Marketing and advertising are critical elements to your success. So why is it the second last chapter in the book? Well, I didn't know where else to put it and I figured that you will have read the entire book before you bought your inn so even located here you will have the benefit of these gems before it's too late.

The purpose of a marketing and advertising plan is to let your target audience know that you exist and to convince them to stay with you. There are a lot of choices out there to accomplish these goals so depending on your budget you might have to be quite selective. The key elements and maybe the only elements of your plan will include a brochure and a website.

A. Your brochure...

Your brochure still remains a key element even though the Internet is has taken over the inn booking world. There are still a lot of folks - and not all of them are old folks - who either don't have access to the Internet or prefer to sit quietly at home reading brochures then placing a call to the inn of their choice and talking to a real live innkeeper and giving their credit card number to a real live person.

The brochure also is still used extensively by chambers of commerce and tourism bureaus in racks at visitor centers and information booths. And, even if someone books in from your website, it's still nice to send them a brochure along with a written confirmation of the booking so they actually have something they can hold in their hands and forget to bring with them on their vacation.

I read over three hundred brochures in preparation for creating ours. How did I round up three hundred brochures you ask? Well we had stayed in over one hundred inns during our traveling days and in getting ready for those stays we had written or called for many brochures from inn books and websites and we had picked up many brochures from chambers of commerce and information booths during our travels in preparation for our next trip. We even stopped in and picked up brochures at inns we spotted along the way.

The one thing I found out is that not one single innkeeper - not one - had a sense of humor or if they had a sense of humor, they didn't let it come out in their brochure. How sad. Everyone felt that they had to take care of "the weary traveler" by taking him "a step back in time to a bygone era" and have "the aroma of fresh-brewed coffee and fresh-baked muffins wafting through the inn to awaken you each morning." Yadda, yadda, yadda.

I felt that I could either prepare one of those boring and mundane brochures or take the whole brochure experience to a different level by introducing a little sarcasm and a little humor into the process. My approach was apparently so refreshing that people actually booked in to our place, so they said, just to meet me. Oh, I'm sure that someone out there thought that I was somehow being disrespectful of the innkeeping fraternity, but the heck with them. I just needed to separate us from the crowd and in the process I attracted people who were of a like mind. It apparently made their stay and my tending to them a mutually enjoyable experience. Having said that, if every brochure was a bit irreverent, there would be nothing special about the bit irreverent brochure. So find your own niche. If you want to take care of the weary traveler - although I don't know why he is so weary having driven up to Vermont from Boston in his Lincoln Navigator SUV in a little over two hours - take care of the weary traveler. I still think there is room for levity and joy in the inn brochure.

Here is the text of our brochure, which included a photograph of the front of the inn and the Sitting Room and a couple of guest rooms and a map:

The Winslow House
"the perfect bed & breakfast in the perfect setting"

The Winslow House is a small, intimate country inn with loads of charm offering its guests the quintessential New England bed & breakfast experience a short, but welcome mile from the hustle and bustle of Woodstock – voted the prettiest small town in America.

We could say, as so many bed & breakfast brochures do, that a stay here would be like a "step back in time" or a "return to a bygone era." However, that would mean you'd have to use an outhouse (when that activity became necessary), bathe in a cast iron tub (probably on Saturday night), read a book in your room by candlelight, try to sleep on a rope bed with a lumpy, horsehair filled mattress, sweat in the summer and freeze in the winter, be awakened by a rooster at 5:00a.m. or so, never brush your teeth, and travel off to your daily activities on a bumpy, smelly horse drawn cart and never exercise (since jogging hadn't been invented yet).

Well, you can forget about the hard times, because the good news is that we have plumbing in our outhouse.

Actually... the beauty of The Winslow House is that it combines the best of the "olden days" (and there were some "bests") with all of today's modern amenities. You can control your own heat and air conditioning. We have queen sized beds with very nice pillows and mattresses, beautifully appointed private bathrooms with your choice of hot and cold running water (or you can treat yourself to a combination of both). Each room has its own color cable television (so the only person you have to fight with about what to watch is your own roommate), a telephone, a clock radio, and a little refrigerator (in each guest room), beautiful hardwood or wide pine flooring, exquisite architectural details and lovely, uncomplicated antique furnishings (true to the period of our carefully restored 1872 farm house). You can pretty much get up and eat when you want to as long as it is between 8:00a.m. and 9:30a.m., and you have innkeepers who truly care about your well-being (we're obviously not in this business to make money so we must be in it for the pleasure of serving our guests).

If only Seneca Winslow could see his farmhouse now. We have every reason to believe that we've "done him proud." And we're sure he'd love the spectacular perennial flower gardens.

But, maybe most of all, what we offer is the attention to detail that makes a stay away from home just plain enjoyable. Like night stands on both sides of the bed, chubby hangers instead of those skinny wire things that leave peaks in the shoulders of your clothes, towel rings right by the showers so you don't have to drip across the floor to reach the towel rack, your own separate sitting area in four of our five guest rooms so that if someone wants to watch TV while the other one wants to read a book or if someone wants to read a book and the other one wants to sleep – you get the idea, and a candlelight breakfast. Of course, as we learned elsewhere, candlelight doesn't make the food taste any better, but it does lend a nice touch to our very tasty breakfasts.

And, if all of that's not enough, we have a little barn on the property which we have set up as an exercise room for those of you who find it necessary to work up a good sweat even when you're on vacation.

Our 25 year collection of magnificent early American antiques and accent pieces - those are the little things sitting around or hung on the walls that make a place truly charming - really does give The Winslow House the authentic flavor of a 19th century farmhouse - without the chores. However, if you do want to pitch in and lend a hand there is always a bed to be made, a bathroom to clean, and a garden to weed.

Do come to The Winslow House - it really is "the perfect bed & breakfast in the perfect setting."

The Village of Woodstock

Your search for the perfect New England village is over - assuming that you have been searching for the perfect New England village. Woodstock really does "have it all" - a beautiful village green, quaint covered bridges, lovely tree-lined streets, and magnificent historic homes.

You can enjoy "walking through the 19th century" on a guided or self-guided village tour - without having to look out for horse stuff. You can browse in the many fine shops and art galleries, visit our museums (a perfect rainy day activity), or go antiquing in the village and in the surrounding area. You can attend theater, concerts, or commune with nature in the Vermont Institute of Natural Science and Raptor Center (known in these parts as VINS) and in the stunning formal and woodland gardens of the Marsh-Billings-Rockefeller National Historical Park. Don't forget the Billings Farm & Museum. A great place to see how life really was in "the good old days."

Nearby are things like the Quechee Gorge, Calvin Coolidge's Birthplace (it really is quite interesting), Simon

Pearce Glassblowing, Silver Lake, and for the hearty among you, the Appalachian Trail and Long Trail...and so much more.

When it's time to eat lunch or dinner, you are in for a treat. The Woodstock area is home to several exceptional eateries from fine dining to casually elegant to casually casual. Lest they change hands and/or chefs, we won't name names here, but we do keep a pile of current menus at the inn and we'll be happy to give you our recommendations.

The State of Vermont

If you've never visited Vermont, what in heaven's name are you waiting for? If you've been here before, when in heaven's name are you coming back?

Vermont is truly a place for everyone and a place for all seasons.

In the Summer (if that's the time you can get away) the Green Mountains are unmatched in their beauty. In the Fall (our favorite time of year) the pure majesty of our foliage is almost beyond belief. In the Winter (if you're the outdoor type) you can subject yourself to the rigors of the finest downhill and cross country skiing in the east (we're real close to Killington, Pico, Ascutney and Suicide Six - that name alone is why we never took up the sport). In the Spring (if a quiet time is your pleasure) come here for great fishing and the rebirth of all things beautiful.

And, in almost any season, back country roads, (nearly) hidden mountain lakes, hiking, fishing, bicycling (but remember, Vermont ain't flat), horseback riding, golf (at the Woodstock Country Club and other public courses), picture taking and, best of all, dreaming and relaxing.

Just let us know what you want to do and we'll point you there.

The Directions

From points West (like Cleveland): Take 90 East to 87 North to 149 North to 4 East and follow the signs to Woodstock

From points Southeast (like Boston): Take 93 North to 89 North to Vermont Exit 1 and follow the signs to Woodstock

From points South (like New York/Hartford): Take 91 North to Vermont Exit 9 and follow the signs to Woodstock

From points North (like Montreal): Take 89 South to Vermont Exit 1 (you know the drill)

The Winslow House is right on Route 4 just 1.2 miles west of the Woodstock village green on the South side of the road. If you get lost – shame on you. But please call us for further directions. Don't worry, we won't tell your friends back home that you called.

The Winslow House
xxx Woodstock Road
Woodstock, Vermont 05091
(xxx) xxx-xxxx

Please take note that even though we did it with humor and some sarcasm, we told the potential guest everything that they needed to know about our inn, our town, and our state. So remember that no matter what journalistic style you choose, be cognizant of what your brochure is intended to do - attract guests.

We subsequently learned that The Winslow House was not built by Seneca Winslow in 1872, it was built by Jesse Safford in something like 1795. We assumed that the previous owners had done their homework when they bought and named the place, but they had made several invalid assumptions with the help of their attorney. We decided to have some fun with this discovery. We prepared an insert to our brochure that opened up with the line "Surprise, Surprise!!!!" and went on to tell the real story of what should have been named The Safford House.

The point of this story is that you really can't believe anything so you need to build into the inn buying process enough time to do your own research into any matter that you deem important. From our point of view it sounded a whole lot better to say that our inn was a beautifully restored 200-year-old farmhouse rather than a beautifully restored 1872 farmhouse. So we began to use the 200-year-old phrase wherever we could. And even though changing the name of the inn would have put us slightly closer to the front of the alphabetical list of inns in the tour books and on the websites, the name was so well entrenched that we left it alone.

Did you notice the quote, "the perfect bed and breakfast in the perfect setting?" Only one guest asked where the quote came from. I told her the truth. The quote came from me. I thought that we had the perfect bed and breakfast in the perfect setting so I quoted myself in our brochure. I think that's legal.

In the design of your brochure remember that some of them will probably end up in racks in chamber of commerce booths and visitor centers. This fact requires that they be the right size to fit in the racks and that the name of the inn be along the top of the brochure so that it is visible.

Two examples will drive this point home. When I filled in for a while in the local chamber's information booth, I spotted a brochure that was all gray - nothing was visible, not a word, not a picture. The innkeepers had put a lovely pencil drawing of their inn (more about pencil drawings a little bit later) half way down the front of their brochure with the name of the inn below the drawing. What a marvelous advertising piece - you couldn't see the drawing or the name of the place because they were below the facing of the rack. I called the innkeepers and asked them to come to the booth. When they got there, I asked them to find their brochure. They ended up taking them home and writing the name of the inn along the top of the front of the brochure until it was time to reprint them.

The other story is of the new furniture maker in town who prepared a lovely short and squat advertising card, which couldn't be seen at all. It was actually shorter than the wooden panel that held the brochures in the rack. I'm sure that he wanted his brochure to stand out in the crowd, but it fell rather short of its mark - no pun intended. He was somewhat crestfallen to learn that we couldn't display his brochure in a way that it could be seen.

Also keep in mind that your brochure may end up being mailed to prospective guests and, therefore, needs to fit into an envelope. Of course, you could leave space on the back of the last section of your brochure for an address and mail it without an envelope or have a specially sized envelope made up for your specially sized brochure, but you will still fall prey to the rack problem if you don't make your brochure the standard size.

One last point about your brochure that will save you a lot of time and money. Don't include anything in the text that might change - like your rates or your policies or your rules. This stuff should be included in an insert. That way your brochure will stand the test of time and all you have to do is write up and print a skinny and relatively cheap insert. You're welcome.

B. Your website...

Your website is the other key marketing piece and, in reality, may be the only other marketing piece you will have. Much of what I just wrote about your brochure applies to your website as well. Make sure that you tell the reader everything that they need to know - where you are, what you have to offer, how to reach you, and if possible a hook (a reason to ignore the other 567 brochures and websites that they have seen and pick your place).

Since the first thing your prospective guests will see is the cover of your brochure or the home page of your website, this is the place to grab their attention - don't waste it.

A pencil drawing of your inn or a photograph or drawing of something other than your inn can be quite attractive, but I always felt that an innkeeper was trying to hide something when this approach was used. One of the main reasons that we chose one inn over another during our travels is because we liked how it looked. Not how an artist made it look. If your inn isn't very nice looking, your guests will know that as soon as they arrive and, at that point, they will feel as though they've been had. Not a nice start. So going way back to the beginning of your search and the development of your search criteria, don't buy an unattractive inn. Or, if you do buy an unattractive inn because it has so many other things going for it, try to do some things to make it better looking - shutters, plantings, different color, window treatment that can be seen from the outside, etc.

Another option of handling the advertising piece for an unattractive inn (that is before you have a chance

300

to make it more attractive) is to take a picture of your inn's best feature - say an angle shot of your front door through your flowering shrubs or through your perennial flower bed. If your inn is right near the road, for heaven's sake, don't show the road in the photograph. And if your inn is next door to a fast food restaurant or a convenience store don't show them either. Come to think of it, why would you buy an inn next to a fast food restaurant or a convenience store? Try not to show power lines, transformers on power poles, etc. But, you get the idea. Do the best you can with what you've got. Make it appealing.

If you think that this last bit of advice is stating the obvious - it isn't and I could show you several examples of brochure or website photographs that absolutely defy all logic and reason. One inn, in particular, with which I am quite familiar happens to be 10 feet from a very busy road and I mean 10 feet. The inn has a relatively nice front porch which the innkeepers feature in their literature - "relax on our sweeping front porch" - or words to that effect. But the picture of their inn shows the very busy road - right there next to the porch. Brilliant marketing strategy.

Let me repeat that when you write the text of your brochure or website be complete - tell them everything they need to know. Looking at other brochures and websites is a place to start, but there is a pitfall to avoid. It's easy to make sure that you include all of the things that the other guys include. The pitfall is what they don't include that you could or should - the hook to get the reader to call you. Take your marketing pieces to another level if you want to stand out in the crowd - and there is quite a crowd.

Also, remember that the one of the real beauties of the web is that it is a visual medium - the almost perfect opportunity to really show off your inn. So don't overload your site with a bunch of words when a bunch of really professional pictures will tell your story so much better. Let's see, what was that old line? Oh, I remember now. A picture is worth a whole lot of words. Or something like that.

Here are some other thoughts to consider in the development of your website:

✓ Make sure that all of your pages are linked to one another - the bottom of each page (or section) should list all of the other pages in your website and they should be live so a viewer can move easily from page to page rather than having to go back to the home page to navigate your website. Again, this may seem obvious, but I could give you plenty of examples where getting to where you wanted to be in a website was quite challenging. Remember that many folks are still not and never will be web savvy. Go easy on them.

✓ If you're going to have an online reservation process, you will need to show your room availability by room, day, and month and this means that you will have to update the information every time you take a reservation or receive a cancellation. This is one of the other reasons that we didn't take online reservations - it's a pain in the butt to update your reservation information on your website every time you take or lose a booking.

But how else will those viewing your website know what is really available?

✓ Use large, clear type. Don't get cute with an exotic type style that some folks will have a hard time deciphering. Don't make the decision to stay with you a challenge.

✓ Go easy on the pictures of you and your pets. Remember that it's not about you - it's about the inn. A nice photograph of you and your significant other innkeeper might give a nice warm touch to your website - or to your brochure for that matter, but keep it simple. Your potential guests are more interested in your guest rooms than in the people who clean them.

✓ If you can afford it, set up your website to enable visitors to take a virtual tour of your inn - it's the next best thing to being there. If you can't or don't want to do the virtual tour thing, at least include a picture of each of your guest rooms. I just received brochures for two inns as part of a planned getaway to the coast of Maine and neither of them includes any pictures of their rooms. I requested brochures because neither of their websites included pictures of their rooms or even described them. Now how am I supposed to choose which inn or which room?

✓ Don't bury your name and your address and your phone number. They should be on your home page as well as on your reservations page or your contact us page.

✓ Have a page devoted to specials and special announcements like mid week packages and don't forget to change the page as needed.

Now that you have created a really neat website, what are you going to do with it? How will you get on all of those search engines? How will you get linked to the local and state chambers of commerce websites? How will you get on that really slick website that features inns that are pet friendly? Or the one that features inns that host weddings - assuming that you want to host weddings? Or the one that features inns that welcome honeymooners with special packages? Or the one that features inns that welcome children? Or the one that caters to …? You get the idea.

Part of your decision-making process will be driven by your advertising budget. So start with the obvious. Put yourself in the position of an inn seeker. What would you do first?

It seems to me that the first thing someone going on vacation does is decide where he wants to go on vacation. I don't think it begins with, "I found this inn that takes pets and kids, Margaret. Let's make a reservation and hope that there is something to do when we get there?"

So begin by getting on the websites that will give you the biggest bang for your buck. If your inn is in a tourist area, that would be the local and state chambers of commerce. You will probably have to join the chambers - which will cost you some annual dues - and then, perhaps pay something additional to be on their websites. Sometimes you can be on the websites without being a member, but you will probably have to pay more for the listing than members pay. We joined the chambers, because it seemed nice to say that we were members of the State of Vermont and the Woodstock Area Chambers of Commerce. It seemed to give us some level of credibility when in reality all we had to do was fill out a form and pay our dues. But, sometimes perception is more important than reality. And part of those annual dues we paid are used for advertising the state and the town. So let the state chamber run the big ads in the national magazines and on television and mail out the fancy, full-color travel booklets and have the major league website and let the local chamber staff the information booth and send its own booklet of area attractions and places to stay. If you are linked to their websites, folks will find you.

The search engines, like Google or Bing, won't cost you anything, but the trick is to be near the front of the pack. If your web master doesn't know how to get you there and keep you there, get yourself another web master.

As far as getting on all of the specialty websites - be careful. Most of them will charge you something for the privilege of joining what they will tell you is their thousands of satisfied innkeepers. Ask them how long they've been around and how many hits they get. Then go on line yourself and see how easy it is to navigate the site. Finally, talk to some of their customers. You can do this by calling an inn or two, pretending that you are a potential guest, and informing the innkeeper where you found them. Then, by being somewhat coy, you can ask how they like the site and how much business it generates. You should also ask what other sites they are on and how successful those sites are. Do your homework before you strike.

As far as the websites that don't cost anything - get on as many of them as you can. The only caveat is that you should avoid any websites that cater to folks who you don't necessarily want to cater to for example www.trashtalkingbeerswillingnudistbikermommas.com. The choice is yours.

I was lucky enough to run my inn before the social media boom. Today just as many folks will look for your inn on Facebook as they will on Google or Bing. Setting up a fan page on Facebook so that people can 'like' your inn is free and easy to do. It's another point of presence on the Internet and allows satisfied guests to spread the word for you. Unfortunately, it also allows unsatisfied guests to take a whack at you. But if you follow all of the advice I've provided you in this book, you won't have any unsatisfied guests.

Only do as much with social media as you are comfortable with and, as I said before, remember it is about their experience not yours. It is easy to go overboard so keep it simple and remember to keep your Facebook page and your website updated. There's nothing worse than finding outdated information on the web. Well, actually, there are plenty things worse than finding outdated information on the web, but you get the idea. If you're going to do it, do it right.

And as far as Twitter is concerned, forget it. I can't imagine why your guests would want to follow you on Twitter.

C. Chamber of Commerce where to stay booklets...

Chamber of Commerce where to stay booklets can be quite valuable so you should give them serious consideration almost regardless of their cost. Remember the chamber does the advertising, they field the phone calls, they do the mailing - all you have to do is take the reservation. The only caveat here is not to spend too much money. In most cases you can have a listing that will be the same size as everybody else's or you can spend some relatively serious bucks and have some sort of a display ad.

Potential guests looking for a nice, attractive, and comfortable bed and breakfast don't expect large display ads. The point of having a listing in this type of booklet is to get them to your website and to the AAA tour book so be sure to mention in your website and in your listing your AAA rating if you have one.

D. AAA Tour Books...

AAA Tour Books are still used extensively, especially by somewhat older travelers who might not be computer literate or computer comfortable. There is some good news and what some might think of as bad news about being in AAA. The good news is that four billion people are AAA members (that's just a guess) and travel all over the place so your listing has the potential of being seen by a whole lot of folks. The bad news is that you have to comply with their standards to achieve their various diamond ratings and - this is a pet peeve - they do not allow you to put your web address in your listing. You can however put your web address in a display ad.

I did not think that their diamond rating requirements were at all onerous and I welcomed their unannounced inspections as a sort of a test as to how we were doing.

This is not meant to be a pitch for AAA, but if you pay to be an Officially Appointed property, part of your listing in the tour books is in red type. We found this to be extremely valuable. Let me repeat that. We found this to be extremely valuable. Even though many inns with which I am familiar had the same rating we did, we were getting many times the number of bookings they were from AAA travelers because our entry in the tour book was in red type. Many times the number of bookings. Apparently some people think there's more to the red listing than just the color. There isn't.

One last thing about AAA. We learned that many guests who found us on the web also checked us out in the AAA Tour Book. We highlighted on our website that we were a AAA three-diamond rated property and many web searchers, knowing that we could say anything we wanted to on our website, also checked us out in the tour book. By the way, I didn't take this personally. I assumed that they did this with all of the inns they were considering as kind of double check.

Lest I get in some sort of difficulty, that's all I will say about AAA, but I encourage you to fully explore what they have to offer and what it costs.

E. Fodor's travel guides...

Fodor's travel guides was worth every penny. Well, come to think of it, it didn't cost us anything. We were a *Recommended* inn, which was quite prestigious and we were quite proud of it. For us, Fodor's ranked third behind the AAA Tour Book and our website as a source of bookings - especially by Europeans. You might want to contact them and see what the current deal is.

F. Other travel books...

Other travel books and journals should be looked at very cautiously, especially the ones that you have to pay to get in. As travelers, we found that, much like a website, when there is no inspector or editor, when you are allowed to say anything you want, when you can hire outstanding photographers with real wide angle lenses who can make a broom closet look like it is fifteen feet by twenty-four feet wide, you might end up being quite disappointed when you arrive at the place.

Check out the actual circulation of these publications and watch out for the infamous "number of readers" statement. Many publications will make an assumption that every magazine or book they sell will be read by three or four other people or some such number as the publication is passed around by the original purchaser. These statements may be statistically valid, but the other three or four or ten people might be the children or grandparents of the person who bought the book and what good are they - as potential travelers, he hastens to add?

Once again, I would recommend that you check with innkeepers who are in these publications and try to ascertain how pleased they are. Call some of them, act dumb - which should not be that difficult since at this point you will have recently become an innkeeper - pretend that you found their listing, which will actually be a true statement, and just start asking questions. Things like, "I found you in The Greatest Inns of All Time, Volume Thirty Seven, East Orange, New Jersey Edition. You sure must get a ton of bookings from being in such a prestigious publication. Oh, and we also found you in AAA and Traveling with Your Hairy Pets. I'm curious, which one of those works well for you so we can subscribe to the one that you innkeeper types like the best?" Or words to that effect. Most innkeepers will be so excited that their phone rang and that you might just make a reservation, they will just prattle on. Take notes.

G. Other places where you can waste your money...

Other places where you can waste your money will keep appearing in your U.S. mailbox or in your e-mail inbox. Even if they're free, be wary. If they cost anything - anything at all - ignore them.

If you get approached by duckhunters.com (and I have no idea if there is such an organization) and for only $25 a month you can be the featured inn every month for the next seven years... Well, you get the idea. Duckhunters.com may not even be a legitimate organization or website and even if it is, my guess is that most duck hunters sleep in tents. You will be amazed at how many websites are out there and how many of them will find you. Be selective and navigate them for yourself.

When the local PAL or the First Baptist Church or Third Spiritual House of Worship or the Sixteenth Church of the Apostle or the Sixty-Third Church of the Holy Order of All Lost Souls approaches you for ads in their annual calendars, it's your choice. It is a given that you will not receive any bookings from these ads, but you might want to be a nice guy. The only problem is that the requests for such ads will keep coming and they will come year after year.

You know those over sized, colorful maps that look like they were drawn by a third grader with an old set of crayons - DO NOT waste your money. Just think about it. By the time a visitor to your area gets his hands on one of those, he's already in your area and most likely already has lodging reservations. If you look closely at who advertises in those things you will see that it is the restaurants, the gift shops, and the tourist attractions - not the lodging establishments.

Newspaper advertising in the main newspaper in a target market area - let's say the Boston Globe if your inn is in New England - is extremely expensive and the chances of getting your money's worth are slim and none. Just think about it - one ad on one Sunday could cost several hundred dollars and could be seen by thousands of people three of whom are looking for a place to stay on their next vacation.

H. Other marketing ideas...

Other marketing ideas that you might want to consider include developing mid-week packages for those times when mid-week bookings are slow; providing guests with discounts when they return in off-peak periods; providing guests with discounts on subsequent stays in off-peak periods if they refer other guests to your inn (if you go down this path, make sure that you don't honor the discount until the referred guest has come, gone, and paid for their stay); offering gift certificates as a way to have your guests spread the word; sending each guest a nice cover letter with their reservation confirmation thanking them for their booking and pitching the inn and area activities and, finally, sending each guest a thank you note.

There are tons of other ideas that you might want to consider - let your imagination, your time, and your personal experiences be your guide. Just keep the cost of these programs in mind as you try to assess their effectiveness.

A few of the inns we visited sent us a periodic newsletter, which often included the comings and goings of the innkeepers and their family members. What a waste. As I wrote earlier, more often than not, we had not become close enough friends in our brief stay to really care if their oldest daughter graduated from college or was expecting her tenth child, or whatever. We probably never even met her and most assuredly didn't remember her name. This goes back to a previous comment - it's not about the innkeeper, it's about the guest. And, from a marketing perspective, this type of folksy information did little to encourage a return visit and isn't marketing about generating business?

And, finally, something else that has come to pass since my innkeeping days and doesn't quite fit in this section and, perhaps, doesn't even belong in this book. But somehow I feel compelled to share with you some comments on the wonderful world of review sites like Trip Advisor and Yelp.

A lot of folks refer to these websites when doing their due diligence on selecting a place to stay. I have found it fascinating how one person will love a place and can't wait to make a return visit or at least tell their friends about it, or, through the use of the web, tell the world about it, and someone else would just as soon as torch the place as they were leaving it. Who are you to believe?

I come down on the side of the old axiom that you can't please everyone. If 34 folks love it and two don't, I'll cast my lot with the 34.

Certainly as an innkeeper, you should ask your guests - at least the ones who aren't making a run for their cars in the morning without saying goodbye - to take a moment and make some positive comments about you and your inn on these sites. It comes under the category of free advertising (so that's why these comments are in the book and in this section).

And remember that you do have the opportunity to throw a written counter punch if you feel that you have been unfairly treated. Just don't make it sound as though you are whining about a crummy guest.

XI. Putting the Inn of Your Dreams up for Sale…

Putting the inn of your dreams up for sale might be a very easy or perhaps a very difficult decision. But, sooner or later you're going to make it and either way it will be an emotion-filled decision. "Ralph, it's time to sell the place. We've had a good run, but if I have to make one more bed, I'm going to kill the guest who slept in it and then I'm going to kill you." Or, "Ralph, it's time to sell the place. For the life of me, I'll never know how you were able to talk me into such a ridiculous move in the first place."

So when that magic moment has arrived, go back to the section of this book on how to buy the inn of your dreams and do everything in reverse.

Actually, it's not quite that simple, but the steps are basically the same: Find a good real estate broker, find a good attorney, and don't let the place go to hell while you're trying to sell it.

This period of time will, perhaps, be your greatest challenge as an innkeeper - running the inn while you are in the process of selling. I alluded to this before, but it really does bear repeating - don't wait until you are mentally or physically or financially spent (no pun intended there) before you put the inn on the market. Have something left in your psyche, in your physical capabilities, and in your wallet to get you through the sales period, the discovery period, and the close.

A. Finding a good dream team...

Finding a good dream team should follow the same pattern. First find a real estate broker who has a good track record of selling inns in your town or state. It just might be the same broker that helped you find and buy your inn or it could even be the broker who sold the inn for the folks you bought the place from, assuming of course that these brokers didn't retire on the commissions they made on that deal. Either way, interview them. Please don't think that you owe it to either of these guys to work with them again. What they did for you or for the seller a few years ago might have been the proverbial flash in the pan. Yours may have been the only deal they pulled off or it might have been their last. You want someone who is actively in the business and has his finger on the pulse of pricing, market conditions, financing, and interested buyers.

If you do choose one of the brokers you dealt with previously, there will be a short learning curve since they will already be familiar with the inn - unless you've really torn it apart and, hopefully, put it back together, since they last saw it.

The same due diligence should apply to the selection of your attorney. If you liked the guy you used previously and if he didn't retire on the fees he earned from your previous deal, use him again - but don't feel obligated to.

Through a unique set of circumstances the seller's attorney when we bought our inn turned up again as the buyer's attorney when we sold our inn. The comprehensive contract that my attorney and I pounded out and negotiated with this guy came right back at us - almost verbatim. It's a good thing that the contract - although quite thorough - was also quite even handed. These things can happen more often than you might think, especially in a small town.

When it was time to sell our inn, we did, in fact, use the broker who the previous sellers had used. I liked his marketing package - among other things - and he knew the inn. Since I had not used a broker when I bought the inn, I didn't have to worry about whether that broker's feelings would be hurt. But had I used a broker and decided not to engage his services to help me sell the place, his feelings would not have been my concern. I wanted to sell and I wanted to sell in a hurry and I wanted the best man I could find to help me do it.

I also used the same attorney that I had used when I bought the place. We had worked well together and his fees were acceptable. He even saved me a few bucks by not appearing at the close of our sale, because there was no reason for him to be there. It was his idea and I thanked him for it.

By the way, after six months of showing the inn to a host of prospective buyers, I switched brokers. I told the broker who I was dumping that I still loved him, but I still owned the inn. It was time to try someone else.

There are two things to keep in mind in this process and they should both be included as clauses in your listing agreement. Negotiate the shortest time period possible for your broker to have an exclusive listing. This will keep his feet to the fire and allow you to change brokers if things don't work out - you don't have to change brokers at the end of the listing agreement period, but you should give yourself the option to. The second thing to include in the agreement - and you shouldn't really have to worry about this because any self-respecting broker will require it - is protecting the broker in case someone he showed the place to during his time as the listing broker comes back in the picture after you've changed brokers. In our case, the broker we had originally listed the inn with was required to provide us with a list of names at the conclusion of his listing period and, of course, he did so.

Be careful here. Make sure that the listing agreement protects him for those interested parties who actually saw the property - not just inquired about it. You should keep your own list of those prospective buyers who actually showed up at your door. The listing broker is entitled to his commission for any deal that he really worked on.

Two more items about the listing agreement: Make sure that the cost of preparing the marketing package and any other advertising is born by the broker and make sure it includes a requirement that your inn is actually advertised a certain number of times in specific journals, websites, newspapers, and so on. Do your homework and make up your wish list. I can hear you now saying something like, "Well of course my broker will advertise my inn." To which I respond, "Don't bet on it unless you make it a requirement." Advertising costs a lot of money and your broker's advertising budget might be near a breaking point when your inn comes on board. If he balks at this requirement, keep looking.

One more thing about advertising. Make sure that the listing agreement gives you the right to approve every ad that your broker intends to run. And read them very carefully. Brokers are salesmen and, here's a news flash, salesmen tend to exaggerate a bit. No, change that. Salesmen tend to exaggerate a lot. Don't allow anything to appear in your ad that you will have to explain away when a potential buyer appears at your door.

And another thing - make sure that your broker requires every prospective buyer to sign a confidentiality agreement before he receives one of your marketing packages even if the prospective buyer and your broker meet for the first time in your parking lot at the time of the showing. Have them take a minute either in the parking lot or in your front entrance hallway or in one of their cars to handle that important bit of paperwork. The only people who the buyer should be legally allowed to share your information with are his attorney, his broker - if he has one - and his financial advisor. Same as when you were the buyer, if you'll recall.

B. Setting the selling price...

Setting the selling price should also follow the same process as you used in determining how much you offered for the place - to some degree. The first thing to consider is how much money do you need to get out of the innkeeping business with at least the shirt on your back. Your mortgage balance, the broker's commission, your attorney's fees, some miscellaneous closing costs, your relocation expenses, your original down payment, and perhaps even some profit should all be factored in along with your sanity - how badly do you want to get out.

Then, when your broker gets done laughing, he will tell you what the place is really worth - but make him prove it with a whole bunch of recent sales as comparables. Here's the classic broker's dilemma - the more your inn sells for, the higher his commission will be, but the higher the sales price the longer it may take to sell. Somewhere between all of those numbers is the listing price.

Keep in mind that if you ask too much - even though you can always drop down to some more reasonable figure - you run the risk of scaring off some potential buyers. Also keep in mind that you don't have to take less than your asking price.

C. Getting the place ready to sell...

Getting the place ready to sell should be done meticulously. Put yourself back into the shoes of the buyer. If the buyer does his job right, he will look the inn over just as carefully as you and your inspectors did when you bought it.

Clean everything, then clean it again. Touch up every smudge. Label your paint cans, although they should already be labeled. Make all of those pesky little repairs that you kept putting off - those are actually the ones that can queer a deal. Make sure that doorknobs and drawer pulls are tightened. Make sure that doors close and drawers slide freely. Make sure that railings and banisters are tight. Make sure that all of your windows open and close properly. Make sure that all of your light switches work and there are no plumbing problems, like leaks.

As best you can, unclutter the place especially the basement and the garage - this of course assumes that you have a basement and a garage. And get rid of any musty odors.

Bottom line - make the entire inn including the building and the grounds look attractive. The buyer should think that all he has to do is move in.

I would strongly suggest that you don't do anything heroic like changing the color of the exterior or installing a new roof or replacing the boiler - things like that. If things like that are needed, they will be factored into the selling price so you're going to pay for them one way or the other and you just might paint the place the wrong color for a potential buyer's taste or you just might not install the buyer's favorite brand of boiler or maybe he always wanted one of those metal standing seam roofs instead of the shingles you installed.

This can be used as a selling tool. "We know the place needs to be painted, but we thought that you as the buyer, would want to select the color. We know it will cost $5,000 for the paint job, so we priced the inn accordingly." However, don't have this discussion unless you have to.

Get your paperwork in order (although it should be anyway) - income and expense logs, room booking reports, reservation deposits, utility account numbers and phone numbers, permits, title work, zoning and planning approvals for that new addition, the latest plot survey, etc. These things will make your marketing package a thing of beauty and will actually save the buyer time and money in the purchase process.

Do yourself a huge favor - don't try to hide anything. If a prospective buyer finds even one thing that appears to be a cover up, everything else will be suspect and I mean everything. It just doesn't pay. Your inn is where it is, your records are what they are, your roof leaks or it doesn't, your boiler heats the place or it doesn't, and on and on.

D. The marketing package...

The marketing package should, in my opinion, be very comprehensive. It should answer as many buyer questions as possible. You and your broker might as well try to eliminate the tire kickers up front.

However, as we discussed before, there are two schools of thought regarding marketing packages - the comprehensive package (tell them almost everything) or the tease package (tell them just enough to pique their interest). Either one can be effective. Which one you prefer could be a deciding factor in the selection of your broker.

The comprehensive package should include a whole bunch of photographs, a site plan, three years or so of income and expense numbers, information about the town - things to see and do and why someone would want to live there - operating permits, lists of where the inn is advertised including websites, and anything else that might convince a buyer to at least go see the place. Throw in a copy of your brochure and don't forget the asking price.

The tease package should contain some photographs, perhaps a site plan unless it shows that the inn is three feet from a freeway on ramp with a gas station on one side and a motorcycle repair shop on the other, some general numbers or perhaps just some percentages - percentage of occupancy, percentage of expenses to income - and information on the area. Of course most buyers who are interested at this point will request the rest of the information that would be contained in the comprehensive package, but at least you won't have shared your numbers with everyone.

In either case, make sure that you proofread the package, whatever the broker places on his website, and any other marketing piece he prepares. It's your inn and to some degree you are responsible for his work product. Don't put yourself in a position of having to explain some stretched truth or major omission.

A point to consider in all of this marketing business is whether the name of the inn should be included in the marketing material. There are pros and cons of keeping this tidbit of information secret. At first, I chose not to include the name of the inn. I'm not quite sure, in hind sight, if that was such a good idea. Who was I trying to keep it a secret from? Your guests or potential guests probably won't see the ads. The other innkeepers in your area will probably learn soon enough that your inn is on the market. And, think about this bit of wisdom, the more people who know that your inn is for sale, the more people know that your inn is for sale. Now, isn't that the exact point of an advertising campaign?

The cast of characters who might be legitimately concerned about the inn being for sale is your staff - although they shouldn't be especially if they have been doing a good job. I would suggest that you tell them the truth. Your problem might be, of course, that they get nervous and find other employment before the sale is finalized. To avoid this situation, you might want to consider promising them some sort of bonus if they stay until the bitter end. What the buyer does with and about them at that point ain't your problem.

E. Showing your inn…

Showing your inn to prospective buyers entails a lot more than just opening your doors and letting them and the brokers (yours and theirs) stroll through the place. Please try to follow some of these "rules:"

If at all possible you should not have a showing when you have any guests. Remember that your guests deserve your almost undivided attention. If it comes to pass that you have no choice, explain to the guests that you are showing the inn to a couple who is planning to rent the entire place for a family gathering. Tell them that, if they don't mind, you would like to allow the couple to quickly peek inside their room. No one ever turned down this request. By the way, make sure that the prospective buyers and the brokers know the story so they can watch what they say as they tour the inn - lest someone say something really stupid or embarrassing in front of your guests.

Make sure that the place is as clean as it has ever been.

Turn on every light in the inn - even if the showing is to take place on a sunny afternoon. It does make a difference.

Have soft music playing in the background. We always played soft classical music during the time that guests would be checking in - mid to late afternoon - and during breakfast. It helped make the scene calm and unhurried. That is not only a good thing for guests, it is probably more important for potential buyers. It sends a "being an innkeeper is not as insane as you might have heard it is" message.

Go along on the tour of the inn with the buyers and the brokers. This will be your chance to answer those questions that the brokers can't because they haven't run the place. There will be plenty of time later for the buyers and the brokers to have private discussions. Don't volunteer anything that might have a negative overtone. Don't point up any flaws. Be smart. Be a salesman, but don't over sell.

After the tour, the buyers and the brokers - maybe just their broker - will, hopefully, want some private time to talk things over. Obviously, you should give them as much time as they want and allow them to tour the inn again without you and your broker tagging along.

Many buyers will want to spend a night or two in the inn - remember, you did as a buyer. It's your choice if you want to charge them for the privilege. But make sure that if you have other guests, the buyers are told to keep their mouths shut and to pretend that they are just guests. I always invited them to tour the inn again at their leisure - after any other guests have checked out or have left for their daily activities - and to knock on my door after dinner if they just wanted to chat about the place and the life of the innkeeper and learn more about the town or whatever. Don't use this time away from the brokers to negotiate or to tell them how difficult it is to be an innkeeper. Be cordial and helpful, but keep your guard up.

F. Negotiating the contract...

Negotiating the contract and actually selling the inn is, literally, the reverse of the process that you went through when you bought the place.

Your attorney and the buyer's attorney will pound out an agreement loaded with all manner of terms and conditions and due dates. Your job is to not allow your attorney to give away the store unless your desire to get out of the innkeeping business is so strong that you actually instruct him to give away the store.

One problem in caving in too quickly on the buyer's demands is that they will keep asking for more and/or they will start to think that there are some hidden problems that you are trying to get out from under. In the former scenario you may end up giving away more that you really need to. In the later scenario they might get skittish and walk - or perhaps run - away.

Keep one thing in mind. Until the close of the sale, you own the place. Oh sure, the agreement might put some constraints on how much you can spend and what you can or can't do, but you still own the place. So make sure that those clauses don't prohibit you from doing everything you have always done to keep it clean and repaired and your guests happy. The deal could always crash - I know of three specific deals that actually crashed at the closing - and you may have to start all over again with a new buyer. How grim is that? But it does happen. So, don't let your inn go to hell.

Make sure that the contract is fair, provides enough but not too much time for the buyer to do what buyers have to do, and allows you to still be in charge.

You could, of course, try to sell the inn without the services of a broker or even an attorney. You'd be nuts, but you could try it. Just follow all of the same steps, do exactly what the broker would have done - determine the selling price, prepare your own marketing package, place your ads on the appropriate websites and in the appropriate journals, screen the potential buyers, have them sign confidentially agreements, arrange the showings, negotiate the sale terms and conditions, etc., etc. It can be done, but remember that while you are trying to do all of these broker and attorney things, you are also trying to run an inn. And remember - always remember - that your guests come first. And, remember that classic line that goes something like anyone who acts as his own attorney has a fool for a client.

A little side story to let you know how things can get screwed up even with the best of intentions. Our broker received a call about our inn from a prospective buyer. He had her sign a confidentiality agreement that only allowed her to share information about the inn including the fact that it was for sale with her broker, attorney, and accountant - just like it was supposed to. So what did this knucklehead buyer do? She sent an e-mail to virtually all of the area innkeepers informing them that she was interested in our inn and because our occupancy percentage was so high, she wanted to know what the other innkeepers' numbers were. Like she was going to get this information anyway. So, immediately our phone was jumping of the hook with calls from the other innkeepers wanting to know the story. Even though Ms. Knucklehead apologized - she obviously had no idea what a confidentiality agreement was or perhaps she hadn't even read the damn thing - and I threatened to sue her for breaching the agreement, the damage was done. The whole town knew our inn was on the market. Fortunately, at the end of the day, no real harm was done.

XII. The Close and the Getaway...

The close and the getaway could be the happiest or maybe one of the saddest days in your life. At this point - for whatever reason or reasons - you will have ended a really special chapter in your life. Remember this was your dream and now your dream has come to an end. At the close, try not to be too depressed or giddy - depending on which end of the emotional spectrum you find yourself. If you are too giddy, the buyer will think that he has been had. Think how you would have felt if the seller had turned cartwheels when you were at your close. If you are too depressed the buyer might actually feel bad for you. Think how you would have felt if the seller had cried at the close when you bought the place. You would have been sad on what should have been one of the happiest days of your life. Keep your emotions in check.

At our closing, I wished the buyers good luck and told them that I hoped that they would be as full as they wanted to be.

The actual machinations of the close are rather perfunctory - just as they were when you were the buyer. Tons of papers prepared by attorneys and bankers are passed around and signed, checks are handed out by the banker, and hopefully, you still have most of the shirt left on your back.

How you handle your last few guests and the potential bookings for the period leading up to the close will be a subject of negotiations between you and the buyer. Remember that we asked for a period of four days between the close and the arrival of our first guest. The couple we sold the place to only asked for two days. We knew that they were nuts, but that was a foregone conclusion since they had - somewhere along the way - decided to become innkeepers.

With all contingencies satisfied, we had actually moved out almost a week before the close and the buyers had moved in a couple of days before the close. This little maneuver required a side agreement - it addressed the fact that if they found something they didn't like that was simply too bad. There was no opportunity for them to crash the deal because they had already gone through their discovery period and had accepted the place. What if they caused some damage though? This would be their problem not ours. Things like that. But the early move in did give them some additional time to get settled in and begin their new life in the inn of their dreams.

The End

Author Biography

After a successful career in the corporate world in his native Cleveland, Ohio, Jeff Bendis and his late wife Kathleen, took advantage of Jeff's early retirement and headed to Vermont to become the new owners of a bed and breakfast inn. Nothing in their past would have led you to believe that they weren't of sound mind. Leaving behind hoards of unbelievers and doubters, their innkeeping odyssey began and the first draft of this book followed shortly thereafter. It could be mentioned here that Jeff graduated from Case Western Reserve University in Cleveland with a degree in business administration and attended graduate school there, but why would that matter? It could also be mentioned that he is a physical conditioning freak, has run a couple of marathons, bikes, kayaks, and occasionally engages in winter sports like cross country skiing and snowshoeing, but why would that matter either? What does matter is that he was a really successful innkeeper and decided to share his experience and wealth of knowledge with the world.

Book Description

An always insightful, often sarcastic, often hilarious, guide into the often enjoyable, often challenging, often rewarding trials and tribulations of innkeeping. If you're an innkeeper, if you've ever thought about becoming an innkeeper, if you've ever stayed at a bed and breakfast, or if you've ever thought about staying at a bed and breakfast you must read this book.

About the Type

As a former corporate guy everything I ever typed was in Times New Roman. So, naturally, when I started working on the manuscript of this book, Times New Roman it was. Then, years later, along came my publisher who rather strongly suggested that I try some other type styles and recommended, among others, Garamond. So, this book is set in Garamond because I like it. I have no idea who Garamond was and why he thought the world needed another type style, but I'm glad that he did. I know I could have looked up his story, but I didn't. The book is also set in 14 pt. type because it's easier to read. In my extensive reading career, I've often put books back on the shelf if the type was too small. There are enough reasons for you not to read this book and I didn't want to add an extra reason to the list.

Words of Praise

"This is a well-written, amusing and informative book. If you're considering becoming an innkeeper, read this book. Then think long and hard if you want to cook creative breakfasts for innumerable guests, make their beds, clean their bathrooms, and be nice to them, even if you have a headache! For the right people, it can be a wonderful and rewarding experience."

Michael Pacht
Co-owner of the Applebutter Inn, Woodstock, Vermont

"A must read for those crazy enough to consider owning a B & B. Entertaining, witty, comprehensive, and brutally honest."

Fred Hunt
Retired banking executive and world traveler

"Just wish we would have had access to this great book before we bought our inn! It's full of wonderful information, lots of humor, great stories, and a real insight in what it's like to be an innkeeper. If you've ever thought about innkeeping as a profession you need to own this book. By far the best book I've read on this subject. Enjoy!!"

Charlotte Hollingsworth
Co-owner of the Ardmore Inn, Woodstock, Vermont

"If George Carlin had written a book on innkeeping, this would be it. Irreverent, yet insightful. Essential reading for would-be innkeepers and an eye-opener for everyone else."

Mary MacVey
Business Communications Consultant

"Buying and owning a bed and breakfast are daunting tasks. Jeff has managed to cover ALL the bases, from beginning your search to running your inn. His straightforward approach, with a dose of humor, will get you through to the wonderful world of innkeeping."

Bob and Sue Frost
Owners of the Canterbury House Bed & Breakfast
Woodstock, Vermont

"With Jeff's creative and humorous mind, it is easy to read his book while learning about what you need to do (or not do) as an innkeeper! The best (and only) book I've read on innkeeping!"

Barbara Barry
Co-owner of the Applebutter Inn
Woodstock, Vermont

Made in the USA
San Bernardino, CA
29 January 2019